What About Law?

Studying Law at University

Catherine Barnard, Janet O'Sullivan and
Graham Virgo

With contributions by:
Mark Elliott
Kevin Gray
Tony Weir

·HART·
OXFORD · LONDON · NEW YORK · NEW DELHI · SYDNEY

HART PUBLISHING

Bloomsbury Publishing Plc

Kemp House, Chawley Park, Cumnor Hill, Oxford, OX2 9PH, UK

1385 Broadway, New York, NY 10018, USA

29 Earlsfort Terrace, Dublin 2, Ireland

HART PUBLISHING, the Hart/Stag logo, BLOOMSBURY and the Diana logo are
trademarks of Bloomsbury Publishing Plc

First published in Great Britain 2011

Reprinted 2013, 2014, 2015 (twice), 2016, 2017, 2018, 2019, 2020, 2021

A catalogue record for this book is available from the British Library.

ISBN: HB: 978-1-84946-085-9

Typeset by Forewords, Oxford
Printed and bound in Great Britain by CPI Group (UK) Ltd, Croydon CR0 4YY

To find out more about our authors and books visit www.hartpublishing.co.uk.
Here you will find extracts, author information, details of forthcoming events
and the option to sign up for our newsletters.

Foreword

The two questions most often asked of a barrister about his or her profession are, 'How can you defend someone if you know they are guilty?' and 'What should I (or my son/daughter) read in order to decide whether to study law?'. This book now provides the answer to the second enquiry, leaving more time for discussing the first.

You can learn something about legal studies by reading the law reports in *The Times* or attending a trial at your local Crown Court or watching classic films such as *Twelve Angry Men*. But like a tourist in a foreign country where you do not speak the language, it can help to have a professional guide. The authors of this volume expertly identify and communicate the essence of the subject: its broad scope, covering a wide range of social, political and moral problems; its intellectually satisfying methods of analysis, based on logic, precedent and judgment; and, above all, its entertainment value.

The law addresses everyday concerns and its reasoning is often no more than applied common sense. But we lawyers do not make it easy for others to understand what we are talking about. Lawyers still have, as Jonathan Swift observed nearly 300 years ago, 'a peculiar cant and jargon of their own, that no other mortal can understand'. This can be confusing, even intimidating, to others. One of the great merits of this volume is that the authors demystify the process. They strip away the obscurities and explain what the study of law is really all about.

I very much hope and expect that the information, and enthusiasm, contained in these pages will encourage potential law students. Our society may not need more lawyers. But we certainly need more lawyers who think clearly about the meaning and the content of the laws that govern all our lives.

Lord Pannick QC
Blackstone ChambersTemple
London EC4Y 9BW

Preface

What About Law? is primarily intended to be a 'taster' for the study of
law as an academic subject, with a view to helping prospective students
decide whether reading law at university is for them. It also aims to provide an introduction to the main subjects students will study for a law
degree. We hope that many other sorts of reader will find something in
it to interest them too, perhaps school careers' advisers or parents wish-
ing to understand what their children are studying, or planning to study,
at university. Indeed, we hope that any intelligent non-lawyer who has
ever wanted to know a bit more about English law will find this book a
valuable tool.

However, this book comes with a health warning: it does not provide
a comprehensive review of the nuts and bolts of the legal system. There
are plenty of such books on the market. Nor is it packed full of useful
tips as to how to be a good student of law (how to write good essays,
how to prepare for exams, etc) or how to become a barrister or solicitor.
Rather, it explores what the law is, how it has developed, how the judges
interpret it and *why* it is that way. It does so by examining seven cases,
each one taken from the subjects forming the 'core' of any law sylla-
bus (criminal, contract, tort, land, equity, constitutional and EU Law).
These seven core subjects are the minimum which students must study,
and pass, in order to be able to undertake their professional training to
become practising solicitors or barristers. Sometimes students consider
these subjects dry and technical. The aim of these chapters is to show
that they are anything but.

In analysing the seven cases, the various authors examine the legal issues raised, the legal reasoning employed by the judges in the different courts, and the relationship between the particular area of law and some of the broader social, political, philosophical, ethical and economic debates. But, of course, each chapter inevitably moves beyond the one chosen case, exploring other aspects of the relevant legal landscape, such as related decisions of other courts as well as legislative developments.

Putting it another way, the aim of this book is to use the cases in the same way as newspapers write features on the 'life in the day' of a particular celebrity: each case is used to illustrate issues which have ramifications beyond the immediate subject in hand. The subjects of many of these cases are not celebrities, certainly not in the tabloid sense of the word, but ordinary people suffering the vicissitudes of life. And because each case is known by the name of the parties (and not by a sterile reference number or date as on the continent) these individuals acquire a certain celebrity status among law students. If you like what you see, you can read the actual cases themselves on the companion website (www. whataboutlaw.com).

As you will discover, the cases studied in the core subjects are the foundations to understanding any branch of law and for learning that elusive skill—how to 'think like a lawyer' (and this certainly does not mean how to charge clients a lot of money). Of course the study of law is academically demanding (this should never be forgotten), but it is also intellectually stimulating, controversial, of daily relevance and very often highly entertaining.

Each of the authors of the chapters in this book is a leading academic and we have, cumulatively, over a century of university teaching and research experience. We hope that we have managed to convey some small part of our own boundless enthusiasm for our subjects—if so, we will have achieved our objective.

Catherine Barnard, Janet O'Sullivan and Graham Virgo (editors)
Cambridge, September 2010

Acknowledgements

This project has had a long gestation period. The editors are extremely grateful to Richard Hart and his team for their enthusiasm for this book, for their support for this rather unusual venture and for all their help in bringing this second edition to fruition. While many of our friends, colleagues and students have given us help, advice and inspiration, we should like to express particular thanks to Albertina Albors-Llorens, Tony Arnull, Caroline Blyth, John Cary, Charles Cook, Phil Fellows, Daniel Francis, David Feldman, Amy Goymour, Jonathan Hilliard, Dominic Hockley, Emily Haystead, Angus Johnston, Magnus Jones, James Lawson, Jake Rowbottom, Jens Scherpe and Rob Veale. We are also most grateful to the various reviewers of this book for their comments and for the feedback from students which we have tried to take into account.

The editors would also like to express sincere thanks to their colleagues and friends, Mark Elliott, Kevin Gray and Tony Weir for writing the constitutional, land law and tort chapters, respectively, and for their constant encouragement and support for this project.

CSB
JAO
GJV

Contents

List of Contributors

Catherine Barnard—Professor of European Union Law and Employment Law, Fellow of Trinity College, Cambridge. Author of *EC Employment Law* 3rd edn (Oxford, Oxford University Press, 2006) and *The Substantive Law of the EU: The Four Freedoms* 3rd edn (Oxford, Oxford University Press, 2010).

Mark Elliott—Senior Lecturer in Law, Fellow of St Catharine's College, Cambridge, winner of Cambridge University Pilkington Teaching prize. Author of Elliott and Thomas, *Public Law* (Oxford, Oxford University Press, 2011 forthcoming) and *Beatson, Matthews and Elliott's Text and Materials on Administrative Law* 4th edn (Oxford, Oxford University Press, 2011 forthcoming).

Kevin Gray—Professor of Law, FBA, Fellow of Trinity College, Cambridge. Co-author of Gray and Gray, *Elements of Land Law* 5th edn (Oxford, Oxford University Press, 2008) and *Land Law* 6th edn (Oxford, Oxford University Press, 2009).

Janet O'Sullivan—Senior Lecturer in Law, Fellow of Selwyn College, Cambridge, winner of Cambridge University Pilkington Teaching prize; previously solicitor at Slaughter and May. Author of O'Sullivan and Hilliard, *The Law of Contract* (Oxford, Oxford University Press, 2010).

Graham Virgo—Professor of English Private Law, Fellow of Downing College, Cambridge, winner of Cambridge University Pilkington teaching prize; barrister. Author of *Principles of the Law of Restitution* 2nd edn (Oxford, Oxford University Press, 2006); *Maudsley and Burn's*

Trusts and Trustees Cases and Materials 7th edn (Oxford, Oxford University Press, 2008) and contributor to *Simester and Sullivan's Criminal Law Theory and Doctrine* 4th edn (Oxford, Hart Publishing, 2010).

Tony Weir—Emeritus Reader in Law, Fellow of Trinity College, Cambridge. Author of *A Casebook on Tort* 10th edn (London, Sweet & Maxwell, 2004); *An Introduction to Tort Law* 2nd edn (Oxford, Oxford University Press, 2006) and *Economic Torts* (Oxford, Oxford University Press, 1997).

1

Introduction to Law

Catherine Barnard, Graham Virgo and
Janet O'Sullivan

STARTING TO THINK ABOUT LAW

Picture this. Laura, who is 17, organises a party at the family home while
her parents are away for the weekend. It gets out of hand. For Laura
and her parents, it is a nightmare. But for a lawyer, there are as many
questions as there are empty bottles strewn the next morning across the
prized living-room carpet.

What if the party was very noisy? It might have caused a nuisance
to neighbours living nearby and those neighbours might have contacted
the local authority, whose noise-prevention officers have powers to close
the party down or reduce the noise in some other way. If the party was
large enough—and loud enough—to cause a serious nuisance across a
wide area, Laura and her guests might even be prosecuted for the crime
of public nuisance and eventually punished.

What if the partygoers damaged the house or stole some of the family's possessions? These are obviously criminal offences, but what
happens if the perpetrators can't be identified? Can guests be forced to
give evidence of what happened? Can they get into trouble if they don't
name names? If the perpetrators are easily identified and have lots of
money, Laura's parents might even consider suing them for compensation to cover the cost of all the damage. If the parents choose not to
bother, but claim instead on their household insurance policy, can the

insurance company recoup some of the money it pays out from those responsible for the damage?

What if one of the invited guests, Mark, was seriously injured when he tripped over a loose paving-stone on the patio—a stone that Laura's parents knew was dangerous and had been meaning to get fixed? He might want to sue the parents for compensation, but would it make any difference to his chances of success if the parents had expressly banned their daughter from inviting anyone to their home while they were away? And what if Mark was drunk or messing about when he tripped, but the paving stone was sufficiently dangerous that he would, more likely than not, have tripped and suffered the same injury even if he had been perfectly sober? Do people nowadays resort too readily to litigation when injured, unwilling to accept that they have no one to blame but themselves for what happened?

How would the arrival of gate-crashers affect the position? What was their legal status while in the house—were they trespassers? If so, what does that mean? They might be guilty of a crime, such as burglary, if they intended to steal property. Could they be forcibly ejected by the hostess's friends, even if this requires physical violence? What if the hostess turned a blind eye to their arrival or appeared to welcome them, but later wanted to throw them out? And what if a gatecrasher is injured tripping on that same dodgy paving-stone?

The internet adds a new dimension to the problem. Perhaps Laura publicised the party on an internet chatroom, or maybe some of her so-called friends hacked into her account and publicised the party without her permission. Would this generate any legal liability in itself? What about any responsibility of the company supposed to monitor the chatroom? Is it asking too much to expect a traditional, national legal system to cope with the challenges of an online world?

Did Laura buy alcohol for the party, even though there are supposed to be laws preventing that happening? Or did she raid the parental drinks cabinet? Are there any laws that penalise *serving* drinks to under-age people at private parties, or any licensing requirements that apply to such private gatherings? We all know about the problem of binge drinking, but some countries have laws imposing 'social host liability'—this means that if a host has served alcohol and then allows an obviously drunk guest to drive home, the host might be liable to pay compensation if the drunk driver later injures or kills someone on the road. Should the same laws be introduced in the UK and, if so, should they apply just to commercial premises, like pubs, or should they apply to private parties too? And should they apply if the person killed or injured is not an innocent third party but the drunk driver himself?

Meanwhile, back at the party, what if some guests did things they deeply regretted next morning? If a woman consented to sex when drunk, but the man knew that she wouldn't have consented if she had been sober, is he guilty of rape? And can a drunken consent to sex really be considered consent? What if a man believes a woman is consenting, but only because he is too drunk to realise that she isn't? The legal age of consent to sex is 16, so what are the criminal law consequences of a 19-year-old man having sex with a 15-year-old girl who said she was 17, or of a 15-year-old boy having consensual sex with a girl his own age? Is it right for the law to attach such overwhelming significance to the age '16' in this context? Is it practicable to have laws that are so difficult to enforce?

As the party descended into chaos, there was a fight and a man was hurt. Can he sue for damages, even though he was a willing participant in the fight? If the fighting spilled out onto the street, can the police arrest the perpetrators for causing a breach of the peace or for drunk and disorderly conduct? Are there any additional protections for under-age suspects?

Finally, the police raided the party and found that illegal drugs were being taken. Is it illegal to take drugs, to share them, or just to supply them? Is it economically and politically sensible to tackle drug-taking using the criminal law?

Laura is clearly going to be in trouble with her parents, but can she be held legally responsible for any of these disastrous events, even if she spent all night cowering in her bedroom, terrified and unable to do anything to bring the party to an end? And should her parents be regarded as legally responsible, even though they were not there and were horrified to discover the chaos when they got home?

* * *

One party, but so many diverse and fascinating legal issues. Some are about what the law *is*, others about *why* it is that way. Lawyers have to think in those terms all the time. For many of the questions, there is no obvious 'right' answer, because the law is surprisingly open to more than one interpretation and because considerations of policy and fairness do not always point in the same direction. Lawyers and law students need to think about all these issues, and this book will give you a taste of the opinions and arguments that result.

We have taken seven cases—one from each of the core subjects that you must study if you wish to start out on the career path of becoming a lawyer. These subjects are essential building blocks for a proper under-standing of law, regardless of whether you go on to pursue a legal career. First, however, we need to provide you with some of the basic tools of the trade to help make sense of the cases that follow. Why not start with a fundamental (and very difficult) question: what is law?

THE TOOLS

What Is Law?

The *Oxford English Dictionary* describes law as:

> The body of rules, whether formally enacted or customary, which a particular State or community recognises as governing the action of its subjects or its members and which it may enforce by imposing penalties.

This definition is perfectly satisfactory as far as it goes, but it does not tell us much about what law really is, either as an academic subject or in the way it works for lawyers and members of the public. So let's think in detail about where law comes from and the role it plays in different sorts of disputes. (Don't forget that although this book focuses on court cases, knowing and understanding the law allows lawyers to settle dis-putes without them ever reaching court or, better still, preventing them from arising in the first place.) We will return to the essential question of what we really mean by 'law' in the final chapter, once you have read the rest of the book. It seems simple, but it is actually one of the most difficult and controversial questions raised by the philosophy of law (known as *jurisprudence*).

The Sources of Law

English law comes from a number of *sources*. First, because we do not have a written constitution in the United Kingdom, the laws with the highest authority in this country are *statutes*, passed by Parliament and given 'royal assent' by the monarch. Statutes, also known as Acts of Parliament, are referred to as *primary* sources of law. These primary laws may be supplemented by *secondary* sources, known as secondary or delegated legislation, usually in the form of Statutory Instruments (SIs). These are the nitty-gritty, detailed, technical rules fleshing out in more detail a provision laid down in a particular Act of Parliament. SIs are subject to less detailed parliamentary scrutiny. To give you an example, the right for parents with children and those with caring responsibilities to request flexible working hours is laid down in general terms in the Employment Rights Act 1996. But you will find all the details in various SIs such as SI 3236/2002 The Flexible Working (Eligibility, Complaints and Remedies) Regulations 2002. However, when adopting Acts of Parliament and SIs, Parliament no longer enjoys the total freedom it once had: it must ensure that the rules do not contravene either European Union law (considered further in chapter 8) or the European Convention on Human Rights.

The statutory rules may also be accompanied by other documents which are not always legally binding but offer guidance to judges and other officials striving to apply these rules. These include planning guidance and codes of practice such as the Advisory and Conciliation Service's (ACAS) Code of Practice on Disciplinary and Grievance Procedures at Work.

The second source of law is the *common law*, much of it made a long time ago by judges. It continues to develop as judges have to decide new and different cases. It is all rather mysterious, because strictly speaking judges don't make new law, they merely declare and apply the existing law when deciding a case (although this is a bit of a chicken-and-egg puzzle because every common law rule must at some point in ancient legal history have been invented for the first time). This *declaratory* theory is certainly accurate insofar as it relates to judges in the ordinary or *lower* courts (we will return to the structure of the courts later). These are judges who decide initially which party wins a civil dispute, or who preside over criminal trials. However, when the losing side is unhappy with the result and takes the case further, to the higher or appellate courts, the senior judges who decide the appeal often do things that look very much like making new law, such as deciding to expand a rule to cover a new area or reverse an earlier rule because it is now out of date or didn't work very well. The appellate judges are adept at being creative with the existing law, managing to respect the declaratory theory while, in reality, changing the law slightly.

The basics of many important areas of law, such as contract, tort and equity (which are considered later in this book), are governed by judge-made law, although even these traditionally common law areas are increasingly being altered by statutory developments. Sometimes this happens when Parliament thinks that the common law is going in the wrong direction. At other times, politicians want to introduce a wholly new law in a particular area. Judges (however creative they are) cannot make major reversals or big changes to the common law—this requires legislation.

A good example of statutory intervention is the Unfair Contract Terms Act, passed by Parliament in 1977, which provided that certain very unreasonable contract terms and notices were no longer to be legally effective. Included among these clauses and notices were those which say that one person is exempt from any liability for negligently causing death or personal injury to another person. The courts had struggled for years to find common law solutions to protect people from onerous exclusion clauses and notices of this kind, but parliamentary intervention was able to do the trick in an instant. From the moment this statute was passed, it replaced all the old common law on the question of the validity of such notices and clauses. When passing the Unfair Contract Terms Act, Parliament had the benefit of guidance from the *Law Commission*. This body, consisting of judges, barristers, solicitors and academic lawyers, considers whether particular areas of law need reform, puts proposals for change out to consultation with lawyers and other interested parties, and produces reports detailing its final conclusions. Parliament is not obliged to implement the Law Commission's recommendations, but sometimes does so.

Today, many statutes are also passed to give effect to the UK's commitments to the European Union. So, for example, in July 1985 the European Community (which is what the European Union used to be called) adopted a Directive on Product Liability requiring Member States to implement domestic legislation providing that manufacturers would be liable, even if not at fault in the traditional sense, for any personal injury or damage to property caused by their defective products. This Directive means the 27 Member States of the European Union all have compatible, harmonised product-liability regimes. The UK government implemented the Directive by passing the Consumer Protection Act 1987.

Most statutes, even those introducing completely new rules, assume and build on the existing common law in some way—they rarely arrive out of a clear blue sky. For example, statutory provisions protect *employees* from being unfairly dismissed, but the question 'who is an employee?' is answered by reference to the common law's understanding of a *contract* of employment. In addition, the common law often still has a role to play when a statute is enacted in a particular area. Judges may need to interpret what a particular statutory provision means and, having decided what it means, this interpretation will then become law in its own right and be applied in future cases.

By now, you will have worked out that existing common law cases, and the rules set down in them, are important in deciding new cases. They not only influence the result in the new case, but also dictate what that result will be, because the fundamental basis of the common law system is the doctrine of *precedent*. To grasp fully the importance of this doctrine, we must first understand the structure of the courts in England.

At its simplest, the structure of the courts (see the diagram on page 10, below) consists of trial judges at the lowest level, then the Court of Appeal and finally the Supreme Court. The doctrine of precedent requires the lower level courts to be *bound* by the decisions of superior courts on matters of *law*—they have no choice but to follow the rule set down in those superior decisions. Don't ignore the words 'of law' in the previous sentence—trial judges often have to decide between conflicting pieces of evidence and work out the *facts* of the case, and in this aspect of their decision-making the doctrine of precedent has no role to play. But where issues of law are concerned, a trial judge is bound by decisions of the Court of Appeal and the Supreme Court, and the Court of Appeal is bound by the decisions of the Supreme Court. In October 2009 the Supreme Court replaced the House of Lords as the highest court. However, decisions of the House of Lords retain their superior status as precedent, a concept that we shall explain later.

In addition, courts of a particular level are generally bound by decisions of other courts at the same level. So, for example, the Court of Appeal is bound by other, earlier, decisions of the Court of Appeal, although on very rare occasions it is possible for the Court of Appeal to overrule one of its own earlier decisions. Likewise, the Supreme Court can in theory overrule its own, earlier decisions, but like the Court of Appeal, it does so only on very rare occasions and for exceptional reasons. On the other hand, higher courts are *not* bound by decisions of lower courts. So, for example, the Supreme Court can, and frequently does, overrule decisions of the Court of Appeal in earlier cases, just as it can reverse the result in the particular case being appealed to it and allow the appeal.

This book focuses on the law of England, which includes the law of Wales. This system is primarily common law based. Scottish law is different. It is derived from Roman law, which is the tradition which also applies in continental Europe. The Scottish system, also sometimes called the *civilian* system (not to be confused with the more common meaning of the phrase 'civil' law as the opposite of criminal law, which is discussed below), is based on formal written Codes prescribing the detail of the law. In contrast to the common law, civilian judges have no lawmaking function at all, other than in interpreting and applying the Code. However, the law of England and Wales, on the one hand, and Scotland, on the other hand, is not as different as would first appear. In areas which have not been devolved to the Scottish Parliament or the Welsh Assembly, statutes passed by the Westminster Parliament in London apply to all three jurisdictions and the interpretation of those statutes by the Scottish courts has persuasive effect on the English courts. Further, and somewhat surprisingly, decisions of the Supreme Court bind the courts throughout the United Kingdom, including Scotland, and (as we shall see in chapter 4) the Supreme Court is the highest appeal court for Scottish cases as well as those from England and Wales.

At present, Northern Ireland's legal system is very similar to that of England and Wales, applying the common law in an identical judicial structure (with final appeals to the Supreme Court), though with some differences in dealing with criminal offences involving terrorism. The Northern Ireland Assembly, which was reactivated in 2007, has legislative power and so in future there may well be significant changes in the legal system and procedure operating in Northern Ireland.

All this discussion of domestic law should not blind you to the variety of other sources of law which have a significant impact on domestic law. We have already mentioned the important influence of European Union law on the United Kingdom (this is considered further in chapter 8). In addition, the European Convention on Human Rights, incorporated into domestic law by the Human Rights Act 1998, provides litigants with an important way of challenging the validity of acts and decisions taken by the government. Other *international law* rules are also important. International law concerns treaties binding on states, such as the Law of the Sea Convention and the UN Convention on the Rights of the Child. Occasionally, English courts may refer to international law to assist in the interpretation of ambiguous provisions of national law.

Classification

We have already seen some of the classifications lawyers use, such as statute/common law and national/EU law. Another important distinction is between the civil and criminal systems, which is reflected in the structure of the court system itself. *Criminal law* is the power of the state to punish people for causing harm or for being involved in other forms of unacceptable conduct. Most minor crimes are dealt with in Magistrates' Courts; more serious cases are heard in the Crown Court by a judge and

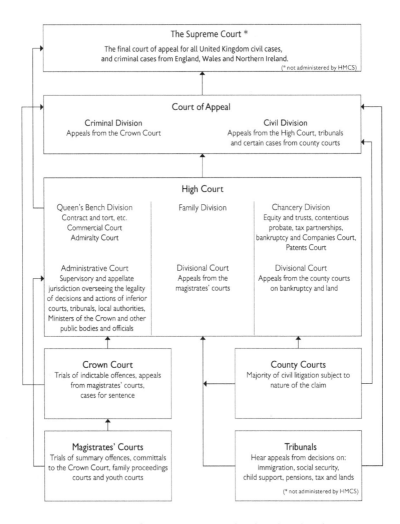

Figure 1.1 Hierarchy of the courts in England and Wales. (Diagram taken from HM Courts Service's website and reproduced with kind permission of HM Courts Service (HMCS).)

jury (see figure 1.1 above). Appeals in Crown Court cases can go to the Court of Appeal (Criminal Division) and then to the Supreme Court. In criminal cases the accused, referred to as the defendant, is *prosecuted* by the state in the name of the monarch (currently the Queen, referred to as *Regina*; in older cases you may see reference to *Rex* for King). In practice, the prosecution is dealt with by the Crown Prosecution Service, a body of professional prosecutors acting in the name of the Queen. The cases are therefore referred to as *Regina* (abbreviated as R) *versus* (abbreviated as *v*) [the name of the defendant]. So, if John Smith is being prosecuted, his case would be called *R v Smith*. It would be written this way too, but when talking about a case lawyers generally say 'and' instead of '*v*', so the case would be called 'R *and* Smith' but, more usually, simply by the name of the defendant ('*Smith*'). If the prosecutor is successful the defendant is found *guilty*.

Civil cases are all those cases which are not criminal, such as cases involving contract, tort, employment, commercial, trusts or property law. Civil cases start in either the County Court, for cases involving smaller sums of money, or the High Court, for cases involving larger sums. The vast majority of civil cases are heard by a judge without a jury (defamation cases being a notable exception). Appeals on the law go to the Court of Appeal (Civil Division) and then, with permission, to the Supreme Court. In civil cases the *claimant* (who used to be known as the plaintiff) sues the *defendant*. If the claimant is successful, then the defendant is held *liable*. For this reason, lawyers often talk about *liability*, saying things like 'these facts give rise to negligence liability' or 'if contractual liability is established, the defendant must pay damages'—remember that this simply relates back to the notion of the defendant being legally responsible.

Civil cases are usually referred to by the names of the parties (eg *Smith v Jones*). On appeal, parties are then called the *appellant* and the *respondent.* When writing the name of a case it is usual to underline or italicise the names. As we saw above, when speaking about a case or reading out the case name, *Smith v Jones* will be referred to as 'Smith and Jones'.

Apart from the different courts which hear the cases and the different terminology used, another major distinction between civil and criminal cases is the burden of proof. In criminal cases, the prosecutor must prove that the defendant is guilty beyond all reasonable doubt: if there is any remaining flicker of reasonable doubt about the defendant's guilt, then the magistrate or jury must not convict. In civil cases, the claimant has to prove a case only to the lower standard of 'balance of probabilities', meaning that the defendant's liability is more probable than not. The higher standard in criminal cases reflects the fact that, if convicted, defendants can lose their liberty and be sent to prison.

The other distinction which is commonly drawn by commentators who write about law is between public and private law. Public law deals with the powers of the state and, in particular the relationships between the different arms of the state, namely the legislature (law-makers), the executive (government, and the arms of the executive such as the police) and the judiciary. In some countries, such as the USA and Germany, these relationships are laid down in a written constitution. In the UK we do not have such a document but the equivalent principles and conventions have developed over the years and form our unwritten constitution, which is considered in chapter 7. Public law includes administrative law, which regulates the relationship between the individual citizen and the state. In this context, the 'state' can take a number of forms (central government, local authorities and agencies).

Private law deals with the rights and duties of individuals towards one another, such as the duty to carry out a contract or to avoid injuring another person by negligent acts or omissions, as well as the remedies which the courts can order when rights are infringed or duties breached, such as ordering the defendant to pay money to the claimant to compensate for loss suffered (damages) or, much less commonly, to stop committing some ongoing harm (an injunction).

Case Law

Citing a Case

When you are studying law, you need to be able to find cases easily. Not all cases are reported in law reports, but those which are have a *citation*. The first case which forms the subject matter of a chapter in this book is the criminal case of *R v Brown and others*. This was a decision of the House of Lords and is reported at [1994] 1 AC 212. [1994] refers to the year of publication of the report (the case was actually decided in 1993). AC is an abbreviation of one set of law reports called 'Appeal Cases' and the numbers mean that *Brown* is reported in the first volume from 1994 on page 212. There are many series of law reports but the Appeal Cases form part of the official law reports, the most prestigious series.

Since 2001 a new, official mode of citation has been developed, called the system of *neutral citation*. This is a universal system: it does not refer to a particular set of published law reports, but rather is a citation which tells you the year in which judgment was given and also which court gave the judgment. This is then followed by a number which is unique to that case. So, for example, a case may have a reference [2010] UKSC 36, meaning that the judgment was given in 2010, in the United Kingdom Supreme Court and was the 36th judgment of that court in that year. The neutral citation is an especially useful way of finding cases online.

The internet has revolutionised the way that the common law system works. For students, life is now much easier, because they can search for a case and find the text of it online, even if they can only remember the name of one of the parties, without having to venture into a law library. There are also online journals and sets of specialist law reports that are never published in paper form. The internet has been helpful in a substantive sense too. The doctrine of precedent means that a new case becomes part of the common law as soon as the court gives its judgment. However, before the internet, the *text* of a new case was hard to find at first and often wasn't published in a law report for several months, even years, after being decided. Now, the texts of many new cases are available on the internet within hours of being decided. It is also much easier for practising lawyers to find every precedent that might have some relevance to their client's case. However, this aspect of the internet is not viewed by everyone as an advantage. For example, judges were not happy when barristers in court began to cite hundreds of cases of very minor relevance to the issue they were dealing with, simply because the barristers had found them online. Eventually a new rule of civil procedure was introduced to limit the number of precedents that either side in a dispute is allowed to cite in court.

Reading a Case

When you have found a case, you need to be able to read it carefully. That means not simply getting from beginning to end but understanding the different elements included.

Most law reports start with a head-note, a summary of the facts and the decision, prepared by a law reporter. It does not constitute any part of the judgment and is not a source of law in its own right. However, the head-note has a use in enabling you to work out what the case is actually about and whether it is going to be relevant to your inquiry. You must never fall into the trap of believing that reading the head-note means that you do not need to read the whole case, although its summary of the *facts* may be beneficial, helping you to focus your energy on reading, thinking about and maybe even criticising the legal reasoning in the judgments that follow.

Studying law in a system based on precedent involves being able to work out precisely what a case decided. This is known as the *ratio decidendi*, or sometimes simply the *ratio*—the 'nugget of law' that the court used to reach its decision on the particular result. Discovering the *ratio* of a case requires you to work out what the key facts were and what rules were applied to those facts. It may surprise you, but this can be a difficult and controversial task, one that lawyers may struggle with long after a case is reported, sometimes for decades. Indeed, the skill of discerning what exactly a difficult case decided and stands for is one which lawyers can spend entire careers perfecting.

Where more than one judge delivers an opinion it is particularly hard to work out the actual legal ruling. These areas of disagreement give lawyers room for manoeuvre later when arguing a subsequent case for their client. They might seek to persuade the judge that the *ratio* of a case was X and not Y. Alternatively, they might argue that the facts of the present case are so different from the earlier case that the earlier case should be *distinguished.*

If you are dealing with a decision of the Supreme Court you may have to read as many as five speeches, and occasionally more. Even a decision of the Court of Appeal may contain up to three judgments. So, although it is common for one or more of the appellate judges simply to agree with the detailed reasoning of one of the others and add nothing more of detail, sometimes all the judges want to give us the benefit of their detailed views.

It gets particularly interesting where there is disagreement among the panel of judges, so that, for example, three or four Supreme Court Justices want to allow the defendant's appeal but one or two would prefer to refuse it. That leaves you trying to work out which judges form the majority and which are in the minority. It is only the judgments of the majority which constitute the law that derives from the case, but a speech given by a judge in the minority (usually known as a dissenting speech or a *dissent*) can nonetheless be well worth reading in detail. Not only does it help you to understand the controversies behind the majority decision and decide whether you agree with it, but it may also turn out to be more important in the future.

For example, the Court of Appeal had to decide in the 1950s whether a negligent accountant could ever be liable to a claimant who suffered financial loss because the claimant relied on incorrect statements made by the accountant, where that claimant was not the accountant's own client (so that there was no contract between them). The majority said that no claim was possible, but Lord Denning dissented and explained in his speech why he thought there *should* be liability in this case and in others like it. More than ten years later, the House of Lords overruled the 1950s decision and said in strident terms that Lord Denning had been right all along.

You may also read part of a judgment which is not strictly relevant to the decision on the facts, but involves the judge expressing his or her opinion on a related legal issue. This is known as an *obiter dictum* (or *obiter dicta* if there is more than one such expression of opinion). An *obiter dictum* does not form part of the *ratio* of the case and does not bind other judges, but it might persuade other judges to adopt that approach in a future case where the particular issue arises.

Courts and Other Means of Resolving Disputes

It is important to be aware that the different levels of courts have different types of judge. The lower courts typically have just one judge presiding (referred to as 'judge' and whose name would be written: Bloggs J). The Court of Appeal sits in chambers of three and the judges are referred to as Lord Justices (so: Bloggs LJ). The two most senior of the Lords Justice are the Master of the Rolls (MR) for civil cases and the Lord Chief Justice (LCJ) for criminal cases. The Supreme Court is the superior court in the UK and is presided over by Supreme Court Justices. The Supreme Court replaced the House of Lords in 2009. (In this context, the 'House of Lords' did not mean all the hereditary and life peers who still make up one part of the Houses of Parliament but only very senior judges appointed to be 'Lords of Appeal in Ordinary', formerly known as Law Lords). The Supreme Court hears appeals only on questions of law.

It is important to be aware that there are other methods of resolving legal disputes. There are other courts throughout the system, like the Small Claims Court which provides a quicker and more informal method of dispute resolution for relatively minor civil disputes. There are also other state tribunals which deal with specialised disputes, such as tax appeals and employment disputes; cases decided in these tribunals can be appealed to the High Court if the losing party wishes to challenge the decision. Another important option in practice, particularly for commercial disputes, is for the dispute to be decided by *arbitration* rather than in the courts. Arbitration will take place where the parties have agreed in their contract that, if there is a dispute between them, then an independent, qualified and often highly specialist arbitrator will be appointed who will decide the dispute and that the arbitrator's decision will bind them. This is particularly useful in resolving complex commercial disputes and it may be cheaper and quicker than having a protracted trial in the High Court.

Some organisations also have their own tribunals to consider disciplinary matters, such as sports tribunals, which deal, for example, with doping allegations involving competitors, and professional bodies, such as the Solicitors' Disciplinary Tribunal which deals with complaints about solicitors. Certain industries and public bodies (such as local government, insurance and pensions) have what is called an ombudsman: an independent and qualified official whose job it is to resolve, if possible, complaints from members of the public without the need for litigation.

At the other end of the spectrum, there are also two key courts in Europe, namely the Court of Justice of the European Union based in Luxembourg and the European Court of Human Rights based in Strasbourg. They are often confused with each other but it is vitally important to remember that these are two completely different bodies with entirely different functions. The European Court of Human Rights gives authoritative interpretations of the European Convention on Human Rights, to which the United Kingdom is a party. The Court of Justice, on the other hand, has less to do with human rights; rather (as we shall see in chapter 8) it hears *references* from the national courts, which are questions as to the meaning and validity of European Union law on, for example, free trade issues.

LEGAL METHOD

The discussion so far might make you think that studying law as an academic subject will only involve looking up rules and regulations in dusty old books, but there is an awful lot more to it than that. This perception of law as an academic subject is based on the popular misconception that there must be a 'right' answer to any legal question if only you look hard enough and read enough books. As you will soon discover, while some aspects of the law are clear, others are far from certain, particularly when dealing with questions of precedent. Lawyers and law students frequently need to tackle some very complex and subtle questions when working out what the law is, or should be, in a given situation. In this section we consider various skills you will need to do this.

Description

The most straightforward aspect of studying law is when you are simply asked to describe the law in one particular area. If you need to consider what the law says on a particular point you will have to look at various books, law reports and statutes to find the current state of the law. So, for example, you may need to describe the law defining the crime of murder, what counts as a valid contract, or when squatters acquire rights over the land they are occupying. It goes without saying that any description you produce needs to be expressed in elegant, often simple, but grammatically correct English.

Sometimes the description of a particular area of the law is straightforward, because it has been accepted and settled for many years. Here it might be sufficient to rely on a reputable textbook for a concise statement of the law. However, the law is never entirely static: legislation is repealed and replaced; old cases are overruled or applied to surprising new areas; new cases are decided in unexpected ways. This is one of the fascinating things about the law—you will be studying a dynamic, developing organism not a fossilised and unchanging text—and means that what once might have been accepted as straightforward law may now be much more controversial. It also means that you can never entirely rely on a textbook, even one that was published relatively recently, for the correct state of the law. Moreover, sometimes there simply is no consensus about what the state of the law is on a particular point, so even the usually straightforward task of describing the law may be in fact prove very complicated.

Applying the Law

Identifying the Nature of the Problem

Although it is of some interest to be able to describe the state of the law, law is never studied in a vacuum. Law is meant to be applied, so when you study law you spend a lot of time applying the law to real or hypothetical problems. This requires, first of all, careful identification of the nature of the problem with which you are dealing. You then need to work out what law applies to the problem and then apply that law to determine the result. This is how lawyers in practice have to approach problems, since they need to advise clients who want their disputes resolved by the law or who want to be able to structure their business or personal affairs to avoid legal difficulties in the future.

The process of applying the law varies, depending on the field of law. For example, a number of the private law core subjects, such as contract, tort and equity, involve, as central issues, the commission of some form of wrongdoing by the defendant, for which the claimant seeks a legal remedy. In such circumstances it is vital to know what the nature of the wrong is, to determine what area of the law you are concerned with. This will require you to identify what is called the *cause of action*. This is the basic set of elements which need to be in place before the claimant can establish that the defendant is liable. For example, let's go back to where we began—to Laura's party and the guest tripping on an uneven patio slab. He suffered a serious injury and now wishes to sue the owner/occupier of the house for damages. He may be able to bring a claim under the Occupiers' Liability Act 1957, but only if he can establish all the elements required by the statute for that cause of action. In this example, the injured claimant would have to show that:

1 he was a lawful visitor on the premises (a more recent, stricter statutory regime applies to claims by trespassers);
2 the occupier failed to take reasonable care to ensure that visitors would be reasonably safe on the premises; and
3 the claimant suffered personal injury as a result of that failure by the occupier.

If the claimant can establish all these things, he will have a cause of action for damages in tort.

However, establishing the cause of action is not necessarily the end of the story, because the defendant might be able to respond by establishing a *defence* to the claim, meaning an excuse recognised by law which would enable the defendant to escape liability. You are probably familiar with some of the defences in criminal law, such as loss of self-control and self-defence, but there are equivalents in civil cases. For example, the defendant may try to prove that the party guest expressly consented to run the risk of tripping on the patio stone, though that is not very likely to succeed. Much more plausible is the defence of contributory negligence, in which the defendant argues that his liability should be reduced in some way to reflect the fact that the claimant was partly to blame for his injuries.

Finally, you will need to consider what type of *remedy* will be available to the claimant if he or she can prove all the elements of the cause of action and fend off the defendant's defences. The most common remedy is financial, awarding damages to compensate the claimant for the loss suffered by the wrong. But for other causes of action different remedies may be available, such as a court order to make the defendant do (or not do) something (an injunction). There are also remedies which enable the claimant to recover money or property from the defendant.

This analysis of the law as involving causes of action, defences and remedies only works for private law subjects involving obligations and property. In this book, these are the foundation subjects of contract, tort, land law and equity. For the other foundation subjects different approaches may need to be adopted, but it is still necessary to identify the nature of the problem carefully and break the law down into its key elements to be able to apply the relevant legal rules to resolve the problem.

Drawing Distinctions

A system based on precedent is not always wholly straightforward, despite the simplicity of its basic premise that like cases must be treated alike. In practice, cases often arise that are very *similar* to an existing case but not absolutely identical. A lawyer then has to decide whether and to what extent the (sometimes subtle) differences matter: is this case nonetheless sufficiently similar to the existing precedent that we should *apply* the same rule, or are the differences significant enough that we should *distinguish* the existing rule and not apply it, maybe recognising a new exception to the existing rule at the same time? This process of drawing distinctions is one of the most important skills for a lawyer, one sufficiently fundamental that we will return to it in more detail in chapter 9. For now, one simple example will give the flavour.

If you promise in a contract not to do something but then do that very thing, the court will normally order you to stop doing what you promised not to do by granting an injunction. However, if the agreement is a contract of work and you promised not to work for anybody other than the employer, then the court will be reluctant to grant an injunction to make you work for the employer, because this would have the effect of making you work for somebody when you do not want to do so; this would be tantamount to slavery. Consequently, in *Warren v Mendy*, the court distinguished the general rule and refused to grant an injunction to make the defendant work for the employer. Instead, the employer was granted a monetary remedy for the breach of contract in the form of damages to compensate him for the loss he had suffered.

Making Predictions

As the previous paragraph showed, there are times when you might be faced with a particular problem and find that there appears to be no statute or case which covers that particular area or, if there is some law in the area, that it is contradictory or confused. Now you need to work out what judges would say if they were faced with the problem. This requires you to put yourself in the position of the judge and survey the existing law to try to find clues as to how the problem would be resolved. Finding the solution requires looking at any rules that do exist, working out the purpose and policy behind those rules, and then, if necessary, drawing analogies from other areas of law to see if they support a plausible conclusion.

The following example will give a taste of this process. It has long been an established part of the law that it is straightforward to sue for damages if the defendant's negligence caused the claimant to suffer personal injury. So if a doctor negligently failed to diagnose the claimant's medical condition correctly, with the result that the claimant is left with a permanent injury instead of being totally cured, the doctor is liable. It was, in contrast, traditionally very difficult, if not impossible, for a claimant to sue a public authority for damages if he or she 'lost out' because that authority negligently failed to perform one of its public responsibilities properly (such as running hospitals, highways, social services, etc). Then in the 1990s the courts were faced with two wholly new sorts of negligence case, dealing with issues that simply did not exist when the precedents were decided. These were claims for damages brought by children in two situations. The first were claims by children who had been subjected to abuse by a parent, step-parent or carer at home, brought against the local authority social workers who, the children alleged, negligently failed to spot or prevent the abuse. The second situation concerned children who were dyslexic but whose dyslexia was not diagnosed during their school days as a result of the negligence of the council's educational psychologists. There were no English precedents covering either of these areas, or even analogous areas, so the lawyers advising the parties had to engage in a lot of (educated) prediction about what the courts would decide.

Interestingly, very few lawyers successfully predicted the eventual House of Lords' decisions on either issue. Even specialist negligence practitioners and academics found the decisions startling and surprising. In 1995, their Lordships decided that children whose future prospects were adversely affected because educational psychologists negligently failed to diagnose their dyslexia were owed a duty of care in negligence and were thus entitled to damages. However, in contrast, the House of Lords decided at the same time that no duty of care was owed to children who suffered ongoing child-abuse when social workers negligently failed to spot what was happening and take them into care. This was mainly because the Law Lords thought that if social workers were to have potential negligence liability hanging over them, this would unduly hamper their independence and decisiveness when dealing with child-protection cases although, as many commentators pointed out, their Lordships had not actually had the benefit of any concrete evidence to back up this view.

Many lawyers believed these results were the wrong way round, and that the law of negligence had got into a position of having, or appearing to have, its values and priorities muddled up. Happily, the European Court of Human Rights has since decided that the abused children did not obtain an adequate remedy from the UK courts when the House of Lords rejected their negligence claims, so the law is now that both sorts of claimant can in theory claim damages (although, of course, to get such damages they must also be able to prove that the defendants were actually negligent—no easy task and one that the tabloid newspapers virtually always overlook when complaining about the 'compensation culture').

INTERPRETATION

Sometimes the meaning of the rules in an area of the law is not clear. As a lawyer, you need to be able to interpret the law before you can describe it and then apply it. Different approaches apply when you are interpreting the meaning of cases and the meaning of statutes.

As we have already seen, when you read a case there may be a variety of questions which arise involving interpretation. It may not be obvious what a case decides because, perhaps, a variety of issues were considered in the case or there was disagreement among the judges and it is necessary to determine which judges were in the majority. The judges' words may also be ambiguous or be context-specific, and so you are required to interpret them very carefully.

Reading a statute may also bring problems of interpretation. The wording of the statute may not be clear, leaving you to work out what the words mean. One of the big questions of statutory interpretation concerns whether the words should be interpreted *literally* or whether the ambiguity can be resolved by considering the *purpose* of the provision. A similar dilemma applies when interpreting the meaning of complex written contracts.

A good example of a case turning on statutory interpretation is one which you may remember from the news in 2009, called *Office of Fair Trading v Abbey National plc and others*. It involved a legal challenge to the hefty fees which high street banks charge a customer if the customer's account goes into unauthorised overdraft. There is a statutory instrument called the Unfair Terms in Consumer Contracts Regulations 1999, which was passed to give effect to an EU Directive designed to protect consumers from unfair 'small-print'. This means terms in contracts between consumers and sellers or suppliers that operate unfairly for the consumer, such as a term enabling the seller or supplier to terminate a contract without reasonable notice or retain the consumer's deposit, without good reason. This was the legislation on which the challenge to bank charges was based (interestingly, the Regulations give enforcement powers to a public body, the Office of Fair Trading, so individual aggrieved consumers don't have to take legal action themselves).

The difficulty was that the Regulations contain an exception. Regulation 6(2) says that assessment of the unfair nature of terms:

> shall not relate (a) to the definition of the main subject matter of the contract, or (b) to the adequacy of the price or remuneration as against the goods or services supplied in exchange.

This is not a model of perfect English drafting! But in layman's language, it is supposed to mean that a consumer is not allowed to allege that the 'core' terms of the contract, the main subject matter and the price, are unfair because these are issues that consumers are well equipped to evaluate before making the contract; they are not tucked away in the small-print. Of course, the banks argued that the fees they charge for overdrawn current accounts form part of the remuneration they receive for providing a banking service and thus fall within Regulation 6(2)(b). So this question was litigated as a preliminary issue, to see whether the Office of Fair Trading could mount a fairness challenge. The first instance judge and the Court of Appeal decided that the bank charges did not fall within the exception in Regulation 6(2)(b) and thus a fairness challenge was possible, on the basis that the exception should be restrictively interpreted to cover just the 'main' or 'essential' price, to maximise consumer protection.

However, to the surprise of many commentators, the Supreme Court took the opposite view and agreed with the banks that the bank charges *were* part of the package of remuneration they received for providing a current account (which is generally free to any customer who remains in credit) and thus fell within the exception. In other words it was not permissible to read the words 'main' or 'essential' into Regulation 6(2)(b). The Supreme Court expressed sympathy with the customers and suggested that Parliament might like to consider passing legislation to prohibit unfair bank charges, but they were not prepared to stretch the statutory wording of the 1999 Regulations to allow a fairness challenge to proceed.

Another example of statutory interpretation is found in *Serco v Redfearn* concerning the interpretation of the then Race Relations Act 1976 (now Equality Act 2010) in the workplace context. This Act prohibits discrimination on 'racial grounds', a phrase which the courts have previously interpreted broadly to cover not just obvious cases in which employees from ethnic minorities are given less favourable treatment, but also to protect white employees who are *instructed* by their employers to discriminate against fellow employees from ethnic minorities. Redfearn was dismissed from his job as a bus driver when it was discovered that he was a local councillor for the British National Party (BNP). The BNP's constitution stated that it was wholly opposed to any form of integration between British and non-European peoples. The bus company justified dismissing Redfearn on health and safety grounds (a lawful reason for dismissal), arguing that its staff and passengers, many of whom were Asian, would be anxious in Redfearn's presence and that he might be attacked at work. Redfearn argued that his dismissal was really on racial grounds, and therefore in breach of the Race Relations Act 1976, but the Employment Tribunal disagreed and found that the 'health and safety' grounds were genuine. However, on appeal, the Employment Appeal Tribunal (EAT) overturned this decision because the Employment Tribunal had not explored whether those health and safety grounds were themselves influenced by racial considerations.

The EAT's reasoning raised the spectre of a provision, which had been interpreted to protect white employees from having to do racist things, being invoked by a racist to protect himself. The Court of Appeal was horrified by this possible outcome. Looking at the objectives of the then Race Relations Act 1976 (now Equality Act 2010), Mummery LJ said that Redfearn's 'sweeping proposition is wrong in principle, is inconsistent with the purposes of the legislation and is unsupported by authority'. He said that it produced the absurd consequence that an employer who, in trying to improve race relations, dismissed an employee whom he discovered had been guilty of racist abuse, would be liable for race discrimination. Redfearn therefore lost his case.

Serco v Redfearn shows how different judges at different levels in the judicial hierarchy can reach very different conclusions on the same set of facts and applying the same legal provisions. It also demonstrates how a simple examination of the dictionary meaning of words may not be sufficient to decide the outcome of a particular case. Mummery LJ recognised this and, when interpreting the statute, called upon the values behind the legislation as well as considering the absurd consequences of ruling in favour of Redfearn. This purposive approach to interpretation is also characteristic of European Union law. Whether the flexibility this brings is invariably an entirely good thing, or whether it sometimes comes at the expense of clarity and certainty in working out the legal rules, is an open question.

IMAGINATION

When asked to list the skills needed to make a good lawyer, few people would think of putting 'imagination' on their list—the law seems far too technical to need such a creative skill. But in fact lawyers need to use their imagination all the time. For example, when a claimant sues a defendant for damages for negligence, one of the relevant issues for the court to decide is whether the defendant breached the *standard of care* expected when doing whatever the defendant was doing when the claimant was harmed. This is an objective test—the question is not whether the defendant was careless by his or her own standards, but rather whether he or she came up to the standard of a *reasonable person* engaged in that particular activity. Traditionally this hypothetical, reasonable person was labelled 'the man on the Clapham omnibus', but today this phrase is considered outdated, so tends to be avoided.

In any event, the lawyer acting for the claimant has a lot more work to do than simply reminding the court of the law and convincing the court that the claimant's version of the facts is the correct one. As well as proving what the defendant actually did, the claimant's lawyer must also show what the hypothetical reasonable person *would have done* in the same situation, which in turn means (because of the objective standard of care) that this is what the defendant *should have* done. The claimant must also prove that if the defendant had followed this hypothetical path instead, the claimant would not have been harmed. This hypothetical version of events is sometimes called the *counterfactual*. Very often this counterfactual enquiry about the standard of care is too obvious even to be noticed: if the defendant failed to stop at a red light and smashed into the claimant on a pedestrian crossing as a result, it is obvious that the hypothetical reasonable driver would have stopped and the accident would have been avoided. But sometimes it is not so obvious. This is where imagination comes in, on the defendant's side as well as the claimant's. After all, this sort of argument is not about the facts (what actually happened), but nor is it really a legal argument either—precedents can only help us so far in working out what the reasonable person would have done in a given situation.

For example, in *Surtees v Kingston Upon Thames Borough Council and another* a foster mother was caring for a two-year-old child; at bath time she left the child sitting on the laundry basket in the bathroom for a moment while going to fetch a towel from just outside. The child managed to knock the hot tap on the basin and badly scalded her foot, so sued her foster mother (and the local authority) for damages in negligence (this may sound bizarre, but if successful the child's damages would come from an insurance policy, not the foster mother's own pocket). The court had to decide whether the foster mother had come up to the standard of the reasonable foster mother in that situation, or whether she had taken an unreasonable risk.

The claimant's lawyer had a relatively easy task, detailing why it was dangerous to leave a two-year-old child in the vicinity of the hot tap, as it only takes a moment to turn it on. But the defendant's lawyer retorted with lots of very imaginative arguments as to why the foster mother had *not* acted *un*reasonably. These included the fact that she was looking after lots of other children, so if she carried the claimant around everywhere she would have neglected the others; that it is not necessarily a good idea to cushion children from *all* risks, because that way they grow up with no idea of how to assess risks and therefore might end up more seriously injured in the future; that carrying the child out of the bathroom might itself have been more dangerous; and that demanding too high a standard from foster parents might put people off volunteering for the role, which would be detrimental to more children in the long term. These imaginative factual and policy arguments convinced both the trial judge and the Court of Appeal, so the child's claim failed.

GENERALISATION

If your study of the law was confined simply to describing, applying and interpreting the law, with a bit of imagination thrown in, you would soon be faced by a very confusing mass of seemingly unconnected legal rules derived from a lot of legal sources. So there is a further dimension to the study of law, which is usefully called *generalisation* or, sometimes, the search for principle. Lawyers spend a lot of time examining a mass of rules and then try to identify a principle which explains those rules and which links similar cases at a higher level of generalisation. The identification of these principles makes the law much more manageable, but also gives a much better idea of the real point of the particular area of law, allowing both patterns and inconsistencies to appear.

This process of generalisation is a bit like looking at a television screen or an Impressionist painting. If you get very close to the screen you can see lots of individual pixels or dots, but you cannot make out a picture. For that, you need to step back, to put the pixels or dots together to see the big picture. In the same way, the process of generalisation of the law requires you to step back to see the bigger picture. Once you have identified some principles, you can then step back even further to link the different pictures together to produce an even bigger picture. This is a bit like looking at an aerial photograph on a website. You could focus on your house in your road, but that will not enable you to see how that road fits in with the neighbourhood. So you can draw back to see the whole town and then back further to see the county, and further to see the country, and further to see the continent and further to see the world.

This sort of generalisation process goes on throughout the law, at all sorts of different level. For example, parliamentary draftsmen, when preparing the wording of new statutes, invariably have to think in general terms, so as to draft statutory wording that deals with problems at a high level of generality: far better than having to include exhaustive lists of every possible example that will be covered by the legislation. Likewise appellate judges, especially in the Supreme Court, often have to generalise in the sense of examining lots of earlier, seemingly disparate, cases and pointing out that they are in fact linked by a principle that had not been recognised before, so as to assist in deciding the particular case that has been appealed to them at the time and to make the law clearer in future cases.

One of the best examples, as we will see in more detail in chapter 4, is the development of the modern law of negligence. In the nineteenth century there were a number of unrelated situations (eg those involving 'occupiers and their guests' and 'horse-drawn carriages and pedestrians') in which the defendant was liable to compensate the claimant for harm suffered as a result of his negligence, but nobody had yet spotted that these different cases might be better regarded as examples of one more general principle. It was not until 1932, in perhaps the most famous case in the English law reports, *Donoghue v Stevenson* (about a snail in a bottle of ginger beer), that the House of Lords examined all of these different cases and synthesised the law, recognising for the first time the general principles that underpin the law of negligence today.

Academic lawyers and law students are frequently better placed to recognise general principles than judges and lawyers who concentrate on dealing with the specifics of the case in front of them. Indeed, judges come in for criticism if they focus too much on the implications of their decisions for other areas of the law. Academic lawyers and students, however, have the freedom to compare one area of the law with another, which often enables them to spot patterns and inconsistencies, connections and general principles that have gone unrecognised by practitioners and judges. A good example is the area of law now known as *restitution for unjust enrichment* (not a core subject in undergraduate law courses, but very important nonetheless). For over two centuries the law recognised a lot of different situations where the defendant was liable to pay something back or return something to the claimant, including where money had been paid to the defendant by mistake. Each case shared the common feature that the defendant's obligation to repay was not contractual (after all, he never promised to make the payment), but beyond this no obvious common thread linking the various examples had been spotted.

It was not until the publication of a seminal book in the 1960s, *The Law of Restitution*, and later academic writing, that these cases were linked at the level of general principle, creating what was, in effect, a new legal subject (a bit like the introduction of new scientific disciplines such as psychotherapy in the nineteenth century and just as hotly disputed). Finally, in 1991 English law officially caught up with this academic progress, when the House of Lords acknowledged in *Lipkin Gorman v Karpnale* that all these different situations could be explained by a single principle to prevent the defendant from being unjustly enriched. Most lawyers think the development of the general principle of unjust enrichment has allowed a better understanding of how the law operates and what it achieves in individual cases.

POLICY UNDERPINNING THE RULE

It is all very well to be able to state what the law is and to be able to apply it to particular problems, but the study of law as an academic subject involves another dimension, namely having regard to the *policy* which underpins the law. This method of legal study is often more theoretical and may also involve engaging with other academic disciplines. For example, we may be concerned with issues of social policy, such as whether a woman, who has cohabited with a man, should have any rights to the house in which they both lived but which was registered only in his name. This is considered further in chapter 5. Elsewhere, lawyers may be concerned with economic issues, in that we are seeking to ensure that the law promotes results which are economically efficient. For example, if you have sold part of your land to a purchaser who made an enforceable contractual promise not to build houses on the land, but who later breaches this promise and builds houses, should you be entitled to enforce that promise and obtain a court order for the destruction of those houses, even at a time of housing shortage?

At other times, lawyers may be concerned with political issues, such as the right balance between freedom of expression and national security, or with ethical issues, such as whether it is appropriate to take body parts from somebody who has just died if it will save somebody else's life, even though the deceased had not given prior consent. Sometimes we may be concerned with philosophical issues, such as whether the law properly respects basic principles of individual autonomy, or with sociological issues, such as whether applying a rule equally to everyone may in fact disadvantage certain groups such as women or ethnic minorities whose social or educational background means that they cannot take advantage of that rule.

These illustrations show that choosing to study law certainly does not close off other avenues of interest in academic terms; far from it, since to master law you really need to understand many other policy issues in society. Much of the real interest in studying and applying law lies in its impact on society. And what is interesting is the extent to which law is, or can be, a vehicle for social change. Take the example of the Sex Discrimination Act 1975 and the Race Relations Act 1976 (now repealed and replaced by the Equality Act 2010). These statutes were adopted at a time when it was commonplace for sexually and racially discriminatory policies to be applied, especially at work. The Acts were significant catalysts of social change because they contained the important statement that the state disapproved of discrimination on the grounds of sex and race. It is hard to prove cause and effect but attitudes to women and ethnic minorities have certainly changed significantly in the last thirty years.

ONE FINAL EXAMPLE

The application of all the different approaches to the study of law outlined above can be illustrated by the following problem which, as hypothetical legal problems often do, might stretch your sense of credulity. David has just been dumped by his girlfriend. He decides to kill her. He goes to a local craft shop to buy some modelling clay and some pins. He moulds the clay into the shape of his girlfriend and then sticks ten pins into it. Why? Because he believes in voodoo and thinks that this will kill her. In fact, it has no effect on her at all. Is David guilty of a criminal offence?

First, we need to describe the law in this area. There is a crime of murder which is committed whenever the defendant kills the victim, intending either to kill or to cause serious injury. Clearly, David is not guilty of this offence because his girlfriend is not dead. But there is another crime of *attempted* murder. This is governed by the Criminal Attempts Act 1981, which creates an offence where the defendant does a more than merely preparatory act with the intention to commit a crime. The Act specifically states that it is irrelevant that it is impossible to commit the offence in the circumstances. Reviewing all the cases which have been decided under this statute, it is clear that none of them relate to trying to kill somebody by voodoo. So the simple description of the law does not reveal whether David is guilty of an offence.

We therefore need to move on to the application of the law to the facts. Analysis of the statute reveals that there are three elements to the offence. First, the defendant must have intended to kill his girlfriend. Although intention can be difficult to define, it is clear on our facts that the defendant wanted to kill his girlfriend and so intention can be identified. But the application of the other two elements is less straightforward. What is meant by 'a more than merely preparatory act' and how should the notion of 'impossibility' be defined? Answering these questions requires the statute to be interpreted. Reviewing the cases which have interpreted the statute merely reveals that 'a more than merely preparatory act' means an act which has gone further than merely preparing for the crime. As David has done all that he believes he needs to do to kill his girlfriend, since he stuck all the pins into the model of his girlfriend, it is certainly arguable that he has done a more than merely preparatory act. In reaching this conclusion, we might perhaps distinguish *Campbell*, where the defendant, who had an imitation firearm with him, was arrested by the police just before he entered a post office. He was charged with attempting to rob the post office, but was acquitted because he had not gone beyond preparing for the commission of the crime of robbery. The result would have been different had he gone into the post office before he was arrested. In David's case, he appears to have got beyond preparing for the commission of the crime. But we would also need to consider any possible defences that David might wish to rely on. For example, if his mental state was wholly unhinged at the time (and a belief in voodoo might suggest it was), then perhaps this would excuse David from criminal culpability?

But the central question remains: if it is impossible to kill by voodoo, can the crime of attempted murder really have been committed? To answer this question we need to predict how the courts would decide a case involving voodoo, an issue which has never come before the courts directly. Since the statute is clear that impossibility to commit a crime is no defence, perhaps the judges would feel they had no choice but to conclude that the offence has been committed. But others might argue that there is a meaningful distinction between the sort of impossibility involved in an attempt to kill using a replica gun (which the defendant believed to be loaded) and the sort of impossibility we are dealing with in the voodoo example.

We would also need to consider whether a conviction would be appropriate, just as the courts would do when deciding the case. In considering this it is useful to identify any rules or principles which can be generalised from the cases on criminal attempts. The general principle appears to be that attempting to commit a crime exists as a separate crime in itself in order to punish defendants who want to cause harm to somebody else and who have done some acts towards the commission of this goal, even if the goal can never actually be achieved. It is the *desire* to reach the goal which is most significant and makes the conduct culpable even though no harm has actually been caused to the intended victim. This would justify conviction in David's case.

We might then to go on to identify the policy which underpins the offence. One policy might be that it is better to arrest and convict a defendant before any harm is committed, so we need a crime of attempt to do this. But this policy would suggest that David should not be convicted because he would never succeed in killing his girlfriend using voodoo. In the light of this clash between policy and principle, we would then need to consider whether the application and interpretation of the law in this case really is defensible. This would turn on whether we consider that it is fair and just to convict a defendant of a crime when he or she has not caused any harm and will not do so using that method. Other issues might arise, such as whether it is a good use of scarce public resources to prosecute someone who has no prospect of causing harm by his chosen method, or whether the mental health system might be more appropriate than a criminal prosecution for dealing with David's situation. So many different questions, suggesting so many conflicting answers: that's what makes law exciting and challenging.

CONCLUSIONS

Learning law is about lots of reading—cases, statutes, textbooks, academic articles—but it is also about thinking: what is the relevant legal rule here? Does it apply to this case or can it be distinguished? Should it apply? If not, why not, and what rule should apply instead? All lawyers need to think—logically, clearly and critically. This is what judges have to do, what practising lawyers have to do when giving legal advice to their clients, and what all law students must do too. The aim of this book is to give you a flavour of this process in action.

Cases

Donoghue v Stevenson [1932] AC 562

Lipkin Gorman v Karpnale [1991] 2 AC 548

Office of Fair Trading v Abbey National plc and others [2009] UKSC 6, [2009] 3 WLR 1215

R v Campbell [1991] Crim LR 268

Serco v Redfearn [2005] IRLR 744 (EAT); [2006] EWCA Civ 269; [2006] IRLR 623 (Court of Appeal)

Surtees v Kingston Upon Thames Borough Council and another [1991] 2 FLR 559

Warren v Mendy [1989] 3 All ER 103

Websites

For many important cases which are freely available: www.bailii.org

For primary and secondary legislation: www.legislation.gov.uk/

For the English and Welsh Law Commission: www.lawcom.gov.uk, and for the Scottish: www.scotlawcom.gov.uk

For links to the many legal resources available on the web: www.law.cam.ac.uk/resources.php

Further reading

On law

Honoré, *About Law: An Introduction* (Oxford, Oxford University Press, 1995)

On legal study skills

Askey and McLeod, *Studying Law* (Basingstoke, Palgrave Macmillan, 2006)

Bradney, Cownie, Masson, Neal and Newell, *How to Study Law*, 5th edn (London, Sweet & Maxwell, 2005)

Finch and Fafinsky, *Legal Skills* (Oxford, Oxford University Press, 2009)

Holland and Webb, *Learning Legal Rules*, 7th edn (Oxford, Oxford University Press, 2010)

McBride, *Letters to a Law Student*, 2nd edn (Harlow, Longman, 2010)

McLeod, *Legal Method*, 6th edn (Basingstoke, Palgrave Macmillan, 2009)

Smith, *Glanville Williams' Learning the Law*, 14th edn (London, Sweet & Maxwell, 2010)

2

Criminal Law

Graham Virgo

We hear about crimes all the time and many of us probably feel that we have a pretty good idea of what conduct is criminal, whether it is murder or rape or theft. It may also be pretty obvious why we want to punish people for committing such crimes. But when you study criminal law you cannot rely on gut reaction: you need to think carefully about how crimes are defined, how they should be defined and why it is appropriate for the state to punish somebody. For example, should people who smoke cigarettes in pubs be punished for doing so? Should we punish people who sell drugs? But why don't we punish people who break a contract, or prostitutes for selling sexual services?

THE ELEMENTS OF A CRIME

When lawyers consider whether a crime has been committed, such as the crimes which may have been committed at Laura's party in chapter 1, they usually break a criminal offence down into three separate elements. First, they consider whether the prohibited conduct and result have occurred. This is known as the external elements of the crime, which are often described by using the Latin term *actus reus*. So, for the crime of murder, the *actus reus* is that the victim is dead and that his or her death was caused by the defendant. Secondly, most crimes also involve a fault element, which is often known as the *mens rea*. Not every crime needs a *mens rea*, but many do, especially serious crimes, because it is the fact that the defendant was at fault which makes him or her particularly blameworthy and justifies the state in punishing the defendant. Relevant fault elements include intention, recklessness and negligence. For the crime of murder the relevant fault element is that the defendant intended either to kill or to cause serious injury. If this cannot be established, the defendant cannot be convicted of murder, although he or she might still be guilty of a less serious offence, such as manslaughter. Once the external and fault elements have been established, the third and final element is whether the defendant has any defences to the crime. For the crime of murder there are a number of full or partial defences which might be available. For example, if the defendant was attacked by the victim, the defendant could plead self-defence. If this defence is success-ful the defendant would be acquitted of the crime completely, so this is a full defence. Alternatively, the defendant might plead defences such as loss of self-control or diminished responsibility. If one of these partial defences is successful the defendant would be convicted of the less seri-ous offence of manslaughter rather than murder.

THE REASONS FOR PUNISHMENT

Assuming that the defendant has been convicted of a crime, he or she can expect to be punished. The criminal law recognises a variety of forms of punishment including imprisonment, fines and community orders. Dif-ferent reasons for punishment can be identified depending on the nature of the punishment, but there are four main reasons why the state wishes to punish a defendant who has been convicted of an offence. First, there is the need to protect the public from dangerous criminals, which can be satisfied by locking the defendant up in prison for a substantial period of time. Secondly, there is the need to deter the defendant and other poten-tial defendants from committing crimes. Thirdly, there is the need to rehabilitate defendants to seek to ensure that they do not commit crimes in future. Finally, there is the need for retribution: society wishes to mark certain types of conduct as wrongful and reassert the accepted social order by punishing the wrongdoer.

REASONS FOR CHARACTERISING CONDUCT AS CRIMINAL

In addition to considering the definition of offences and the reasons for punishment, criminal lawyers also consider another crucial question, namely, why certain conduct is criminal and other conduct, which we might dislike, is not treated as criminal. In considering this question there are two separate principles which are involved and which contradict each other. The first is the principle of autonomy. According to this principle, individuals should be free to do whatever they like. But if we allowed this principle to operate without any check we would end up with a society which is lawless and where anarchy prevails. Society needs rules to operate by and so the autonomy of individuals needs to be restrained in some way. We can do this by means of a second principle, which is called the welfare principle. According to this principle, the needs of society must prevail over the interests of individuals. Of course, if we allowed this principle to operate without check we would end up with a totalitarian state where the interests and rights of individuals would always be subordinated to the interests of the state. Whenever we consider whether or not certain conduct should be criminalised we are really considering to what extent, if at all, the autonomy of individuals should be restricted for the benefit of the state and the protection of other individuals. We sometimes describe this restriction on autonomy in other ways. One way is by reference to the doctrine of utilitarianism, where the interests of the majority are more important than the interests of the individual. Also, there is the doctrine of paternalism, where the state intervenes to restrict the autonomy of the individual because the state is acting in what it considers to be the best interests of the individual.

This tension between autonomy and welfare is illustrated by a number of long-running debates in the criminal law. One of the best examples concerns the use of certain types of drug. If we wished to adopt an approach which is simply based on the autonomy of the individual, we would allow all drug-taking to be legal since it would be up to the individual to decide if they wanted to take drugs. However, the state has determined that there are certain types of drug the possession of which should be criminalised because of the dangers posed by drug addicts to other people (the utilitarian argument) and to themselves (the paternalism argument).

The implications of these three distinct issues of the definitions of offences, the reasons for punishment and the reasons for criminalising certain conduct were raised by the very important decision of the House of Lords in a case called *Regina v Brown*.

FACTS OF *BROWN*

Brown concerned a group of more than 40 sadomasochistic homosexuals. Some of these men were sadists who obtained sexual satisfaction from causing pain. Others were masochists who enjoyed having pain inflicted on them. The activities were wide-ranging, but essentially involved branding, piercing and beating sensitive parts of the body. Certain features of the men's activities need to be emphasised. They occurred in private; injuries were inflicted but they did not result in any permanent disability; no infection was caused; the participants had safety words to use to ensure that the activities did not get out of hand; no medical attention was required; and no complaint was made to the police. Crucially, all of the participants consented to the activities.

The police discovered the activities of this group in the course of a separate investigation, called Operation Spanner, into the sale of obscene videos. In the course of this investigation the police discovered private videos of the sadomasochistic activities carried out by Brown and his friends and consequently the participants were charged with various criminal offences.

THE KEY OFFENCES

The defendants were charged with two specific offences contrary to sections 47 and 20 of the Offences Against the Person Act 1861. To be convicted of the section 47 offence it must be shown that the defendant assaulted the victim so as to cause him or her actual bodily harm. This offence can be broken up into four distinct elements, all of which need to be satisfied to convict the defendant of the crime:

1 Assault: this means either causing the victim to apprehend immediate and unlawful harm to the person (known as common assault) or unlawfully touching the victim (known as battery).
2 Actual bodily harm (otherwise known as ABH): this means that the victim suffered an injury which interfered with his or her health or comfort but was more than transient or trifling. So, for example, this would include a broken finger and bruising which was painful to the touch.
3 Causation: that the actual bodily harm was caused by the defendant's conduct.
4 The fault element: the defendant must have intended to assault or batter the victim or foresaw that this might happen as a possibility.

If the defendant is convicted of this offence he or she can be sentenced to imprisonment for a period up to five years.

The other relevant offence in *Brown* was maliciously wounding or inflicting grievous bodily harm contrary to section 20. This offence can also be broken up into a number of distinct elements:

1 Either wounding, which means doing something which penetrates all the layers of the victim's skin, so a pin-prick could count as a wound; or
2 Inflicting grievous bodily harm, known as GBH. This injury is defined simply as serious injury. It is clearly worse than ABH and includes broken limbs as well as serious internal injuries. This harm needs to be inflicted. The meaning of this word 'inflicts' has proved to be controversial but it now seems that it simply means that the defendant caused the victim GBH.
3 The fault element for this offence is malice, regardless of whether the defendant has wounded or inflicted GBH. Malice here means that the defendant foresaw the possibility of some harm occurring, but that harm need not be as serious as the harm which did actually occur. So, for example, if the defendant punched the victim in the face thinking that the victim would only suffer bruising, but her nose was

badly broken, the defendant could be guilty of the section 20 offence because he has inflicted GBH and foresaw the possibility of some harm being caused.

The maximum sentence for this offence is five years' imprisonment, just as for the section 47 offence, even though that offence involves less serious harm. However, in practice, if the defendant is convicted of a section 20 offence he or she is likely to get a longer sentence than if he or she was convicted of the less serious section 47 offence.

THE ISSUE IN *BROWN*

The key issue for the courts in *Brown* was whether it was appropriate to convict the defendant sadists of harming the masochist victims where the victims wanted to be harmed. In other words, should the consent of the victim operate as a defence? You might be surprised to learn that, even though the relevant criminal offences were defined by statute, the answer to this question turns on the interpretation of the common law rather than statute. English law accepts that, as a general rule, where the victim consents to harm, then that is a valid defence. So, for example, if the defendant tattoos the adult victim at her own request, the victim's consent means that no crime has been committed. This defence of consent even extends to cases where the victim cannot be shown to have specifically consented to the harm but that harm occurs in circumstances where the victim can be deemed to have consented to it. So, for example, if the defendant slaps the victim on the back as a greeting at a party, that is the type of touching to which everybody can be assumed to have consented. Similarly, if the defendant is playing football with the victim and trips the victim up in order to get the ball, that would usually be the sort of touching to which all football players consent, at least if the defendant has not gone beyond what a player could have reasonably been regarded as having consented to by taking part in the sport. But should any limit be imposed upon the type and circumstances of harm to which the victim can consent? That is the key issue with which the judges in *Brown* had to grapple.

The Trial

The defendants were tried in a Crown Court before a judge and jury. In such a trial the judge has to decide questions of law, such as the proper interpretation of elements of the crime, but the jury has to decide questions of fact in the light of the judge's directions and rulings about legal questions. In *Brown* the jury was asked to consider whether the elements of both the sections 47 and 20 offences had been satisfied to justify a conviction. For the most part this was simply a question of fact. But there was a key question of law, namely, that if, as the defence argued, the victims had consented to the harm, then, because of the extreme circumstances in which that harm was caused, was this consent a valid defence? The judge ruled that it was not and so, even if all the victims did consent, it followed that the defendants would be guilty. Following this ruling the defendants pleaded guilty and various sentences of imprisonment were imposed on them, ranging from one to three years.

The Court of Appeal

Following the defendants' conviction they wanted to appeal against the judge's ruling that the defence of consent was not available. This involved appealing to the Court of Appeal (Criminal Division). The argument before the Court of Appeal focused simply on a question of law rather than fact, namely whether the actual consent of the victims meant that the defendants could not be found guilty of the crimes. The judges reviewed earlier cases and concluded that they were bound by these authorities to rule that the victim's consent was not a valid defence. Consequently, the defendants' appeal was rejected. However, their sentence was reduced to between three and six months because they did not know that their conduct was criminal.

The House of Lords

The defendants then appealed to the House of Lords. Three of the five judges decided that the appeal should be rejected and the other two dissented, concluding that the appeal should be allowed. The decision of the majority prevails and so the appeal was rejected, which meant that the defendants' convictions were affirmed.

Since, however, there were three speeches given by the majority, it is not immediately obvious what counts as the 'official' reason for rejecting the appeal. It is, therefore, necessary to analyse these speeches very carefully, and by doing so it is possible to identify a central principle which justifies the decision of the majority. As we saw in chapter 1, this is called identifying the *ratio decidendi*, otherwise known as the *ratio*. The *ratio* of *Brown* is as follows:

• Where the victim has suffered harm which is actual bodily harm or worse, then the victim's consent to that harm is no defence.
• But this principle is subject to an exception, namely that the consent can operate as a defence if the circumstances of the harm can be justified by a good reason.

Since, on the facts of *Brown*, the harm was at least actual bodily harm and because satisfaction of the sadomasochistic libido was not considered by the majority to be a good reason for causing such harm, it followed that the victims' consent was not relevant and the defendants were properly convicted.

The majority identified four key reasons in support of this decision.

Earlier Authorities

Although this was a decision of the House of Lords, which was not bound by earlier decisions of lower courts such as the Court of Appeal, the judges in the House of Lords considered it important that their decision was consistent with such earlier authorities. These earlier cases were interpreted as recognising that the consent of the victim to actual bodily harm or worse could be justified only if the conduct was consistent with public policy. So, an earlier decision of the Court of Appeal had held that causing harm in the course of a fight in public was not an acceptable reason even if the victims had consented. This case had recognised that acceptable reasons for consenting to harm would include medical interventions and properly conducted sports. However, the judges in the House of Lords could have decided to overrule these earlier cases if they thought that the principles involved were not acceptable. Indeed, it is even possible for the House of Lords to overrule its own earlier decisions if it is felt that those decisions were incorrect or no longer appropriate.

Technical Reasons

The majority accepted that it was easier to differentiate between no injury and some injury than it was to distinguish between degrees of injury. Consequently, it was accepted that the appropriate line to be drawn between when the victim's consent should always be a defence and when it should only be a defence if the conduct was consistent with public policy is the line between battery and actual bodily harm, rather than between actual bodily harm and grievous bodily harm. This is, however, highly dubious reasoning, because the criminal law distinguishes between injuries constituting actual bodily harm and grievous bodily harm all the time, since it is the difference between these degrees of injury which underlies the separate offences of section 47 and section 20.

Policy Reasons

A number of policy reasons were identified by the majority for their decision. These included:

- the dangers of more serious injury being caused if the defendant's activities became too exuberant;
- the dangers of infection being transmitted, particularly of the HIV virus; and
- the danger that young men would be corrupted by involvement in sadomasochistic activities.

But all of these factors involve potential harm, none of which was found to have occurred on the facts. It is difficult to justify the decision in *Brown* on the basis of what might have happened, rather than what did actually happen, particularly because the defendants had introduced various safeguards to ensure that very serious injuries were not caused and that any diseases were not transmitted. Further, if there had been any evidence that young men had been corrupted into performing sado-masochistic activities, this would suggest that they were not consenting, which would unquestionably constitute an offence against the person, and may also involve a sex offence in its own right.

Morality

None of these reasons is therefore altogether convincing. However, careful reading of the majority speeches reveals a fourth reason for the decision, namely that the majority perceived the case as involving conduct which was so immoral that it could not be tolerated by society and had to be punished. For example, Lord Templeman said that '[p]leasure derived from the infliction of pain is an evil thing' and Lord Lowry spoke in emotive terms of activities resulting from 'perverted and depraved sexual desires'. Whether reliance on gut reactions to perceived immorality is a sufficient reason to criminalise conduct is a difficult question. The danger of such an argument is that the notion of what is immoral is virtually impossible to define and depends very much on personal perceptions and beliefs rather than legal principle. It is difficult to see, therefore, that this is a sufficient reason in its own right to justify conviction.

APPLICATION OF THE DECISION

Despite concerns about the reasons behind the decision of the majority, we are left with *Brown* representing the law in England as to when the victim's consent can operate as a defence. When you are considering whether an important decision is correct, it is always useful to test the implications of that decision by applying it to hypothetical situations in an attempt to determine whether the results are acceptable or absurd. In considering the application of *Brown* it is important to consider those circumstances where harm might be considered to be justified by public policy and those where it might not.

Good Reasons for Consenting to Harm

In a case decided before *Brown*, the Court of Appeal recognised that a victim could validly consent to harm involving actual bodily harm or worse where the harm occurred in the course of properly conducted games and sports, lawful chastisement and correction, reasonable surgical interference, and dangerous exhibitions, which would presumably cover the case of an incompetent knife-thrower at a circus who misjudges the throw and wounds his assistant.

The test of properly conducted sports encompasses boxing, because such a sport must be conducted within the Queensbury Rules, which provide that there must be no hitting below the waist, gloves must be used and there must be a referee. This is distinct from the old practice of prize-fighting, where the fight occurred without rules and where, as a matter of public policy, the consent of the participants was not sufficient to negate criminal liability. That boxing is a legitimate activity was confirmed in *Brown*. It appears therefore that there is a distinction between fighting without rules, where the participants' consent is no defence, and boxing, where the consent of the parties means that no crime has been committed.

The boundary between unacceptable and acceptable fighting is difficult to draw, particularly because it has been held that conduct characterised as 'horseplay' is acceptable. This was recognised in a case called *Jones*, which involved a fight in a playground during which one boy was thrown into the air and suffered a ruptured spleen when he fell to the ground. It was held that the victim's consent was a defence because 'boys would be boys and would always engage in rough and undisciplined horseplay'. This was applied in a later case called *Aitken*, which was decided not long before the House of Lords handed down judgment in *Brown*. This was a decision of the Courts Martial Appeal Court, which is the equivalent of the Court of Appeal (Criminal Division) but which hears appeals from disciplinary decisions involving the armed forces. The case concerned a group of drunken RAF officers who celebrated the end of their exams by pouring white spirit over their fire-resistant suits and setting light to them. One officer was doused with white spirit which, once set fire, caused 35 per cent burns to his body. Aitken was found to be not guilty of inflicting grievous bodily harm, because he assumed that the victim consented to the activity and, crucially, the victim's consent could be considered legitimate because the participants were engaged in rough and undisciplined horseplay. Bearing in mind that this case was decided not long before *Brown* there appears to be an inconsistency developing, especially given that the activities in *Brown* were carefully controlled whereas those in *Aitken* were not and so were much more dangerous. It is difficult to avoid the conclusion that the context of the activities in each case played some influence in determining whether or not the conduct was considered acceptable.

The law relating to one of the other recognised situations where consent can be considered valid has in fact changed. It has been recognised that parents can use force to chastise their children. Since this exception was recognised in *Brown* it appears that parents could use force to cause actual bodily harm and the child could still be deemed to have consented to the harm, so no crime would have been committed. The law has since changed. By section 58(1) of the Children Act 2004 the defendant has no defence of chastisement if the injury caused is at least actual bodily harm. It follows that chastisement of children now falls within the principle recognised in *Brown* and so chastisement is only a defence to a battery, where no significant injury is caused, and not to assault occasioning actual bodily harm, where the injury is more than merely transient or trifling.

Bad Reasons for Consenting to Harm

Following *Brown* it is clear that the consent of the victim to actual bodily harm or worse will be relevant only if the conduct can be justified by reference to public policy. We have seen that fighting without rules and satisfaction of the sadomasochistic libido by homosexuals do not satisfy this test. What else will not satisfy it? What if the sadomasochistic activity occurs within a heterosexual relationship, eg between husband and wife? Although the facts of *Brown* did not involve heterosexual people, does the *ratio* extend to them? It appears that the *ratio* in *Brown* is not confined to sadomasochistic activity amongst homosexuals and so all such activity would appear to be criminal, regardless of the sexuality of the participants. This is consistent with an earlier case called *Donovan* where a man caned a woman to give him sexual pleasure. It was unclear whether she had consented to this, but it was accepted that, if she had been consenting, this would have been no defence because he had caused her actual bodily harm.

A useful hypothetical example against which the application of the principle in *Brown* can be tested concerns a boyfriend and a girlfriend who are in love and the girlfriend asks her boyfriend to give her a love-bite, which he does. Assuming that the love-bite results in a bruise to the girl's neck which is painful to the touch, and so constitutes actual bodily harm, can her consent be regarded as legitimate within the *Brown* principle? It cannot be assumed that this is acceptable conduct; a positive reason needs to be identified for such conduct. If no such reason can be identified, then giving a loved one a love-bite would be a criminal offence. This is, presumably, absurd, and we will see later that the motive of the biter may be enough to make the conduct acceptable. Similarly, what about a defendant who pierces the victim's ear to enable her to wear an ear-ring. Is that a crime? It does constitute actual bodily harm, but can a good reason for the conduct be identified? What if other parts of the body are pierced? What if the defendant is a schoolfriend who uses a needle to pierce the victim's ear without first sterilising it? When, if ever, should such conduct be treated as criminal within the principle recognised in *Brown*? We are forced to engage with such issues following *Brown*.

THE DISSENTING JUDGES

When you are seeking to analyse and criticise the law it is always useful to consider the judgments of dissenting judges, even though their views do not represent the law, because they can provide important arguments for criticising the decision of the majority. Both of the dissenting Law Lords in *Brown*, Lords Mustill and Slynn, shared the revulsion of the majority as to the nature of the defendants' conduct and characterised it as immoral, but they considered that this was not a sufficient reason to convict the defendants. Lord Mustill in particular sought to identify the rationale for determining when the victim's consent cannot be considered to be legitimate by reference to earlier decisions, and he concluded that no rationale existed. Rather, he considered that these cases turned on the application of vague principles of public policy and value judgments. He, with Lord Slynn, sought to identify a workable principle for such cases. Both judges accepted that there reaches a point where the nature of the injuries caused are such that public policy should treat the victim's consent as invalid, but this should only occur where the harm involves serious injury. Where lesser harm is involved the consent of the victim should be sufficient to operate as a defence. Although the approach of the minority does not represent the state of English law, it is an approach which is arguably more principled and therefore easier to apply than that of the majority.

THEORY: AUTONOMY VERSUS WELFARE

The debate about whether the approach of the majority or the minority in *Brown* is to be preferred goes right to the heart of the criminal law since it turns on the question: what are we seeking to do when we punish? This raises some deep issues about the philosophy of law. We saw earlier that there is a tension in the criminal law between the autonomy of the individual on one side and the welfare of society on the other. This tension is illustrated best by the issues in *Brown*. An emphasis on autonomy would suggest that the defendants in *Brown* should have been acquitted, since the recognition of the autonomy principle means that the defendant should be free to do what he or she wants to do. If this involves causing harm to others then the defendant should be free to do that. This argument can be strengthened by reference to the autonomy of the victim so that, if the victim wants to be injured, then he or she should be allowed to consent to that. However, the welfare principle would appear to support the decision of the majority, on the basis that the conviction of the defendants was for the benefit of society. But where was this benefit? There was nothing to suggest that the conduct of the defendants was harmful to society since no member of the public, outside the group of sadomasochists, was in danger from this type of conduct. The welfare principle must, consequently, be interpreted in a somewhat different way so as to justify the conviction. This interpretation of welfare would encompass the morality of the defendants' conduct. This interpretation is consistent with the approach of a former member of the House of Lords, Lord Devlin, who wrote a book entitled *The Enforcement of Morals*. Lord Devlin argued that there was a need for the criminal law to exist to ensure that certain standards of morality are maintained. This approach focuses on the paternalism of criminalising this sort of conduct, namely that it is considered to be in the best interests of the defendants and society generally that sadists are convicted for causing harm. There is no doubt that Lord Devlin would have supported the approach of the majority in *Brown*.

Against the philosophical approach of Lord Devlin is the approach of other philosophers of law, especially HLA Hart and John Stuart Mill, who advocated, to varying degrees, that the criminal law should intrude only to ensure that people's interests are not adversely affected. This emphasis on adverse effects suggests that, if the victim consents to being hurt, the hurt is not adverse and so should not be criminalised. This approach clearly focuses on autonomy rather than welfare and would result in an acquittal in *Brown*. This begs the question as to whether any limit should be imposed as to the degree of harm to which the victim should be allowed to consent. Would the answer differ if the victim suffers from a rare psychiatric condition which makes him believe that one of his limbs is repulsive and needs to be amputated? What if the victim wants to die?

Brown is thus a decision which is founded on morality and the concept of paternalism. In other words, the state seeks to protect certain types of people from themselves where their conduct does not accord with what is regarded as acceptable and normal, whatever that means.

SUBSEQUENT EVENTS: MOTIVE AND RISK

Even though *Brown* is a case which suggests that the welfare principle prevails over that of individual autonomy, events subsequent to *Brown* indicate that there is a move away from this approach. This section will examine the judicial developments following *Brown*. This illustrates an important feature of the study of law, namely that it is not sufficient to focus on the principles derived from leading cases; it is also necessary to examine what has happened to those principles subsequently. It may be found that these subsequent developments have moved the law on dramatically.

One of the significant decisions following *Brown* was *Wilson*, in the Court of Appeal. Although this was a decision of a lower court, which could not overrule a decision of the House of Lords, it is possible for the Court of Appeal to interpret the principles derived from a decision of the House of Lords and apply them in such a way that we are better able to understand the rationale of those principles. That is exactly what happened in *Wilson*, which concerns a moving love story involving an elderly couple. Mr and Mrs Wilson wanted to show their love for each other by bodily adornment. After discussing the matter they agreed that Mr Wilson would brand his initials on his wife's buttocks: A (standing for Alan) on one and W (standing for Wilson) on the other. They agreed that Mr Wilson would use a heated knife to do this. The wife never complained about this conduct. Indeed, she wanted it. She went to her doctor for a medical examination; he saw the scarring and complained to the police. Mr Wilson was prosecuted for assault occasioning actual bodily harm and was convicted. He appealed to the Court of Appeal and his conviction was quashed. The decision of the House of Lords in *Brown* was distinguished for a number of reasons, including that the wife was a willing participant, that the branding was analogous to tattooing which is acceptable, and that this conduct was done in the privacy of the matrimonial home, in which it was not for the courts or the law to interfere, so that there was no public interest in prosecuting the husband for this conduct. However, there was one reason which appears to be the most significant, especially as a way of distinguishing the facts of *Brown* from those in *Wilson*. This was the motive behind the activity. In *Brown* the motive was to get pleasure from pain and this was not considered to be an acceptable reason. However, in *Wilson* the wife got no pleasure from the experience of branding; it was the consequence of the branding which she wanted. Consequently, the motive was a sign of their affection for each other. The motive was love rather than pain and love is consequently a perfectly acceptable motive for causing injury to another.

This emphasis on motive is significant. If we return to the example of a boyfriend giving his girlfriend a love-bite, although there may well be pleasure in the activity it is not pleasure which derives from pain, but is pleasure which derives from love. Consequently, it appears that it is not a crime to give somebody a love-bite.

A further example of the retreat from *Brown* is to be seen in a series of cases involving the transmission of HIV. In the first of these cases, *Dica*, the defendant, who had AIDS, had unprotected sex with two women in the course of which he transmitted HIV to them. The defendant was charged with maliciously inflicting grievous bodily harm contrary to section 20 of the Offences Against the Person Act 1861. It was held that the disease constituted grievous bodily harm and that the defendant had inflicted this on the victims. He was also aware that he had the disease and that he might transmit it to the victims in the course of having unprotected sex. The crucial issue, however, concerned whether the defendant's conduct was unlawful, bearing in mind that the women had consented to have sex with him. Did it follow that the victims had consented to the disease? For, if they had consented, the defendant could not be found guilty of the offence. One argument which was adopted was that, even if the victims had consented to the disease, this was not a legitimate consent within the *Brown* principle, since there was no social utility in consenting to such a disease. The Court of Appeal in *Dica* rejected this argument by distinguishing *Brown* again. The principle in *Brown* was considered to be relevant only where the harm had been deliberately inflicted and not where, as may have been the case in *Dica*, the victims had consented to the risk of the harm being inflicted. Consequently, in any case where the victim consents to the risk of harm rather than wanting the harm, the victim's consent is legitimate and the defendant would not be guilty. So, in *Dica*, if the victims had contemplated the possibility that the defendant might have a sexually transmitted disease and were prepared to take that risk by having unprotected sex, the consent to the risk would mean that the defendant would not be guilty. This raises a difficult question of policy as to whether the victim in such a case should be required to bear the burden of taking the risk of the defendant having unprotected sex with him or her. Dica was subsequently retried and was found guilty, presumably because he had falsely told the victims that he did not have the disease and so they did not in fact consent to the risk of the disease. A subsequent case, *Konzani*, has placed the burden of risk-taking squarely on the defendant by holding that the victim's consent to the risk of the disease must be a fully informed consent. So, if the defendant knew or suspected that he had the disease but did not reveal this knowledge or suspicion to the victim, that victim's consent to the risk of the disease would not be considered to be fully informed and would not therefore be relevant.

This review of the decisions following *Brown* indicates that the law has developed dramatically. Today the victim can legitimately consent to injury where the motive for the injury is regarded as acceptable or where the victim is consenting to the *risk* of injury. It is only where the defendant wants the injury to be inflicted for no acceptable motive that the victim's consent will not be considered relevant.

HUMAN RIGHTS

There is one further dimension to the decision in *Brown*, involving the application of the European Convention on Human Rights. Following the decision of the House of Lords, the defendants appealed to the European Court of Human Rights. This was on the basis that the conviction of the defendants interfered with their fundamental human rights under the European Convention. In particular, the defendants relied on Article 8, which recognises the right to respect for private and family life. They argued that this encompassed a right to express their sexuality as they wished, even if this involved sadomasochism. Article 8 does indeed protect the right to expression of sexuality, but the European Court confirmed that the conviction of the defendants by the English courts did not infringe the European Convention. This was because states which are parties to the Convention are allowed to derogate from the right under Article 8 where it is 'necessary in a democratic society' for the protection of health and morals. So, even the European Court of Human Rights adopted a paternalistic approach in preference to one which respected the autonomy of the individuals to express their sexuality as they wished.

LAW REFORM

Having reviewed the decision of the House of Lords in *Brown*, its application and its implications, we should now consider whether that decision itself is justifiable. This requires students of the law to engage critically with the decision and consider whether reform of the law is necessary. You might consider that the decision of the majority in *Brown* is correct and that there is no need to reform the law. However, if you conclude that the decision is unsatisfactory, you need to consider how the law should be reformed and whether this should be left to the judiciary or should be a matter for Parliament.

The question of reforming the law in this field has been considered by the Law Commission. As we saw in chapter 1, the Law Commission was established in 1965 to review the law in certain areas and, if the law is found wanting, make recommendations for reform to the Government. The Law Commission prepares reports for consultation and, having reviewed the responses, prepares a final report. The Law Commission produced a consultation paper in 1995, soon after the decision in *Brown*, on the relevance of the victim's consent where injury has been caused. Its preliminary conclusion was that the victim's consent to personal injury should be regarded as valid save where the injury is seriously disabling or involves death, and even then the victim should be allowed to consent to the risk of injury or death where it is for a legitimate reason such as medical treatment. Unfortunately, the Law Commission did not proceed with this project to a final report to be presented to Parliament.

The Law Commission's preliminary proposals would seem to be a satisfactory compromise between the need to respect the autonomy of the individual defendant and the victim and the need to protect those parties. Where the injury is seriously disabling or worse it should be appropriate for the state to intervene through the mechanism of the criminal law to protect defendants and victims from themselves, for in an extreme case, such as that of Armin Meiwes, a German national, who advertised on the internet for a willing victim to come forward to be killed and eaten, the criminal law should make clear that such conduct is unacceptable in a civilised society. In that case a victim did come forward and allowed himself to be killed and eaten and the German court in May 2006 held that Meiwes was guilty of murder, regardless of the victim's consent. Of course, issues of consent to one's own death raise big and difficult questions concerning euthanasia, suicide and assisting and encouraging suicide. These issues essentially concern the legitimacy of consent and when engaging with them the law student needs to take account not only of legal rules but also moral and ethical considerations.

CONCLUSIONS

Although *Brown* raises some issues of quite technical law, ultimately the analysis of this case raises a very simple question, namely whether it is appropriate to convict a defendant of a serious crime involving personal injury where the victim consented to that injury. The case can be analysed on a variety of different levels. First, there is the basic analysis of what the case decided and the identification of the arguments for and against the decision. Secondly, the practical implications of the decision need to be considered by reference to hypothetical examples and subsequent decisions. Thirdly, the decision needs to be considered critically by considering whether a workable principle can be identified and whether that principle is acceptable with reference to theoretical and social policy considerations. Ultimately, you need to ask, 'If I were one of the justices sitting in the Supreme Court how would I decide the appeal in *Brown*?'

Cases

Aitken [1992] 1 WLR 1006
Attorney-General's Reference (No 6 of 1980) [1981] 2 All ER 1057
Barnes [2004] EWCA Crim 3246; [2005] 1 WLR 910
Brown [1992] QB 491 (Court of Appeal); [1994] 1 AC 212 (House of
    Lords)
Coney (1882) 8 QBD 534

Dica [2004] EWCA Crim 1103; [2004] QB 1257
Donovan [1934] 2 KB 498
Emmett (1999) *The Times*, 15 October
Laskey, Jaggard and Brown v UK (1997) 24 EHRR 39
Jones (1986) 83 Cr App R 375
Konzani [2005] EWCA Crim 706
Wilson [1996] 2 Cr App R 241

Further reading

Ashworth, *Principles of Criminal Law*, 6th edn (Oxford, Oxford University Press, 2009) 307–15

Devlin, *The Enforcement of Morals* (Oxford, Oxford University Press, 1965)

Hart, *Law, Liberty and Morality* (Oxford, Oxford University Press 1963)

Law Commission Consultation Paper No 139 (1995) *Consent in the Criminal Law*

Simester and Sullivan's *Criminal Law: Theory and Doctrine*, 4th edn (Oxford, Hart Publishing, 2010) 432–46, 747–66

3

Law of Contract

Janet O'Sullivan

INTRODUCTION

I wonder how many contracts you have made today, before sitting down to read this chapter. Perhaps you bought a sandwich from the supermarket, travelled on public transport, opened a bank account or sold an unwanted gift on an internet auction site? You may even have bought this book today. Meanwhile, all over the world, other people are booking tickets and holidays, commissioning building work, leasing flats or signing employment contracts for new jobs, while small businesses and giant corporations are borrowing money and employing staff, acquiring premises and equipment, even taking-over other companies. The law of contract is at the heart of all these situations, the same basic principles whether it is a simple, oral contract to purchase a book or a complex financing transaction spelt out in hundreds of pages of detailed terms and conditions. (It surprises some people to discover that, with notable exceptions, most contracts can be made orally and are no less valid for not being written down.) Admittedly, you may not notice any sort of contract when you buy a book—you simply hand over your money and the shopkeeper hands over the book—but you do in fact make an invisible contract, one which, for example, obliges the shopkeeper to give you your money back if all the pages fall out of the book the first time you open it.

To a lawyer (at least one with a traditional outlook), a contract is typically an agreement between two (or sometimes more) parties who make *binding promises* to each other, each party's promise given in exchange for the other's. In this context, the adjective *binding* means that if the promise is not honoured, the law becomes involved and provides some redress for the other party (as opposed, for example, to the sorts of promises parents make to children about treats in return for good behaviour). Many simple contracts are like the book-purchase example, where the seller and the buyer don't actually spell out any promises to each other, because the goods and the money are handed over simultaneously (although the seller, whether he likes it or not, is *treated* as having made certain promises about the quality of what he is selling, because these are implied into the contract by a statute called the Sale of Goods Act). But in virtually all other sorts of contract, there is a *gap* in time between the making of the contract and its ultimate performance, ie the date when everything is finally done as the contract requires. So the parties promise each other that they will do something in the future. For example imagine you pre-ordered this book on the internet two months before its publication date. The moment you clicked the 'I agree' button, the internet seller promised to deliver the book, and you in turn promised to pay for it, even though both obligations would not actually be performed for two further months.

SOME CRUCIAL IDEAS ABOUT CONTRACTUAL REMEDIES

The crucial point is that these promises (to deliver, to pay the price) are regarded as legally 'binding' from the moment the contract is made, not merely at the later date when performance is due. In other words, if the seller changes his mind and decides not to send you the book when it is published, you have a legal right against him and not merely a right to complain, a right to a *remedy* if your complaint doesn't persuade him to change his mind, enforceable in the civil courts. In fact in English law, the courts rarely actually *compel* a contract-breaker like this seller to honour his contract and send you the book, but that is not usually a problem (after all, you have not paid anything yet). Imagine that the seller was offering the book for a bargain price of £5 to anyone who pre-ordered it, instead of the usual selling price of £9.99. When he failed to deliver it to you, you had to obtain the book from your local book shop for £9.99, so the seller's *breach of contract* meant that you spent £4.99 more than you would have done if he had honoured his promise. Thus you would be entitled to *damages* of £4.99 from the seller. Identical rules apply even if the figures involved are multiplied by millions and the transaction a complex, commercial one.

All this explains why people and companies bother to make contracts at all. Imagine X is a soft drink manufacturer and Y is a commercial grower of tomatoes. X wishes to ensure a supply of tomatoes to make tomato juice, sales of which peak at Christmas time. So X makes a contract with Y in June, to purchase from Y 10,000 kilos of tomatoes to be delivered in October at an agreed price per kilo, the price to be paid on delivery of the tomatoes. Both parties, being rational, make the contract for a good reason—X to feel secure about a supply of tomatoes in October at a price it is happy with, Y because it wants to make a profit and is confident that the cost of growing and harvesting the tomatoes will be less than the price. The contract allows both forward planning and risk allocation, *because* the law treats it as valid and binding immediately, even before any part of the contract has been performed or any sums spent preparing to perform it. Indeed commerce is built on the understanding that contracts create enforceable obligations and corresponding expectations *immediately*, not at some unidentifiable later date when the other party first acts or incurs expenditure in reliance.

Commerce also relies on the fact that Y's promise to deliver the tomatoes is a very *strict* concept, not merely a promise to take reasonable care to deliver them or only to deliver them if has a plentiful supply. You will recall from chapter 1 that defendants are generally only liable in tort where they are at fault in some way: in contrast, liability for breach of contract does not depend on *fault.* Put another way, you can be in breach of contract merely because circumstances beyond your control prevented you from doing what you promised. So in our tomato example, the law would not allow Y to ignore its promise or to increase the contract price merely because, for example, there is an unexpected drought, tomato yields are badly affected and their market price soars accordingly. This may seem 'hard' on Y, since it is not Y's *fault* in a moral sense that it cannot honour the contract, but think back to the reasons why the parties wanted to make a contract in the first place. Y took the risk that it could perform for less than the contract price, hoping to make a profit (which it would have done if the market price had moved down instead of up). X made the contract to allow for forward planning, for the security of not having to worry about the risk of the market price moving up because of problems like a poor harvest (and was prepared to take the risk of the market price moving down to achieve this security). So it is crucial that the law holds the parties to their contract in these unexpected conditions, 'holds' not in the sense of requiring Y to deliver the tomatoes, but to pay *damages* to X instead, representing the difference between the contract price and the October market price.

At this point it is worth mentioning another important aspect of a remedy for damages, the requirement of *mitigation*, that the claimant must mitigate his or her loss. This means that claimants must act reasonably to keep their losses to a minimum; more accurately claimants cannot claim damages for an amount in excess of what they would have lost if they had acted reasonably. So in our tomato example, X will only be entitled to the difference between the contract price and the *market* price, not between the contract price and the *highest* price of tomatoes on the date of delivery. Likewise a tort claimant who is injured by the defendant's negligent driving may claim damages if she suffers a broken arm, but if she deliberately and unreasonably refrains from seeking medical help and for this reason the arm develops gangrene, she cannot claim damages to compensate her for the gangrene—she has failed to mitigate her loss.

Now some misguided law students regard the law about contractual remedies as if it is an unimportant add-on to the legal rules about contracts, a discrete module that can safely be ignored. They think of other areas as the 'real' parts of the law of contract. It is true that the law of contract is concerned with much more than just remedies. To name just a few important issues, the law of contract determines whether a binding contract has been formed at all, what exactly the terms of the contract are and what those terms mean, whether an apparent contract is invalidated by something improper that one of the parties did (maybe he bullied the other party or made a false statement about the contractual subject matter), what happens where one or both of the parties were contracting under a mistake, whether one of the contractual promises has been breached and, if so, what effect does this have on the rest of the contract. Nonetheless, those misguided students are really missing the point. From what we have seen already, it is clear that the *remedy* for breach of contract is a crucial part of the legal regime supporting contracts—indeed, it is meaningless to envisage contractual *rights* without a legally enforceable remedy for breach of contract, meaningless to learn about the formation of contracts without understanding the law's response when a contractual obligation is breached.

For this reason, the rest of this chapter is concerned with a fascinating case called *Ruxley Electronics and Constructions Ltd v Forsyth*, which is about the usual remedy for breach of contract, namely an award of damages. As you will see, it started life as a small run-of-the-mill claim in the County Court about some domestic building work, but ended up (because of a series of appeals brought by one party, then the other) being resolved by the highest court in the land, the House of Lords, whose decision is now a very important precedent shaping the law of contract for the future. This is a really satisfying feature of English law—it is not necessarily the big money cases that raise the important issues of legal principle.

THE CASE

The Pool Was Too Shallow

Stephen Forsyth commissioned Ruxley Electronics, a small company run by a builder, to build a swimming pool in the garden of his house in Kent. The contract price for the pool and its enclosure, some of which was to be paid during the construction and the rest on completion of the work, totalled just over £70,000 (this simplifies the facts slightly, but not materially). The contract originally specified that the pool was to have a maximum depth of 6 feet 6 inches, but the depth specification was increased some time later, at Forsyth's request, to 7 feet 6 inches, apparently because he was a tall man and wished to feel confident that he would not hit his head when diving.

When the work was completed, Forsyth discovered that the pool had a maximum depth of only 6 feet 9 inches and that it was only 6 feet deep at the crucial entry point for dives, some distance from the end of the pool. So when he received his final bill for the remainder of the contract price (approximately £39,000), he pointed to this breach of the contractual specification and alleged a number of other defects in the work, and refused to pay. Ruxley sued him for its money (plus interest) and Forsyth *counterclaimed* for damages. This means that Forsyth didn't just defend himself against Ruxley's action for the balance of the price; he also went 'on the attack' and claimed damages from Ruxley. It also means that it is easy to get confused when reading reports of the case, because Forsyth is officially the *defendant,* even though most of the discussion concerns his counterclaim for damages and it is of course usually a *claimant* who claims damages.

Notice that, although Ruxley and Forsyth were each claiming *money* from the other, the claim and the counterclaim were for fundamentally different remedies. Ruxley's claim was for the sum of money agreed by the parties as the contract price for building the pool. In this sort of claim, sometimes also called a *debt* action, the role of the court is very simple, merely deciding whether the sum claimed is in fact due. In contrast, Forsyth's counterclaim was for *damages* for breach of contract, where the court has a further job to do once it has decided that there has been a breach of contract: it must also *calculate* those damages, work out how to convert 'loss' into 'money'. As we will see, this can be a highly complex, controversial process.

The judge at the Central London County Court examined all the evidence, listened to the witnesses and decided that there *was* a breach of the depth specification, but that the pool as constructed was nonetheless perfectly safe to dive into. He also decided, however, that Forsyth had not proved any of the other defects in the pool that he was alleging. What did these findings mean for both the claim and the counterclaim?

The straightforward part was that Ruxley's claim for the balance of its contract price succeeded. The law says that, in general, one party cannot resist paying the price unless there was a 'substantial failure' to perform the relevant contractual obligation by the other party (or, put the other way round, you must pay the price if the work was substantially performed). There are some exceptions to this rule: certain, unusual contractual obligations are said to be 'entire', in other words they must be performed entirely before the other party is obliged to pay anything at all. A good example might be a contract to paint a portrait—the painter cannot deliver a 90 per cent completed painting, lacking only ears, and demand payment of 90 per cent (or indeed any part) of his price. But this exception did not apply to our swimming pool contract. Ruxley's breach of the depth specification was not a 'substantial failure' and Forsyth could not withhold the balance of the price.

Contractual Damages—A Brief Discussion

What about Forsyth's counterclaim for damages to *compensate* him for the fact that the pool was shallower than Ruxley had promised in the contract? This is where we need to step away from the swimming pool for a moment and introduce some basic principles about legal compensation. The rationale for any award of damages is to compensate the innocent party for what he or she has lost, but the notion of 'loss' does not mean exactly the same thing in all branches of the law. If you are the victim of a *tort* (eg you are run over and injured by a negligent driver), you will be entitled to damages *to put you into the position you were in before the tort occurred.* Of course, money can not literally repair broken bones, but it can compensate you for your lost wages, pain and suffering,

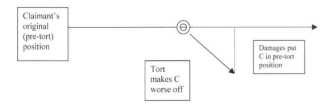

Figure 3.1 Damages in tort

'lost amenity' in the sense of being able to enjoy your work and leisure activities, as well as paying for any expenditure you incurred as a result of the tort. The focus in tort is backward looking, to restore you to the pre-tort position, and can be represented diagrammatically as shown in figure 3.1

In contrast, the aim of damages for breach of contract is subtly but significantly different. It was explained in an early Victorian case called *Robinson v Harman* as follows:

> The rule of common law is that where a party sustains a loss by reason of a breach of contract, he is, so far as money can do it, to be placed in the same situation, with respect to damages, *as if the contract had been performed.*

So this is forward looking: what would your position be if the other party had performed, not breached, the contract? Sometimes a breach of contract actually causes you loss in the tort sense, but very often the only adverse effect is on your expected profit. The significance of contractual damages is that they are paid even if you are not actually worse off than you were before you made the contract, but merely if you are not *as much better off* as you would have been if the contract had been performed (rather than breached). As in our earlier examples about the book ordered from the internet at a bargain price and the tomato grower that must pay its customer the difference between the contract price and the (higher) market price. Of course, sometimes a breach of contract actually leaves you worse off, instead of making your expected profit, and you can claim the difference. (See figure 3.2.)

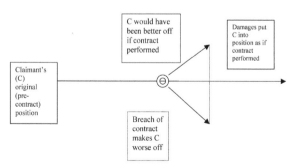

Figure 3.2 Damages in contract

This contractual notion of damages is said to be compensating the fact that you didn't get the performance you were entitled to expect from the other party, and so is commonly called the *expectation measure* of damages. All this is relatively easy in theory, but how do the courts actually put a *value* on this expectation measure?

How to Value the Contractual Expectation

Traditionally there have been two different ways of doing this valuation exercise. The most obvious way, which works perfectly well when dealing with contracts for the sale of marketable commodities like our book and tomatoes examples, is to award the *difference in value between* (i) what, if anything, the claimant actually received and (ii) what the claimant would have received had the contract been performed. Notice that the more profitable the contract would have been, the greater the amount of damages awarded to the claimant; in contrast where the contract price is the *same* as the market price, the difference in value and thus the damages will generally be nil. So going back to our internet book example, imagine that the internet seller was not offering the book for sale at a bargain price, but only at its market price of £9.99: if the seller fails to deliver the book to you, you can simply buy it at the same price elsewhere, so your damages (assuming you have not yet paid for the book) are nil.

Sometimes, however, the difference in value approach is not appropriate, generally in the sort of case where the claimant cannot simply go to market and purchase substitute performance. For example, in *Radford v De Froberville*, Mr Radford owned a very large house in Holland Park, London, which was divided into flats let to tenants and which had a big garden (used by the tenants). He sold *part* of the garden to the defendant, Mrs De Froberville, who was planning to redevelop the plot by building a new house on it. One of the contractual terms of the sale was that she promised to build a brick boundary wall between her plot and the rest of the garden, of a thickness and height specified in the contract. But in breach of contract she did not build the wall or any other sort of boundary (having failed to redevelop the plot at all). What was the appropriate measure of damages for Mr Radford? The difference in value between his property with the boundary wall and without it was negligible, but that wasn't really the point. He *wanted* the wall and so had obtained from Mrs De Froberville a promise to build it, but he was now going to have to spend his own money if he wanted a wall. The judge explained why the difference in value measure would be inappropriate, giving an example of:

> a man with a garden by the sea or a river, subject to inundation on rare occasions by freak floods. He sells a part of his garden as part of the sale and stipulates that the purchaser shall erect a flood wall on the property purchased to protect both properties. If the purchaser fails to build the wall and the court is satisfied that the plaintiff intends to build it on his own land what the defendant has failed to build on his, why should he be limited to the amount by which his land is diminished in value as a saleable asset by the possibility of an occasional flood? He is interested in cultivating his garden, not selling his property.

In this sort of case, the courts recognise that the difference in value measure is inadequate to value the claimant's lost expectation, so use instead another approach, namely the cost of actually putting right the breach of contract. This second approach is generally known as the '*cost of cure*'.

Often the cost of cure and the difference in value produce identical results (eg when you can 'cure' the breach by purchasing substitute performance in the market place), but sometimes they produce dramatically different figures. This brings us back to Mr Forsyth's shallow pool, which was a striking example of the two conventional methods of assessing damages producing dramatically different figures and, more to the point, *neither* of which seemed quite right.

Back to the Poolside

The cost of cure was a staggering £21,650, since the only practical way of increasing the depth of the pool to conform to the specification would be to remove the existing pool, excavate further and construct a new pool. On the other hand, the judge's somewhat surprising conclusion was that there was *no* difference in market value between the pool as built and the pool as it should have been built (indeed it is somewhat artificial to think of built-in swimming pools as having a 'market value' at all, separate from the property in which they are constructed, so it is by no means clear precisely what the judge meant by this finding, but for the purpose of this chapter we will put these factual doubts to one side and continue).

Why is it that neither of the two conventional measures seems to fit the facts of *Ruxley*? The cost of cure 'feels' too large, because it ignores the fact that Forsyth obtained a perfectly serviceable, well-constructed pool, entirely suitable for swimming, paddling and lounging next to, but merely shallower than the depth specified. It would over-compensate him to award the full cost of cure, particularly as Forsyth was highly unlikely to use the money to rebuild the pool. On the other hand, the difference in value (nil) 'feels' inadequate: after all, Forsyth did not get what he paid for, and it is irrelevant that what he paid for was no more valuable than what he got. After all, he did not make the contract to enhance the value of his house. In the words of Lord Mustill:

> It is a common feature of small building works performed on residential property that the cost of the work is not fully reflected by an increase in the market value of the house, and that comparatively minor deviations from specification or sound workmanship may have no direct financial effect at all. Yet the householder must surely be entitled to say that he chose to obtain from the builder a promise to produce a particular result because he wanted to make his house more comfortable, more convenient and more conformable to his own particular tastes; not because he had in mind that the work might increase the amount which he would receive if, contrary to expectation, he thought it expedient in the future to exchange his home for cash. To say that in order to escape unscathed the builder has only to show that to the mind of the average onlooker, or the average potential buyer, the results which he has produced seem just as good as those which he had promised would make a part of the promise illusory and unbalance the bargain.

The reason for the law's traditional emphasis on market value when measuring expectation damages for breach of contract is because of the historical background to the modern law of contract. The classical rules of the law of contract were first understood and conceptualised as such in the nineteenth century, in a wholly *commercial* context. To a Victorian lawyer, the ethos of the law was to interfere as little as possible in the parties' freedom of contract, while the paradigm contractual situation involved two gentlemen (note the gender!) of roughly equal bargaining-strength negotiating and then making a contract to sell a carriage or a business. This is self-evidently not the only contractual model in the twenty-first century, in particular because of the growth of contractual relationships between consumers and big businesses. Today, almost all such contracts are made on non-negotiable printed forms, often virtually identical across the particular market sector; Parliament has, in turn, intervened with statutory controls on certain sorts of undesirable, one-sided contractual terms in consumer contracts.

In the area of contractual remedies, the traditional assumption that the parties were contracting merely for profit-making, commercial motives (as in our tomatoes example) does not fit comfortably in the context of consumer contracts, where it is perfectly rational to be motivated for reasons other than a desire for profit. The recognition of this in the field of building contracts led to the adoption of the 'cost of cure' measure in the first place, but *Ruxley* forced the law to confront whether more flexibility might be needed than just the two familiar approaches.

The County Court's Judge's Decision and the 'Middle Ground' Award

The County Court judge refused to award the cost of cure. He said:

> Not only am I not satisfied that Mr Forsyth intends to build a new pool at a cost of £21,560, but in addition it seems to me that this cost would be wholly disproportionate to the disadvantage of having a pool whose maximum depth is 6 ft as opposed to 7 ft 6 in. In those circumstances I find that it would be unreasonable for Mr Forsyth to carry out this work at such a cost.

However, the judge did award Forsyth a small sum in damages (£2,500) as a sort of *middle-ground* award, being neither the difference in value nor the cost of cure. This, the judge said, was to reflect his *lack of amenity* in not having a pool of the correct depth, saying that it is:

> a perfectly reasonable requirement to wish to make deeper dives or to have a greater depth of water and one can sympathise with any pool owner who

makes a legitimate request for a specified depth of water and does not get the depth he contracted for. There is, accordingly, a lack of amenity brought about by the shortfall in the depth of water, but this lack of amenity is not easy to quantify.

The judge did not analyse further the theoretical basis of this lost amenity award, but that is unsurprising. After all, it is a commonplace, everyday matter for County Court judges to award damages for lost amenity to *tort* claimants who have suffered personal injury, reflecting their reduced ability to enjoy life as much as before the injury. As a way of valuing expectation damages for breach of contract, however, an approach based on 'lack of amenity' was new and controversial.

On Appeal to the Court of Appeal

In any event, Forsyth was unhappy with the result of the County Court decision. You will remember that Ruxley's claim for the balance of the purchase price succeeded, so Forsyth actually had to pay £39,000 plus interest, less the £2,500 damages for his counterclaim. He there-fore appealed to the Court of Appeal, arguing that the judge should have awarded him the full cost of cure on his counterclaim. This time, his argument was successful. The Court of Appeal felt considerable sympa-thy for Forsyth, presenting him as the long-suffering, innocent victim of cowboy builders and stressing that he wanted a deeper pool because he was tall and feared diving in shallow water. With this view of the merits of the case, it is perhaps unsurprising that the Court of Appeal decided (though only by a majority of 2:1) that his damages should be the full £21,650 cost of cure (Dillon LJ agreed with the County Court judge, but his was a minority view). Staughton LJ said:

> In the present case Mr Forsyth has without question suffered a loss; he has a swimming pool which is less well suited to diving than the one he contracted for. What money will place him 'in the same situation . . . as if the contract had been performed?' The answer, on the facts of this case, is the cost of replacing the pool. Otherwise, a builder of swimming pools need never per-form his contract. He can always argue that 5 ft in depth is enough for diving, even if the purchaser has stipulated for 6, 7 or 8 ft, and pay no damages.

The reasonableness or unreasonableness of rebuilding the pool, and Forsyth's intentions in that regard, were not regarded by the majority of the Court of Appeal as relevant. As Mann LJ put it:

> There can be instances where the cost of rectifying a failed project is not reasonable, as, for example, where no personal preference is served or where there is no preference and the value of the estate is undiminished. In my judgment this is not such a case. The bargain was for a personal preference.

On Appeal to the House of Lords

With the score at one-all, Ruxley wanted to appeal to the House of Lords, then the highest court in the land. It is worth noting that a civil litigant did not have an automatic right to appeal to the House of Lords if he or she disagreed with the Court of Appeal's decision, and the same applies now to the Supreme Court. The litigant must obtain permission to do so, known as *leave to appeal*. Sometimes this is granted by the Court of Appeal itself, but normally the Court of Appeal refuses leave to appeal and the litigant must apply to the Supreme Court itself for permission, by filing an application for permission to appeal. The Court decides whether to allow or refuse an application, depending on whether the case involves a point of law of general public importance that ought to be considered by the Supreme Court. In our swimming pool case, the Court of Appeal refused leave (the judges naturally thought their decision was correct and should not be challenged further!), but Ruxley successfully petitioned the House of Lords for leave to appeal. This small County Court dispute had, by this stage, generated a point of law of considerable public importance and battle lines were drawn.

The appeal to the House of Lords, like many final, decisive battles in long military campaigns, was very much a *tactical* contest. It is crucial to appreciate that, in civil litigation, the loser generally pays the winner's legal costs as well as his or her own, so if Ruxley won this appeal, Forsyth would be responsible for its costs as well as his own. Bearing in mind that the dispute had already lasted seven years since Forsyth first declined to pay the final invoice for the pool, those costs were potentially astronomical. The other important tactical point was that Ruxley had always been happy with the County Court judge's middle-ground award of £2,500 and were only appealing against the Court of Appeal's decision to award the full cost of cure (concentrating only on why the cost of cure was inappropriate). More significantly, Ruxley had offered to *settle* the case on this basis (ie to abandon the appeal and 'call it a draw' if Forsyth would accept £2,500), but Forsyth consistently refused this offer. From a costs point of view, this stubborn stance put Forsyth in a dilemma when it came to his *arguments* in the appeal, because the rules of civil procedure say that if a litigant refuses an offer to settle a case but then is *not* awarded *any more* than the other side were offering, he or she is treated as having 'lost' and must pay the other side's costs. So Forsyth was forced to argue, somewhat counterintuitively, that the reason the House of Lords should stick with the cost of cure was because their *only* other alternative was to award him the (plainly inadequate) difference in value measure, namely nil. Only if that argument succeeded would he get his costs paid by Ruxley.

All this meant that, bizarrely, for tactical reasons *neither side* offered any argument or analysis whatsoever about the theoretical basis or practical implications of the loss of amenity 'middle-ground' award, even though this was central to the 'point of law of general public importance' which the appeal was meant to consider, namely the appropriate way of valuing Forsyth's lost expectation.

The House of Lords evidently viewed the merits of the case very differently from the Court of Appeal, presenting Forsyth as a pedantic, demanding client, trying to find technical breaches of contract to avoid paying for good work carried out by honest contractors. For example it was revealed in the House of Lords appeal that Ruxley had already agreed to reduce Forsyth's bill because of unfounded allegations of defects and (more damning still) that Forsyth first raised the question of the depth of the pool three days after the commencement of the trial (amending his pleaded case accordingly), many years after the completion of the work!

Viewing the case in this light, it is not surprising that the House of Lords unanimously decided that the Court of Appeal had been wrong to award Forsyth the full cost of cure *and* (undeterred by the lack of submissions on the point from either side) that the *middle-ground award* for *loss of amenity* favoured by the County Court judge had indeed been a perfectly proper way to value that elusive notion of Forsyth's lost expectation from the breach of contract. As Lord Mustill said, once the possibility of a middle-ground award for loss of amenity is recognised,

> the puzzling and paradoxical feature of this case, that it seems to involve a contest of absurdities, simply falls away. There is no need to remedy the injustice of awarding too little by unjustly awarding far too much.

So Forsyth's tactic failed and he was left paying his own legal costs as well as all of Ruxley's.

THE HOUSE OF LORDS DECISION IN MORE DETAIL

Let us look in more detail at the House of Lords decision. First, why was the cost of cure refused? The House (unlike the Court of Appeal) stressed that the cost of cure should not be awarded where it would be *unreasonable* for a claimant to insist on reinstatement, 'as where, for example, the expense of the work involved would be out of all proportion to the benefit to be obtained'. Their Lordships cited an old American case as an extreme example of this principle in operation, called *Jacob & Youngs v Kent.* This involved a contract for the construction of a new house, in which the owner had insisted in the contractual specification that the builder should install plumbing using pipes of 'Reading manufacture', but the builder had mistakenly installed practically identical pipes made by a different manufacturer. The owner's counter-claim for damages reflecting the cost of replacing the pipework was rejected: the famous American judge Cardozo J expressed the view that a claimant 'is entitled to the money which will permit him to complete, unless the cost of completion is grossly and unfairly out of proportion to the good to be attained'. In the same way, their Lordships held that it would be grossly unreasonable and disproportionate to incur the cost of demolishing the perfectly adequate existing pool just to build a new and deeper one, so Forsyth's loss should not be *valued* at the cost of reinstatement.

In addition the House relied on the County Court judge's refusal to believe Forsyth's evidence that he intended to rebuild the pool as another factor indicating the unreasonableness of the cost of cure. Lord Lloyd said 'if, as the judge found, Mr Forsyth had no intention of rebuilding the pool, he has lost nothing except the difference in value, if any'. For tactical reasons, Forsyth was now willing to give the House an *undertaking* to rebuild the pool if they let him keep his cost of cure damages, but even this did not make any difference: it could not make the unreasonable reasonable and would not 'be allowed to create a loss, which does not exist'.

But if a cost of cure award of £21,650 was 'wholly disproportionate' to the true value of Forsyth's lost expectation, the House went on to explain why the difference in value measure (nil) was *also* inappropriate on the facts. Remember this measure looks at the difference between (i) the market value of the pool as constructed and (ii) its market value if it had been built to the correct specification.

The House of Lords' reasoning was very simple: it is for the particular individual making the contract, not the notional average punters who create the market value, 'to judge what performance he required in exchange for the price. The court should honour that choice'. It ought to be irrelevant that the average person would not have been bothered by the shallower pool, because Forsyth had contracted for a pool of a particular depth in the contract to satisfy *his own* preferences. Lord Mustill pointed out that, for example, contracts to install features such as

> lurid bathroom tiles, or a grotesque folly . . . may be so discordant with general taste that in purely economic terms the builder may be said to do the employer a favour by failing to install them. But this is too narrow and materialistic a view of the transaction. Neither the contractor nor the court has the right to substitute for the employer's individual expectation of performance a criterion derived from what ordinary people would regard as sensible. As my Lords have shown, the test of reasonableness plays a central part in determining the basis of recovery, and will indeed be decisive in a case such as the present when the cost of reinstatement would be wholly disproportionate to the non-monetary loss suffered by the employer. But it would be equally unreasonable to deny all recovery for such a loss.

So, having rejected both the cost of cure and the difference in value measures, their Lordships gratefully looked back to and adopted the County Court judge's middle-ground award for *loss of amenity*. Only two members of the House made any attempt to explain the theoretical basis of the award.

Lord Mustill viewed it as reflecting the *consumer surplus*. This is an important idea that needs explanation. What it means is the amount by which the particular claimant values performance of a particular obligation, over and above the amount by which the average person would value it. In other words, it recognises that an individual can, for personal reasons, value something over and above its market value—this extra value is the consumer surplus. For example, an old gold wedding ring might be worth £100 on the market, but if that ring was a family heirloom, once your great-grandmother's wedding ring, then you will value it at much more than £100. So if you make a contract with a jeweller to repair or clean the ring, but in breach of contract he loses or destroys it, then damages of £100 will not adequately compensate you for what you have lost. The same applies to a set of wedding photographs, which have a limited market value in terms of the paper and printing costs, but are worth vastly more to the bride and groom.

Although the consumer surplus had been discussed at length by academics as being an important consideration when valuing a claimant's expectation fully, Lord Mustill was the first Law Lord to acknowledge the concept. He said, '[T]he law must cater for those occasions where the value of the promise to the promisee exceeds the financial enhancement of his position which full performance will secure.' This is a very significant statement, forming part of the process we have already mentioned of bringing contract law into the twenty-first century and recognising that people who make contracts are not all motivated entirely by profit considerations. So, for Lord Mustill, the £2,500 loss of amenity award was best regarded as an example of the consumer surplus—the average pool purchaser placed no value on the depth of the pool, but Mr Forsyth did.

Lord Lloyd, on the other hand, explained the £2,500 award as damages for Forsyth's 'distress and disappointment'. Damages for mental distress or disappointment are not generally awarded for breach of contract: this is not surprising bearing in mind the commercial roots of English contract law, since commercial parties are not expected to react emotionally to a breach of contract! The courts have, however, recognised for some time a couple of limited exceptions to this general rule, one of which is where the contract's *sole object* was to give pleasure, peace of mind or freedom from distress. A good example is a holiday contract: if your holiday is a complete disaster and does not accord with the promises made to you in the contract, you will be entitled to recover damages for distress and disappointment, not just a cold, financial calculation of the difference in value between the lovely holiday you were promised and the grotty one you actually had. For example, in the recent decision of the Court of Appeal in *Milner v Carnival plc (trading as Cunard)* damages were awarded for mental distress when a luxury cruise that should have been the 'holiday of a lifetime' went disastrously wrong. In *Ruxley*, Lord Lloyd stressed that the swimming pool contract was one to provide 'pleasurable amenity' and so was able to treat the middle-ground award *in this case* as falling within the exception.

So, although both Lords Mustill and Lloyd expressly approved of the loss of amenity award, they did not adopt the same reasoning in doing so. Lord Lloyd's approach had the advantage of being built on existing precedent, but there are strong arguments of principle for preferring Lord Mustill's consumer surplus analysis. Lord Lloyd was only able to rely on existing caselaw about contracts to provide 'pleasurable amenity' or 'freedom from distress' because, fortuitously, this case involved a swimming pool, something designed to give pleasure. But there may be many instances where a consumer surplus exists, and should be recognised, that do *not* fall into this exceptional category. For example a domestic homeowner may have specified for a particular heating system, roof tile or floor plan, which they value even though failure to comply with the specification will not cause a reduction in the market value of performance. Lord Lloyd himself recognised that a 'distress' award would not be available for some defects, such as a difference in level between two rooms creating an irritating step when the customer had expressly contracted for a flat floor. There is no obvious 'pleasurable amenity' here and yet there is certainly a consumer surplus that should be compensated. So this issue was not conclusively resolved in *Ruxley,* leaving a 'question mark' over precisely what the case decided, to be pondered by commentators and judges in the future.

In fact, some commentators felt uneasy about a more fundamental aspect of the decision in *Ruxley*, namely the court's restriction on the cost of cure measure. It has been argued that, whilst it may be right to deny the cost of cure in certain situations (eg where the landowner has *died* since the contract was made and it is clear that his next of kin will be selling the property immediately), consumer cases where there is simply 'disproportion' between the cost of cure and the apparent value of what has been lost do not necessarily warrant the same treatment. In other words, despite the obvious lack of merits of Forsyth's own counter-claim, perhaps a general test based on whether the loss is disproportionate to the cost of cure is not sufficiently *respectful* of consumers' contractual expectations in domestic building cases.

For example, the 'disproportion' approach may well have unfortunate implications in the ordinary case of a domestic building contract. First, does it give the right signal to contractors? Assume, for example, a contractor doing domestic building work where, as in *Ruxley*, the employer is not on site supervising his every move. If the contractor monitors the work properly, keeping the employer informed at every stage, he risks spotting mistakes and defects which he will then have to spend money remedying. If, however, he ploughs on with the work, so that any defects are quickly buried in the fabric of the construction, this maximises the chances that the cost of curing such defects will be high, in comparison with the difference in market value, and thus rejected as disproportionate. Perhaps the principle encourages a culture of inefficiency and provides no incentive, indeed a positive disincentive, for builders to monitor work or keep the employer informed. Secondly, the vagueness of the 'disproportion' principle makes the position of a claimant complaining of bad workmanship uncertain and risky, and (where the cost of cure is high) enables a contractor to 'hold out', offering a low sum which he asserts will adequately compensate the employer for his loss of amenity. As Forsyth's barrister observed after the House of Lords decision, '[M]any a [building owner] may well accept such sum rather than undergo the uncertainty of litigation'.

WHAT HAS HAPPENED SINCE *RUXLEY*?

Ruxley was decided almost fifteen years ago, so for an all-round picture of the case it is important to consider how it has been applied and interpreted as a precedent in subsequent cases. In fact it has been cited and discussed many times, in all sorts of cases, but just by looking at two very different examples will give you a flavour of its development and influence.

Very soon after *Ruxley* was decided, it was applied by the Court of Appeal in *Freeman v Niroomand*. Mr Niroomand commissioned a builder to carry out building work at his semidetached house, namely constructing a porch at the front and an extension to the rear. The dispute involved the porch, which the contract specified should mirror the porch on the adjoining house and should be constructed of cavity wall brickwork (to minimise staining from the elements). When the porch was built, it did match the porch next door, *but* it had not been constructed with cavity walls. As is all too common, the market value of the house was not altered by the addition of the porch, *whether or not* it complied with the contractual specifications. To cure the breach, the porch either had to be demolished or have its internal dimensions considerably reduced by the addition of an inner layer of brickwork. For this reason Mr Niroomand gave evidence that he did *not* wish to rebuild the porch and thus did not *ask* for the cost of cure, but only claimed a *Ruxley* 'middle ground' award from the defendant builder, representing the value of his unfulfilled expectation (essentially the risk of a weather-stained porch). The Court of Appeal sympathised and awarded him £130 in damages, adopting Lord Mustill's *consumer surplus* reasoning in the process. Notice that Lord Lloyd's justification would *not* have worked on the facts, as a contract to construct a porch cannot be explained as one which has 'pleasure, peace of mind and freedom from distress' as its object!

A few years later, the House of Lords had another opportunity to consider damages in the consumer contract context, although not this time concerned with a building contract. In *Farley v Skinner* the claimant, Mr Farley, was interested in purchasing a property in Sussex (near Gatwick Airport) as a quiet, relaxing house to live in once he retired. Keen to check that the house was suitable for this purpose, he employed Mr Skinner, a surveyor, to look over it and expressly asked him to report on whether aircraft noise was likely to be a problem. In breach of contract, Skinner negligently reported back that it was unlikely that the property would be noisy. Therefore, Farley bought the house, only to find to his horror that the property was seriously noisy: aircraft 'stacked' in the air just over the house at busy times (mornings, early evenings and weekends), spiralling there until a landing slot became free! Despite the fact that the trial judge found that the price Farley paid reflected the aircraft noise problem (so his *financial* loss was nil), he nevertheless awarded Farley £10,000 for his 'loss of amenity'. The House of Lords unanimously affirmed this award, although suggesting that the amount awarded was at the 'high end of what was appropriate'.

Some of the Law Lords adopted Lord Lloyd's rationalisation of the *Ruxley* middle-ground award as falling within the exceptional category of contracts (such as holiday contracts) made with the object of providing pleasure, peace of mind and freedom from distress, for which damages for distress were available. It was then a simple matter merely to expand the exception very slightly to cover cases like this, where pleasure/freedom from distress was not the *sole* object of the contract, but was nonetheless an important object (after all, Farley contracted with the surveyor to check for other defects and problems with the house, not solely to consider the noise issue). Lord Scott, on the other hand, preferred Lord Mustill's approach, unhesitatingly endorsing the concept of the consumer surplus and allowing relief on this basis: Skinner's breach of contract prevented Farley from obtaining the peace and quiet that were extremely important to him.

So after two House of Lords cases and numerous lesser decisions, we are still not entirely certain how to rationalise 'middle-ground' awards of this kind or what the relationship is between the 'consumer surplus' and damages for distress allowed in exceptional cases. Perhaps by the time you study law, this issue will have been clarified by the Supreme Court, but experience suggests that, by then, new cases will have arisen with yet more factual twists, leading instead to refinement and possibly even complication of the relevant legal rules.

WHAT IF THE BUILDER HAD *SAVED* MONEY BY BREACHING THE CONTRACT?

One notable feature of the facts of Ruxley was that the builders did not appear to have *saved* any money by building the pool too shallow, or at least that was not mentioned in the pleaded facts. But in other cases, a contracting party might very well save a lot of money by breaching his contract, or even make a big profit by deliberately breaching one contract in order to enter into a more favourable one with someone else. Should this be taken into account when calculating the claimant's damages for breach of contract?

The traditional answer to that question in English law has always been a resounding 'no'. Damages for breach of contract have always been purely compensatory, calculated (as we've seen already) to put the claimant into the position he would have been in if the contract had been properly performed—in other words, based solely on the claimant's loss not the defendant's gain. So the rule has always been very clear—damages are not meant to strip profits away from contract-breakers or to punish contract-breakers. Their only role is to make good the claimant's loss.

There are very good reasons for contractual damages being compensatory only. For example, the requirement that claimants must mitigate their loss when suing for damages (act reasonably to keep their loss to a minimum) only makes sense in a damages regime that is loss-based. Economists offer another explanation, namely that the law should allow contract breakers to keep any profit they make from the breach provided they compensate the other party's losses, as this is the most 'efficient' outcome. Imagine A contracts to sell B 100 kilos of widgets for £100 when the market price is £110 (for some reason, legal examples about generic goods nearly always involve imaginary items called 'widgets'!). Then someone else, C, offers to pay £150 for the widgets (in other words, more than the market price). Economists regard it as rational for A to break his contract with B and sell to C instead, because this is said to be an *efficient* outcome. This way, A is happy because he has made £50 more than he would have done, C is happy because he has got the widgets, and B should be *neutral*, because she has got £10 damages *and* keeps the £100 price, so can mitigate her loss by buying widgets at their market value.

This economic approach looks very neat, but not everyone is happy with the idea behind it. After all, it treats A as if he had an entirely free choice between performing his contract with B or breaching it and paying damages, when he actually made a *promise* to B to sell the widgets. It seems to underplay the importance of respecting contractual promises. After all, breaching a contract is 'wrongful', although not as serious a wrong as a criminal offence or a tort. It also underplays B's expectation when making a contract: B almost certainly isn't 'neutral' about receiving £10 damages rather than the widgets she ordered, not least because of the hassle involved in finding another supplier of widgets. Finally, and more fundamentally, it just troubles many lawyers that a defendant can make a profit from a breach of contract and yet be allowed to keep that profit—surely, they argue, the law should respond to this 'unjust enrichment' of the defendant by depriving him of his profit and paying it to the innocent claimant.

These objections have led some judges and commentators to argue that damages for breach of contract should, in some circumstances, be calculated by reference to the defendant's gain and not solely the claimant's loss. This is difficult and very controversial territory. The argument generally begins by suggesting that the law already does recognise 'gain-based' damages and so it is time for it to 'come clean' and admit that damages are not purely compensatory.

This is tricky because sometimes an award of damages *looks* as if it is depriving a defendant of some or all of his profit, but that profit is just being treated as a way of valuing the claimant's loss. For example, what if A sells some of his land to B for development and B promises not to build more than 20 houses on the site? If B breaches that covenant and builds 25 houses, the extra houses may have no adverse financial effect on A at all, and yet B has made more profit than he should have. English law has long recognised that B must pay damages to A in this situation and what's more those damages *will* be calculated by reference to a proportion of B's extra profit. But that approach to damages is perfectly consistent with a *compensatory* approach. B has gone ahead and built the extra houses in breach of contract without A's permission, but if

B had asked A's permission to release him from the contractual restriction, A would probably have granted that permission *at a price*. So B's breach *has* deprived A of something of value—the opportunity to charge for release of the '20 houses only' restriction. And the same compensatory approach applies even if it is clear that A would not have agreed to release B from the contractual restriction at any price. Indeed, the fact that A would not have agreed at any price suggests that it is *particularly* important to him to prevent B building extra houses, so it is counterintuitive to suggest that A has suffered no loss in such circumstances. After all, if you lose your legs as a result of someone's negligence and claim damages in tort, the fact that you would not have sold your legs for any amount of money does not mean that you have suffered no loss!

A further argument sometimes offered in favour of gain-based damages for breach of contract is that they would be a useful additional tool to help the law to protect contractual expectations properly, even where the claimant has suffered no obvious financial loss from the breach: the same sentiment, in other words, behind the decision in *Ruxley*. This is a very laudable aim, *but* if the real problem in the law is insufficient respect for contractual expectations (so some losses are overlooked or inadequately respected), would it not be better to attack that problem directly and concentrate on valuing contractual expectations properly, rather than turning to the defendant's gain instead?

An old American case called *City of New Orleans v Fireman's Charitable Association* provides a good example. The claimant paid the defendant to provide a fire-fighting service for five years, with the contract specifying how many men and horses should be kept available and how much hosepipe. At the end of the contract period, the claimant discovered that the defendant had failed to keep available as many men or horses as specified, or the length of hosepipe that had been promised, thereby saving itself over $40,000. However, the claimant could not show that the breach had prevented the defendant extinguishing any fires, so the Supreme Court of Louisiana held that the claimant had suffered no loss and thus was not entitled to damages.

Many commentators have argued that this is the perfect example of a case in which damages should be based on the defendant's profit, because otherwise the claimant goes under-compensated. But if you stop and think for a moment, it is obvious that the Supreme Court of Louisiana got it wrong—the claimant *has* suffered a loss, because he did not get the level of contractual performance he had bargained and paid for. This problem should be tackled directly: if the problem is failure to compensate properly, the answer is to expand the notion of loss to enable the law to compensate more fully, not concentrate on the defendant's profit instead.

However, the House of Lords in *Attorney General v Blake* agreed that the defendant's gain might occasionally be relevant to calculating damages for breach of contract, although only in very exceptional cases where a compensatory remedy would be inadequate. George Blake was a spy for the British intelligence services, but he was also a double agent working for the Soviet Union. He was convicted of treason and imprisoned, but later escaped from Wormwood Scrubs prison to Moscow. There in 1989 he wrote his autobiography, which contained some old information about his career in British intelligence. The information was no longer confidential by this time: if it had been, the Crown could have recovered Blake's profits in a different type of legal action for breach of confidence, but this was of course not available. Nor was its disclosure damaging to the public interest, *but* by releasing it Blake was in breach of his *employment contract*, in which he had promised, 'not to divulge any official information gained as a result of [his] employment' (this promise continued in effect beyond the time his employment ended). So the Crown (in the person of the Attorney General) sued for *breach of contract* to get its hands on Blake's profit from publishing the book.

The House of Lords held in 2000, by a 4–1 majority, that because the facts were so exceptional, the Crown *could* recover the profits made from Blake's breach of contract, even though it had not suffered any *loss* from that breach. The reason given by Lord Nicholls was that the traditional remedies for breach of contract were *inadequate* on the particular facts of the case:

> It will only be in exceptional cases, where those remedies are inadequate, that any question of accounting for profits will arise. No fixed rules can be prescribed. The court will have regard to all the circumstances, including the subject matter of the contract, the purpose of the contractual provision that has been breached, the circumstances in which the breach occurred,

the consequences of the breach and the circumstances in which the relief is being sought. A useful general guide, although not exhaustive, is whether the [claimant] had a *legitimate interest* in preventing the defendant's profit-making activity and, hence, in depriving him of his profit. It would be difficult, and unwise, to attempt to be more specific.

He went on to explain what the Crown's *legitimate interest* was:

The context is employment as a member of the security and intelligence services. Secret information is the lifeblood of these services. In the 1950s Blake deliberately committed repeated breaches of his undertaking not to divulge official information gained as a result of his employment. He caused untold and immeasurable damage to the public interest he had committed himself to serve.

Many lawyers have criticised this decision and its reasoning. Although it is obvious why the House of Lords disliked George Blake and wanted to find a way of making him give up his profits, it looks as if this instinct was based on a desire to punish him over again for his previous treachery in the 1950s. But this was an action for Blake's *breach of contract* in publishing his memoirs in 1989, which wasn't actually a particularly serious breach of his former employment contract. So it is not obvious why the Crown's interest *is* legitimate here.

More to the point, the decision does not just affect George Blake, but (because of the doctrine of precedent) makes this sort of remedy potentially available in other cases as well. A number of judges have already struggled in subsequent cases, trying to decide whether or not their facts are sufficiently 'exceptional'. Lord Hobhouse dissented in *Attorney General v Blake*, warning of the danger of introducing an element of uncertainty into commercial transactions, which would make it hard for lawyers and their clients to predict in advance when such a remedy would be awarded. He said:

I must also sound a further note of warning that if some more extensive principle of awarding non-compensatory damages for breach of contract is to be introduced into our commercial law the consequences will be very far reaching and disruptive.

So now if another *Ruxley*-type case came along in which the builder *had* saved money, a sharp barrister would probably try to argue that the facts fell within the *Attorney General v Blake* exception. This probably wouldn't succeed, but the law of contractual remedies is so dynamic and controversial that you never know!

CONCLUSION

I hope that this chapter has shown that there is much more to contractual remedies than just the boring mathematical bit tacked onto the end of a course on the law of contract. As a topic, it reminds us very sharply that good lawyers must be able to focus on complex arguments and make fine distinctions, whilst at the same time recognising the shared general principles and common problems that can link apparently unconnected situations like ordering books, building swimming pools, buying houses near airports and spying for the enemy.

Cases

Attorney General v Blake [2001] 1 AC 268
City of New Orleans v Fireman's Charitable Association 9 So 486 (1891)
Farley v Skinner [2002] 2 AC 732
Freeman v Niroomand (1996) 52 Con LR 116
Jacob & Youngs v Kent (1921) 129 NE 889
Milner v Carnival plc (trading as Cunard) [2010] 3 All ER 701
Radford v De Froberville [1977] 1 WLR 1262 *Ruxley Electronics & Construction Ltd v Forsyth* [1996] AC 344

Further reading

O'Sullivan and Hilliard, *The Law of Contract*, 4th edn (Oxford, Oxford University Press, 2010)
Harris, Ogus and Phillips, 'Contract Remedies and the Consumer Surplus' (1979) 95 *LQR* 581
Hedley, '"Very Much the Wrong People": The House of Lords and Publication of Spy Memoirs' [2000] Web *JCLI*

4

Tort

Tony Weir

You may not be familiar with the term *tort*, but you are bound to have come across lots of tort cases in the newspapers. It derives from the French word for 'wrong' and, in English law, means a *civil wrong*. Criminal cases are pursued by the state against the wrongdoer, with punishment of that wrongdoer as the principal aim; tort cases, on the other hand, involve one individual (the claimant) *suing* another individual (the defendant) whom the claimant alleges has done him wrong in some way, principally with a view to obtaining financial compensation. The same set of facts sometimes gives rise to criminal *and* tort liability, but more often than not the wrongdoing involved in a tort case is not serious enough to attract criminal sanctions.

The case chosen here to illustrate the law of tort in operation is *McFarlane v Tayside Health Authority.* This is a House of Lords case from Scotland, which is of interest in itself, because in many respects Scots law differs considerably from its English relative south of the border, yet the House of Lords was the final appeal court for Scottish cases as well as English ones, as the Supreme Court is today. The Supreme Court must therefore apply Scots law from time to time, so it helps that there are usually senior Scottish judges amongst the Supreme Court justices. *McFarlane* is a very important case for English lawyers too, because the law of tort it considered is virtually identical north and south of the border.

McFarlane involved a bouncing baby born, owing to the fault of a doctor, to parents who had decided they had enough children already, so it could equally well figure in books on family law, or even medical law. The reason the case appears in books on tort is that the parents were suing the hospital for damages, compensation for the cost of bringing up the baby. It therefore sits in the tort books alongside other cases whose main feature is that the claimants—mainly those injured in industrial or highway accidents—are seeking damages as compensation for the harm they have suffered owing to the misconduct of the defendant or, in our case as in many others, the defendant's employee (a wrongdoer's employer is very often sued as well as, or instead of, the individual wrongdoer, because the law makes employers *vicariously liable* to pay damages wherever an employee commits a tort in the course of his or her employment; employers commonly have insurance to cover claims of this kind). Sometimes such harm is caused deliberately, but usually it is the result of carelessness, or *negligence*, as lawyers like to call it.

Just as there are a number of separate crimes (such as murder, theft and rape), similarly there are various separate torts. Of these the tort of negligence is by far the most important in practice, but you may well have heard of some of the other torts, such as defamation and nuisance. To bring a claim in negligence, the claimant must establish certain basic elements. These are first, that the defendant owed him a *duty of care* (which, as we will see later, is so self-evident in most straightforward cases that it goes without saying, but which occasionally gives rise to problems in unusual situations); secondly, that the defendant *breached* that duty by behaving unreasonably or carelessly; thirdly, that the defendant's breach of duty *caused* the claimant to suffer, fourthly, legally recognised *harm*. Lawyers tend to use the word 'negligence' in two ways: as shorthand for the second element just mentioned, careless conduct on the part of the defendant, and also (more properly) to denote the whole 'tort', the cause of action which is established if the claimant establishes all four elements.

McFarlane is a case of 'negligence' in this sense, and it is of particular interest because the outcome is not quite what one would expect in view of the accepted rules of negligence as a tort. The alleged facts were that the claimants, husband and wife, decided that four children were enough and that the husband should submit to a vasectomy, like some 8,000 other Scotsmen each year. The doctor reported that the operation, which he performed quite properly, had been successful and that normal marital relations could be resumed. Alas, the doctor was wrong in this (having misinterpreted the husband's sperm tests carried out after the operation) and the wife conceived. The pregnancy and birth, though painful as always, were quite normal, and baby Catherine McFarlane was in perfect health. But it costs a lot of money to bring up a child (an average of £165,000 has been suggested). Who was to bear this cost, the parents whose child it was, or the health service whose fault it was that the child had been born at all?

If the case had arisen in England it would never have reached the House of Lords for, in 1984, the House had declined to review a decision of the Court of Appeal which had held that there was no objection to such a claim. Although the Court of Appeal case concerned a disabled rather than a healthy child, so its decision as to a healthy child was arguably *obiter* (not binding), and although the court rendered its decision immediately after the barristers had finished their submissions, without taking any time taken to consider its implications, the decision was treated as conclusive thereafter and was followed for fifteen years. But Scottish courts are not bound by the English Court of Appeal and, unlike their English counterparts, Scots applicants such as the McFarlanes needed no leave to appeal to the House (the rules are slightly more complicated now for appeals to the Supreme Court). In the event, the House of Lords held unanimously that the McFarlanes' claim must fail.

THE MOST FAMOUS TORT CASE

Seventy years earlier, in 1932, Scotland had produced the most famous case in the tort of negligence—the 'snail-in-the-ginger-beer-bottle' case of *Donoghue v Stevenson*. Mrs Donoghue alleged that she had been poisoned by a foreign body, to wit a very dead snail, lurking in a bottle of Stevenson's ginger beer bought for her by a friend in a café. The Scottish court held that, even if she could show that Stevenson had been careless, her claim must fail since he owed her no duty in law to take care of her: she had not actually bought the product. The House of Lords, by a majority, held that the manufacturer did indeed owe her a duty to take such care.

Why is this case regarded as so important? After all, by 1932 there were plenty of situations in which a defendant would be liable if he caused harm negligently, but they were regarded as isolated, unconnected instances that just happened to have similar characteristics, not linked at a conceptual level to form one general tort of negligence. At the time most lawyers thought that *Donoghue v Stevenson* merely added one more such isolated pocket of liability and was no more than a small step forward for 'consumer protection', of little or no significance outside that area. But the case is as famous and important as it is today because its reasoning went beyond that narrow view, when Lord Atkin, with some aid from the Sermon on the Mount, delivered himself of a *general* statement regarding the situations in which one person would be held to owe another a duty to be careful not to injure them. There need not be a contract between the parties, it was enough if there were 'neighbourhood' between them, and one's neighbour was not just the person next door, though such persons are very close, but anyone close enough that injury to them was reasonably foreseeable if one mismanaged whatever one was doing.

As the case indicates, liability in the tort of negligence depends, among other things, on the defendant's having been under a 'duty of care'. Whether or not such a duty exists is a matter of *law*, the subject of legal argument that can be decided in principle without hearing any of the evidence. This is in sharp contrast to the question of whether or not the duty has been breached, ie whether the defendant had actually been negligent by falling below the proper standard of conduct, which is a matter of *fact* to be proved by witnesses. This distinction was more obviously significant before 1965, when juries were still used to decide negligence cases, because questions of law remained for the judge to decide and thus it was open to the judge to hold that there was no duty of care on the facts as pleaded, however careless the defendant might have been, so that the case failed before getting as far as a jury. Nowadays negligence cases are invariably decided by a judge alone, but the distinction between questions of law and questions of fact remains a very important one in practice.

THE 'DUTY' QUESTION

Mrs Donoghue had, we suppose, suffered injury to her person, and the same was true of Mrs McFarlane, what with the pregnancy and confinement. Where the injury is physical in nature, the 'duty' question is not often discussed, at any rate where, as in both *Donoghue* and *McFarlane*, the defendant's conduct actually created the danger, as opposed to merely failing to prevent it: Stevenson actually despatched the noxious bottle into the world and the doctor in *McFarlane* said that sex was now safe (from babies anyway). So there was not much discussion of the mother's claim for the pain of pregnancy and parturition. Indeed, in cases of highway or industrial accidents the existence of the duty is never questioned—it is too obvious that road-users owe each other a duty to drive carefully, and that an employer is under a special duty to look out for the safety of his employees—but the question does arise in novel cases, especially if the judges want to exonerate the negligent defendant from liability for the foreseeable harm he has caused, for then 'no duty in law' is almost the only device they can deploy.

THE KIND OF HARM

Tort lawyers often say, somewhat illogically, that the existence of the duty, or its scope or ambit, depends on the nature of the harm that resulted from breach of the duty. In *McFarlane* there were two types of harm: the wife had suffered not only physical harm, harm to her body, as a result of the unwanted pregnancy but also financial harm, in having to pay for the baby's upkeep, while the husband had suffered only harm of the latter kind. The real issue was the cost of bringing up the child. This was problematic because our law of tort has always been less ready to award compensation for a loss which is merely financial than for damage which is physical in nature, harm to person or property. In other words, the claim 'You wounded me' has always been held stronger than 'You cost me'. Of course, where the tort has caused the claimant to suffer personal injury or property damage, its economic aspects—lost wages, cost of cure, repairs and so on—are every bit as compensable as pain and suffering and loss of amenity, but it is different if the only harm is financial, not consequent on physical damage to person or property: this is commonly called *pure* financial loss, and it is less readily compensated in tort. Some judges regarded the financial loss in *McFarlane* not as 'pure' but rather as consequential on the personal injury to the wife, and therefore compensable on normal principles, but a majority of their Lordships treated the harm to the mother as regards the pregnancy and birth as quite distinct from harm in the sense of the cost to both parents of bringing up the baby.

DAMAGE AND LOSS

This distinction between physical damage and pure economic loss makes some commentators uneasy—after all, they are both kinds of harm—but it seems perfectly justifiable, even in a society which seems to put money above all else. Consider, for example, the word 'dangerous'. It is applied only in situations where the potential harm is of a physical variety, where there is a risk of injury to person or property, and since the counterpart of 'danger' is safety, it is not too surprising if the law puts safety first. To put it another way, health is more important than wealth: we don't have a National Wealth Service—indeed, we have the very opposite, in the form of Her Majesty's Revenue and Customs.

RECOVERY FOR PURE FINANCIAL HARM

For thirty years after *Donoghue v Stevenson* it was assumed that there was no prospect of claiming in the tort of negligence for pure financial loss due to mere carelessness, as opposed to deliberate lies (deceit) or failure to do what one had been paid to do (breach of contract). Then, in 1963, the House of Lords held that such a claim might lie. In *Hedley Byrne v Heller and Partners* the claimant lost money as a result of a misleading credit-reference given, gratuitously, by the defendant bank on one of the claimant's customers. What the bank did—certifying that the customer was in a good financial position when it was anything but — was careless and negligent, but it was not *dangerous*, since the only loss that could and did result from the claimant's relying on the reference and giving credit to the customer was purely financial.

As in *McFarlane*, as we shall see, the House of Lords in the banking case was agreed as to the result—that there could be liability in negligence for causing merely financial harm—but their Lordships differed in the reasons they gave and consequently as to the circumstances in which liability would attach. The five different speeches emphasise different points. Could the defendant foresee that the recipient of the information would rely on it? Was it on a business rather than a social occasion? Was the defendant an expert on the matter in issue? Was the relationship between the parties 'equivalent to contract'? Did the defendant undertake responsibility for the statement in question?

As the law developed, it became less important whether the defendant had spoken or acted, and more important that there be a 'special relationship' between the parties, characterised by an 'undertaking of responsibility' on the part of the defendant. The fact that different reasons were given for the decision made it easier for later courts to expand its scope, to the point that in 1995 a solicitor who failed to draw up a will as instructed by his client was held liable in *White v Jones* to the client's daughters who would have inherited had the will been drawn up as it should have been. The disappointed daughters won, despite the facts that the solicitor neither spoke nor acted, and seemed to be in no very special relationship with them, and that, even supposing that he could be said to have assumed responsibility for drawing up the will, they surely did not rely on his doing so, foreseeable though the harm to them was. In other words, although he undoubtedly assumed responsibility *to his client*, the father, it is quite another thing to say that he assumed responsibility, in any meaningful sense, to *the daughters*. One can easily see that rather surprising decisions may 'follow' from a previous decision, especially one in which several different reasons are given for the same outcome.

APPLICATION IN *McFARLANE*

Now, in *McFarlane* it was plain that there was a 'special relationship' between the parents and the doctor, that he was a specialist who undertook responsibility and that he knew they would be relying on what he told them. It is true that they didn't pay for the treatment, so there was no contract, but after *Hedley Byrne* that was unimportant. It had been held for centuries that doctors owe their patients a duty of care, and though the cases have generally involved harm to the patient's person rather than his pocket, Lord Devlin in *Hedley Byrne* said that that made no difference. Since the birth of the child was the 'very thing' that the defendant was retained to prevent, it was not easy to say that it fell outside the scope of his duty of care; and since it is notorious that children are expensive, the loss could not possibly be described as too 'remote'. Furthermore, several of the judges said that it was immaterial whether the claim rested on *Donoghue* or on *Hedley Byrne*. As Lord Bingham put it in a later case, 'An orthodox application of familiar and conventional principles of the law of tort would, I think, have pointed to' imposing liability in *McFarlane*. So how was this avoided?

FAIR, JUST AND REASONABLE

The majority in the House of Lords invoked an element which their predecessors in 1990 had added to Lord Atkin's statement of the requirements for finding a duty of care. The 1990 case—*Caparo v Dickman*—was again one of pure economic loss: a shareholder interested in taking over a company was suing the auditor whose carelessly favourable statement about its profitability in its annual accounts, a publicly available document, induced him to pay too much for further shares. In rejecting his claim, their Lordships said that in addition to 'foreseeability of the harm' and 'proximity between the parties' (= neighbourhood) it must be found that it would be 'fair, just and reasonable' to impose a duty (= make the defendant liable).

The first two of these elements were plainly satisfied on the facts of *McFarlane*. The doctor could hardly have been closer to the husband in performing the operation, which he knew would, if its outcome were carelessly misreported, affect the wife. The harm was evidently foreseeable—indeed, what happened was the very thing the doctor was retained to prevent—but the majority of their Lordships held that it was not 'fair, just and reasonable' to impose liability on the careless doctor for the cost of upbringing.

THE REASONS GIVEN IN *McFARLANE*

The reasons given by their Lordships were rather varied. Some members of the House of Lords were content to rely on the formula that it was not 'fair, just and reasonable' to impose on the medical services liability for the cost of bringing up a healthy, though unwanted, child, or that to make the doctor liable to pay for the maintenance of a healthy child for eighteen years was disproportionate to his fault. Less time was spent on justifying the decision than on dismissing arguments which had been raised against it. These included the argument that the (provable) harm of having to pay for the child's upbringing should be offset by the (intangible) joy of parenthood. This was regarded as impracticable and unprincipled: after all, a person disabled from working by a negligent driver does not have his claim for lost earnings reduced just because he can now relax and watch daytime television.

THE SPEECH OF LORD STEYN

Lord Steyn did not care much for the reasons given by his colleagues:

> To explain decisions denying a remedy for the cost of bringing up an unwanted child by saying that there is no loss, no foreseeable loss, no causative link or no ground [for] reasonable restitution is to resort to unrealistic and formalistic propositions which mask the real reasons for the decisions. And judges ought to strive to give the real reasons for their decision.

He held that when there were thousands of people in the kingdom who desperately wanted a family and paid good money in the vain hope of achieving it, it would be contrary to the principle of distributive justice to give damages to the parents of a healthy child they did not want (but kept). Furthermore, he said:

> Instinctively, the traveller on the Underground would consider that the law of tort has no business to provide legal remedies consequent upon the birth of a healthy child, which all of us regard as a valuable and good thing.

Lord Millett said much the same. He said that 'plaintiffs are not allowed, by a process of subjective devaluation, to make a detriment out of a benefit' and that 'it is morally offensive to regard a normal, healthy baby as more trouble and expense than it is worth.'

DISTRIBUTIVE JUSTICE

Lord Steyn referred to 'distributive justice', a rather unattractive term often attributed to Aristotle's distinction between what is fair between claimant and defendant on the one hand and what is fair between different classes of claimant or potential claimant on the other. Thus Lord Steyn suggested that when deciding on a claim made by parents who didn't want a child one should bear in mind the many other people who do want a child and can't have one. He might also have mentioned another constituency, namely sick children who would be deprived of proper treatment if the limited resources of the health service were deployed to pay for the upbringing of children in perfect health.

PSYCHIATRIC HARM

The term 'distributive justice' had surfaced in the House of Lords a few years previously in one of the cases arising out of the Hillsborough disaster in Sheffield when 95 football fans were crushed to death when the police negligently allowed too many of them to enter the stadium. Many claims were brought by relatives of the deceased victims, who had been shocked by what they witnessed, with their own eyes or on television, but almost all their claims were dismissed. The harm here was psychiatric, not physical: to the mind, not the body. Harm of this kind might well seem at the other extreme from pure economic loss, but it, too, is subject to restrictive rules: in particular, the claimant, unless himself physically endangered, must have been physically close to the shocking event and emotionally close to the person primarily affected. But there was some authority that the second restriction did not apply to those who went to the rescue of those actually injured, and clear authority that employers owe their employees a special duty not to cause them injury, so there was a problem when claims were brought by members of the police force, shocked by having to deal with the dead and dying, since they were rescuers suing their employer, the negligent police authority. Could the courts really bring themselves to award damages to the police when they had refused to compensate relatives of the deceased victims, members of the public whom the police are supposed to protect? To award damages might be fair as between the policemen and their employers, but it wouldn't seem right as between policemen and the relatives. Likewise, in the *McFarlane* case, it didn't seem right to award damages to parents of a child they didn't want (though now dearly loved) when so many parents wanted children they couldn't have, however much they paid.

EFFECT ON THIRD PARTIES

That the courts do and should consider the effect of their decisions on third parties is shown by another recent case. In *Tomlinson* a young man ignored signs prohibiting swimming in a reservoir in a public park and was badly injured in the water. The Court of Appeal held the occupier liable because, knowing that the prohibitions were ineffective, it had failed to erect a physical barrier which it had resolved to erect and which would have prevented all access to the water. A unanimous House of Lords, in unusually vigorous judgments, reversed the Court of Appeal's decision: to block access in this way was not fair to innocent holiday-makers who wished to sit beside the water, and the local authority had, in deciding to effect a physical barrier, overreacted to the fear of being held liable to injured trespassers.

TORT AS DETERRENCE

To be held liable is unpleasant, even if one has insurance against such liability (as is required of employers and motorists, among many others), so the risk of being held liable may act as a deterrent. Indeed, it follows from the doctrine of precedent that decisions which impose liability are apt to affect third parties: court decisions may affect the behaviour of the public, or a relevant section of it, just as much as statutory prohibitions. Given that tort liability is commonly imposed for conduct which is dangerous, it may well be conducive to safety if third parties, especially public bodies and firms conscious of risk management, respond to the decision. So tort law certainly has *some* deterrent effect. But there may be better devices, in particular those enforced by the criminal law. A statute or regulation can state precisely what must be done on pain of penalty (eg that a guardrail must be provided where persons work more than two metres above the ground) but all a judge can say—and that after the event—is that the employer or occupier must take reasonable care of the safety of his employees or visitors. Indeed, the existence of sanctions other than damages was one reason why the House of Lords reversed a decision of the Court of Appeal which had held that where a claimant's 'constitutional right' had been infringed by malicious conduct on the part of a public officer (in the case, a prison officer who insisted on reading the prisoner's privileged mail), there was no need to prove any damage at all.

DETERRENCE AND COMPENSATION

If the primary, though by no means the sole, function of tort law is to award compensation for harm due to culpable conduct, there are dangers in overemphasising its deterrent aspects: since compensation looks to the harm suffered by the claimant and deterrence looks to the conduct of the defendant, compensation and deterrence do not quite go hand in hand. Accordingly, to focus on deterrence may lead one to downplay the importance of the harm in relation to the conduct: one might be tempted to impose liability on those who have acted negligently so as to deter others from doing likewise, even if the harm in the case is not obviously attributable to their negligence. After all, the defendant's carelessness might well have caused harm even if it did not obviously do so in the particular case, and might, unless repressed now, do so the next time. Does some such idea lie behind the fact that the common law seems to treat damage to property very much like injury to the person, although people are surely more important than their property and should have greater protection? After all, anything which can damage a thing could have injured a person. Again, one might think that *unless* we hold people liable for breaching their duty of care, even if it is not clear that the breach caused any harm, people similarly situated might be able to ignore their duty with impunity.

TWO RECENT CASES

Two cases from the start of the twenty-first century are indicative. In *Chester v Afshar* a doctor failed to inform his patient, as he was duty-bound to do, of the risk of paralysis inherent in the proposed operation, which tragically materialised even though the operation was performed impeccably. Had she been informed, the patient would *still* have had the operation, though not then and there because she would have wanted to go away first to consider and research the possible risk, and that risk would have been the same on whatever day she eventually had the surgery. The minority in the House of Lords would have absolved the doctor on the ground that his breach of duty did not increase the risk of harm, but the majority gave judgment for the patient, even though they said that this was inconsistent with the conventional principles of causation, because otherwise doctors could ignore their duty with impunity. Similar considerations led to a unanimous decision in *Fairchild v Glenhaven Funeral Services* to impose liability on all the successive employers who had carelessly exposed the claimant to asbestos fibres, although only one of them could possibly have triggered his cancer: in certain circumstances, especially where it is impossible to identify the precise cause, you are taken to have caused harm if your misconduct increased the risk of its occurrence, for otherwise your breach of duty would have no legal consequences at all.

Analogous are cases where a defendant who had acted in a manner apt to cause physical harm has been held liable for harm of a different kind not otherwise compensable. In *Page v Smith*, for instance, the defendant was held liable when his slightly bad driving caused a minor accident in which the claimant, though not physically injured at all, was (unforeseeably) shocked enough to take to his bed. Again, it was held in *Anns v Merton LBC* that the buyer of a badly built house was entitled to damages, but only if the house was 'imminently dangerous' so that it could have collapsed and injured him physically, though it didn't, and all he lost was some money. That decision also held that if the house was dangerous the local authority was liable for negligently permitting it to be built. The risk of such liability was later felt to induce planning authorities to be overcareful and unduly scrupulous, thereby delaying the construction of buildings in an unacceptable manner. *Anns* has since been overruled. One reason for the overruling was that there was a statute on the books which provided the purchaser of a jerry-built dwelling with a claim against the builder.

STATUTES AND JUDGE-MADE LAW

That statute (the Defective Premises Act 1972) applied only to *dwellings*, homes for people; *Anns*, had it not been overruled, would have applied to all buildings, including office-blocks. This indicates a distinction between statutory and judge-made rules which deserves further reflection. In *McFarlane* itself no statute was involved, and our choice of it to illustrate the law of tort might lead one to suppose that tort law is largely judge-made. The supposition is quite false: almost all tort suits involve, and frequently turn on, a statute. This is true not only of those cases where a workman sues for breach of a safety regulation and his claim is based explicitly on the statutory rule, but also of cases where statute has intervened to reverse or modify rules laid down by judges. Thus in every case involving death or more than one defendant or injury to which the claimant's fault has contributed or which occurred on the defendant's premises or which is due to a defective product or the act of an animal—and that is a lot of cases!—the outcome depends on some statute or other.

Statutory rules and those laid down by the judges are very different in nature and operation. Judge-made rules are applied *by analogy*—a decision involving a dog may well be applied in a case concerning a cat, since cats and dogs are analogous (in some ways), but a statute which refers to a dog could never be applied to a cat, for a statute applies only to what is covered by its wording, whatever the courts hold the words to mean. Again, while both Parliament and the courts speak by a majority, often a very slim one, Parliament speaks with one voice, and its very words are law. One cannot imagine five different versions of a statute, but a court may speak with five different voices, and while it is the actual holding which is binding rather than the words the judges use, it is the reasons they give which will be ventilated in subsequent cases.

THE EFFECT OF *McFARLANE*

We have seen that the decision in the case of the misleading banker's reference, in which there were five different speeches, has been applied in situations very far from the facts of *Hedley Byrne* itself. There were five different speeches in *McFarlane* also, and though it can hardly prove equally seminal, it has left some unanswered questions. Thus while we know that a doctor whose fault is responsible for the birth of a healthy baby need not pay for its upbringing, what if the child is born because of a defect in a contraceptive device carelessly manufactured, or sold, by the defendant? What if the child is not healthy, but handicapped? Are these also situations in which it would not be fair just and reasonable to make the defendant pay?

The actual decision in *McFarlane* displeased two classes of critic—those who objected to the displacement of the normal rules of tort law, and those who thought it was unfair on the parents. Two years after *McFarlane*, the Court of Appeal held in *Parkinson v St James and Seacroft University Hospital NHS Trust* that if the child was disabled, the extra cost of upbringing attributable to the disability could be claimed, and shortly after that the same court held in *Rees v Darlington Memorial Hospital NHS Trust* that where the extra cost was due not to any disability in the child but to the disability of the mother, that too was compensable. Both parties in *Rees* appealed to the House of Lords so, less than four years after *McFarlane*, the House, with seven judges instead of the usual five, was invited to change its mind about its original decision. All seven judges held that *McFarlane* should not be overruled, and allowed the defendant's appeal. But then four of them did something very remarkable: they held that though, under *McFarlane*, the parents of the unwanted child could not claim *damages*, ie full compensation for their loss, they should nonetheless receive a *lump sum* of £15,000.

DAMAGE AND THE INVASION OF RIGHTS

This decision to award £15,000 is simply extraordinary, as the minority emphasised with great vigour. The only explanation is that the claimants had suffered a wrong in that their right to organise their life and plan their family had been negligently infringed, and that while *McFarlane* had declined to award compensation for the consequent harm (the standard consequence of wrongful conduct), still something should be done about it. It is true that in recent years we have become increasingly used to people claiming that their rights have been infringed. In fact, however, the common law always did award money when certain basic rights had been infringed (even without negligence or consequent harm): the right to freedom of movement, to physical integrity and to undisturbed possession of property were protected by the tort of trespass, and the right to one's reputation was (over)protected by the tort of defamation (libel and slander).

Now, since the enactment by the Human Rights Act 1998 of the European Convention of Human Rights, the number of protected rights has been greatly increased, but the person complaining of infringement of one of the new rights (including the right to 'respect for family life') may have to forgo damages and be content with a declaration that his grievance is justified. Future McFarlanes will do better than that—they will get £15,000. The £15,000 was said (but not held) to be payable whether the child is healthy or disabled, with the implication that (contrary to *Parkinson*) even where the child is disabled, only the £15,000 is payable. But *McFarlane* and *Rees,* which endorsed it, were concerned only with the healthy child, so there are some untidy ends, as well as an unprecedented precedent.

THE UNWANTED BABY ABROAD

There seem to be unwanted babies and claimant parents all over the world, and in *McFarlane* the House of Lords considered a few decisions from abroad. Subsequently the High Court of Australia, after very full argument, declined (by a majority) to follow *McFarlane* and awarded full damages in the case of a healthy child. In Germany the Constitutional Court split on the question whether to treat a child as harm was consistent with the constitutional requirement of respect for the human being, but now it is accepted that the harm is not the existence of the child but the cost of maintaining it, and the courts, treating the doctor's negligence as a breach of contract, award damages to the mother, though not the full amount where the child is healthy. France is different, as usual, for it holds that to have a healthy child is not damage at all, which is a very sensible view. But then the French court did something remarkable, not possible in England: it held that the *child itself* could sue if (a) the doctors had failed to recognise that it would probably be handicapped and (b) the mother, if informed of this, would have proceeded to a lawful abortion. Now there is certainly something odd and unpalatable about letting a person claim on the basis that if the defendants had done their duty he would not have been born at all, but be that as it may, the decision caused public outrage and legislation was passed in great haste: it was the *state's* job to provide for disabled persons, regardless of the reason for their disability, and doctors were to be liable for the parents' personal harm only, ignoring the extra cost of the child. Subsequently, however, the High Court in the Netherlands has held that the disabled child can indeed claim for being born if the doctors carelessly failed to inform his mother that he was likely to be born disabled, and she would, if so informed, have proceeded to an abortion. Whether this approach enhances or reduces the dignity of the disabled claimant, and how it affects the perception of disabled people in society, are impossibly difficult questions to answer, indeed even to address in civil legal proceedings.

CONCLUSION

It is hardly surprising that courts in different countries, faced with the same problem, reach different conclusions. Nor is this entirely due to the fact that they may be operating in different social and legal contexts and traditions. After all, even in a single system such as ours, quite cogent decisions of trial judges may be reversed by a divided Court of Appeal, and unanimous decisions of the Court of Appeal, seemingly the last word, may be overturned by three members of the Supreme Court, unpersuaded by the very plausible speeches of two determined dissentients. There is therefore no point in pretending that the ultimate holding in any debated case is at all inevitable or obviously 'right'. But disputes must be resolved and cases decided: there must be a decision one way or the other so that citizens can be advised where they stand (and perhaps press for remedial legislation). Meanwhile, the ultimate decision is authoritative, however minoritarian or objectionable. It is necessary, therefore, to know what the law is (for the time being), but it is also very desirable to know how it comes to be the way it is and how easily it might have been otherwise. And that is one of the things that makes the study of law as interesting as it is.

Cases

Alcock v Chief Constable [1992] 1 AC 310
Anns v Merton London Borough Council [1978] AC 728
Caparo Industries v Dickman [1990] 2 AC 605
Chester v Afshar [2004] UKHL 41
Donoghue v Stevenson [1932] AC 562
Fairchild v Glenhaven Funeral Services [2002] UKHL 22
Hedley Byrne & Co v Heller and Partners [1964] AC 465

McFarlane v Tayside Health Board [2000] 2 AC 59
Page v Smith [1996] AC 155
Parkinson v St James and Seacroft University Hospital NHS Trust [2001]
    EWCA Civ 530
Rees v Darlington Memorial Hospital NHS Trust [2003] UKHL 52
Tomlinson v Congleton BC [2003] UKHL 47
White (or Frost) v Chief Constable [1999] 2 AC 455
White v Jones [1995] 2 AC 207

Further reading

Atiyah, *The Damages Lottery* (Hart Publishing, Oxford 1997)
Cane and Atiyah, *Atiyah's Accidents, Compensation and the Law*, 7th
    edn (Cambridge, Cambridge University Press, 2006)
Weir, *An Introduction to Tort Law*, 2nd edn (Oxford, Oxford University
    Press, 2006)

5

Land Law

Kevin Gray

INTRODUCTION

William Blackstone was the first ever Professor of English Law, being appointed to the newly established Vinerian Chair in Oxford in 1758. He wrote four monumental volumes of *Commentaries on the Laws of England*, a work which still ranks as one of the most remarkable attempts to rationalise and expound the law for the benefit of university students and, more generally, for an intelligent citizenry. However, Blackstone concluded the second volume of his *Commentaries* (which was devoted to the law of property) on an extremely gloomy note, recording his fear that this volume 'has afforded the student less amusement and pleasure in the pursuit, than the matters discussed in the preceding volume' (*Blackstone Commentaries*, vol II (1766) 382). Blackstone's evident disenchantment with the law of property—and particularly with the law of land—inaugurated a myth which has since coloured the perceptions of entire generations of students as they embark on their exploration of land law. Many have approached the encounter with a weary resignation born of some apprehension that the law of realty (as it is often known) will be dry, dusty and dull in comparison with the more vivid entertainment offered by, say, the law of crime or tort.

How wrong such perceptions turn out to be! True it is that property matters are, at least initially, more technical than many other areas of law. It is also fair to say that the land law of Blackstone's day was deeply marked by the mind-numbing complexities of a rapidly disintegrating feudal order. But the reality of realty—so to speak—is that 'all human life is here' (if we may borrow a phrase once employed by the *News of the World*). If you want sex, lies, violence and vitality—the full gamut of human strengths and frailties—it is all here. Moreover, there is something for everyone: something for the theorist, the technician, the pragmatist, the romantic and the cynic alike. The reason is not hard to search out. The law of property is not ultimately about land or things. It is about ourselves; it is about the way in which we perceive our relationship with the external world; it is about the rapaciousness with which we choose to seize the resources and opportunities offered by that world. Here is an arena in which the agony and ecstasy of life are played out against a backdrop of abstract proprietary concepts.

THE PROBLEM OF PROPERTY

For the student, the challenge of property is deeply internal. Property law is, effectively, a kind of applied psychology. The law of property poses fundamental questions to which the answers lie not outside, but inside, oneself. How absolute or sacrosanct should property entitlements be? How much room is there for notions of fairness in the allocation of property rights? What is the proper balance between justice, certainty and efficiency? Is property law simply about excluding other people from resources which one values or is it more about a sharing of socially valued resources with others? How do human rights and property rights interact? On what grounds can one's property be taken away or confiscated? What is property anyway? The answers to such questions depend upon the private, latent, barely conscious assumptions and perceptions which each of us brings to the study of property. Yet our responses to these ancient questions have implications which go far beyond the immediate resolution of property disputes. Our conclusions impinge upon a whole range of modern debates—about personal privacy, civil liberty, distributive justice, social exclusion and environmental welfare—debates which are central to the way in which we live our lives. Property questions are profound; their reach is universal; their power to engage is immense. Small wonder that even Blackstone, in one of his more cheerful moments, recognised that there is 'nothing which so generally strikes the imagination, and engages the affections of mankind, as the right of property' (*Blackstone Commentaries*, vol II, 2).

In the case of land, the factor which intensifies the explosive cocktail of proprietary emotion is the truism that there is a strictly limited supply of the commodity. Particularly in the context of land, property becomes the obsessive concern of a lifetime: ask anyone with a mortgage or, for that matter, anyone who sleeps in a doorway. Indeed you, the reader, are already a fully fledged expert on property, for you have spent most of your life engaged in the constant and instinctive—often subconscious—identification of things as being either your own or someone else's. Nor will you ever escape the long reach of land law, for this body of rules has something to say about every aspect of your daily life. What right, for example, do you have to be in the place where you are reading this book? Do you own the space in which you are sitting? Are you a tenant? Are you a licensee (or permitted visitor)? Are your parents entitled to throw you out of the family home? Or are you, perhaps, a squatter or trespasser in someone else's premises? You are never, in fact, immune from classification in land law terms. As the American jurist, Max Radin, once said, '[t]o go to sleep in one's bed is as much and as little of a legal act . . . as signing a deed' (Radin, 'The Permanent Problems of the Law' (1929–30) 15 *Cornell LQ* 1 at 3). Even when you rest six feet under, land law can still tell us your precise legal status in relation to realty.

THE CASE (*CHHOKAR v CHHOKAR*)

An Ordinary Family Home

But let me transport you far away from these musings to a street in West London and to an everyday story of ordinary people living in Southall. The central characters in this drama are a husband and wife, Mr and Mrs Chhokar. The beguiling normality of the suburban context should never, of course, blind us to the volatility of emotion, the duplicitous scheming and the bizarre twists of fate that often flourish in such settings: always expect the unexpected! The tangled narrative of the Chhokars' life together was to end up in the Court of Appeal in the 1980s and to lead to a ruling which, somewhat improbably, invoked the authority of an unreported decision of a Venetian court some four centuries earlier.

Two years after their marriage in 1975 the Chhokars bought a house in Clarence Street in Southall for a price (in today's values) of £120,000. The deposit of £10,000 came from their joint savings and the remaining £110,000 was borrowed by Mr Chhokar from a building society. The Chhokars were typical participants in what soon became Thatcher's 'property-owning democracy' or, as Lord Diplock more accurately described it in *Pettitt v Pettitt* (1970), 'a real-property-mortgaged-to-a-building-society-owning democracy'. The Chhokars' purchase was doubtless founded on hard work; their aspirations were upwardly mobile; they had a young child for whom they were striving to create a better life.

Legal title to the Chhokars' home was registered at the Land Registry in Mr Chhokar's name alone (although, in the confusion of the purchase, his wife initially believed that it had been registered in their joint names). The rights of the building society were, incidentally, merely those of a secured creditor. This meant that, although the money which it had lent to Mr Chhokar ranked immediately as *his* money for the purpose of the purchase, the building society was entitled, in the event of any default, to recover the outstanding loan money by forcing a sale of the home. Herein lies the essence of mortgage-fuelled house-purchase. The borrower is enabled to acquire a major capital asset (usually by means of instalment payments over a mortgage term of some 20 or 25 years), while the lender's rights are confined to the eventual return of the loan principal plus any interest which has accrued on this sum. Of course, land (together with any house which is part of the land) tends to inflate in value over time, with the result that the modern mortgage operates as a very remarkable engine of wealth creation for the borrower. By purchasing a home with externally sourced funds, the borrower is allowed to ride up on the steadily increasing capital value of the land, thereby achieving a tax-free windfall in which the lender takes no share beyond the contracted return of loan money with interest.

Legal and Equitable Ownership

Right at the outset we meet our first difficulty in the Chhokar saga—
where exactly did Mrs Chhokar fit into the ownership picture? So far as
the Land Registry was concerned, Mr Chhokar was quite plainly the sole
registered proprietor of the matrimonial home. There was not a scrap of
documentation anywhere to suggest that his wife owned *any* share in that
home. Yet it was beyond dispute that at all relevant times Mrs Chhokar
had handed her wages over to her husband, with the result that both the
initial deposit on the house and the subsequent mortgage payments had
been generated by the earnings of both. No matter how the registered
(or 'legal') title is held, it seems intuitively *unfair* that joint contributory
effort should not be recognised in some form of shared ownership. But
here the legal ownership of the Chhokars' home had already crystallised
definitively in the husband's name alone.

At this point an extraordinarily significant branch of English jurisprudential doctrine comes into play. For centuries the courts have
recognised that ownership can sometimes exist on two parallel planes.
In such cases, 'legal' ownership (or ownership 'at common law') comprises merely the superficial documentary record of ownership (usually
as evidenced by title deeds or by the proprietorship entered in the Land
Register). Viewed in this way, 'legal' ownership is only the external
face of proprietary entitlement. It is, in many ways, a nominal kind of
ownership, signifying simply that someone is the *caretaker* or *custodian*
of the land. 'Legal' ownership is not even that important, since it does
little more than reflect the fact that the name of a particular transferee
has been inscribed (sometimes quite fortuitously) on a deed of transfer.
More vital by far is the 'equitable' (or 'beneficial') ownership of the
asset in question. The jurisdiction of equity—originating in the court of
the king's Chancellor in medieval times and later exercised by the Court
of Chancery—came to recognise that 'legal' ownership is not necessarily conclusive of the allocation of proprietary entitlement (see chapter 6).
Equity's central contribution to English jurisprudence has always been
the idea that conscience-based obligation takes priority over strict legal
right. Unlike the common law (which is moved by the sheer outer form
of documentary titles), equity looks to the inner reality of transactions.

Accordingly, in appropriate circumstances, equity answers its primary call of conscience by engrafting a corrective image of entitlement—a species of 'equitable' ownership—upon the ownership which exists at common law.

In this way equity is able to supplement the common law by responding more flexibly and sensitively to the need for fair dealing and just outcomes. It would be wrong, however, to suggest that equity intervenes in *every* circumstance in which a person in the street might identify a particular outcome as unfair. To go down this path would simply lead to chaos. But one of the standard cases where equity *does* interpose its own view of ownership occurs where a legal title to property is purchased using money contributed by some person or persons who are omitted from the legal ownership. In a world where money talks loudly, it is intrinsically unlikely that money contributors will have intended to part with substantial amounts of cash otherwise than in the expectation of some form of ownership. In these circumstances it seems 'inequitable' for the purchaser of a legal title to deny the ownership rights of the very persons who made his acquisition possible. Accordingly, in the absence of any proven contrary intention, equity regards the purchaser as a mere 'trustee' (or custodian) who holds his legal title 'on trust' for those who directly funded his purchase (each in proportion to their respective money contributions). The fair return expected by the money contributors takes the form of shares of 'equitable' (or 'beneficial') ownership under the 'trust'. In effect, 'legal' ownership is reserved for the person nominally entitled to the property, while a parallel form of 'equitable' ownership—ultimately the more important kind of ownership—is recognised in those whose efforts, in reality, facilitated the purchase. So forceful is equity's mandate of conscience that the trust which arises here requires no documentary existence. It subsists as an 'implied trust', hovering—as it were—in mid-air, but in no sense diminished or weakened by its lack of visible paper form.

When this doctrine of trusts is applied to the facts of the *Chhokar* case, it readily yields the conclusion—undisputed by all parties concerned—that although Mr Chhokar owned the matrimonial home 'at law', ownership 'in equity' was divided between husband and wife in equal shares by virtue of their joint contributions of money. (Ongoing

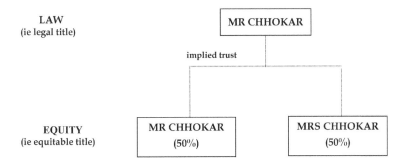

Figure 5.1 Ownership in law and equity by Mr and Mrs Chhokar

mortgage payments are effectively treated as a discharge by instalments of the initial purchase price.) The overall effect was therefore that, while Mr Chhokar (as 'legal' owner) retained the bare right to sell or otherwise dispose of the home, the money value inherent in that home was shared equally between husband and wife as co-owners of the 'equitable' (or 'beneficial') interest. These parallel versions of ownership can be expressed in the graphic form, as shown in figure 5.1

A Dreadful Deed

So far so good. You have just survived a first (and not entirely easy) encounter with the technicalities of the law of property. But the same cannot be said for the Chhokar family, because from here on storm clouds begin to gather over their heads. Tolstoy wrote famously that 'all happy families are alike but an unhappy family is unhappy after its own fashion'. Domestic discord struck the Chhokars in an inimitable sequence of events. In 1978, just as their second child was on the way, Mr Chhokar suspected his wife of infidelity, although no evidence was ever found to support such an assertion. Nevertheless, Mr Chhokar devoted himself single-mindedly to a strategy which was designed to rid himself of his wife. He took her to India for a short holiday and, while there, he confiscated her return ticket and came home alone, leaving her destitute. Somehow Mrs Chhokar, heavily pregnant, managed to borrow enough money to make her way back to London: we are told that her husband was 'surprised to see her'. Mr Chhokar then embarked upon a scheme which he hoped would not only disembarrass himself permanently of his wife, but also siphon-off a sufficiently substantial portion of the value of the matrimonial home to enable him to start a new life elsewhere without her. To this end he met a Mr Parmar in a bar somewhere in London. There, as Ewbank J was later to say, he had 'a discussion that might take place in similar circumstances in relation to property . . . asserted to have fallen off the back of a lorry'.

The upshot of this conversation was an agreement to sell the Chhokars' home to Parmar for £165,000, a sum which was patently a gross undervalue. The transaction was planned behind the back of Mrs Chhokar, who was led to believe that Parmar, during his inspection of the premises, was merely a prospective lodger. Parmar was fully aware of Mr Chhokar's fraudulent intent and together they agreed that completion of the house transfer should occur while Mrs Chhokar was in hospital having her next baby. Such plans never, of course, run smoothly. Mrs Chhokar's baby was tardy in making its appearance and completion of the transfer had to be postponed for some four days after the expected date of delivery. Notwithstanding this inconvenience, the duplicitous transfer eventually took place while Mrs Chhokar was still in the maternity ward. Mr Chhokar immediately repaid his outstanding mortgage debt and set off for India with a cash windfall of some £50,000. Two days after completion Parmar put the house on the market for £240,000—ie £75,000 more than the price he had paid to Mr Chhokar. When, a day later, Mrs Chhokar emerged from hospital clutching her new-born child, she found the locks changed at her home and, on trying to gain access, was beaten up by Parmar's heavies. Parmar threatened to throw the baby out of a window and he and his thugs proceeded to break every window in the house and vandalise the lavatory in an attempt to render the house uninhabitable by Mrs Chhokar.

An Unforeseen Outcome

At this stage the scoreline could not but register the fact that some of the participants in this story had fared rather better than others. Parmar had got the house and the prospect of a massive profit on resale; Mr Chhokar had got no wife, a large cash bonus, a new life incognito, and probably a new woman; whereas Mrs Chhokar had got two small children and no home and was therefore compelled to live in a hostel. But how fundamentally the circumstances of life can alter! As the Bard of the North once put it, 'the best laid plans of mice and men gang aft agley'. Two entirely unforeseen developments occurred which were to confound the expectations of Parmar and his feckless accomplice. A few months after the fraudulent transfer Mrs Chhokar—a brave and resourceful woman—managed to move back into her former home in Southall, still unoccupied, and to reinstate there a semblance of family life with her two children. Then even less predictably—and after an absence of two years—Mr Chhokar reappeared on the scene. The prodigal husband, it turned out, had wasted his substance in riotous living, had secretly returned to England, and had been working on the buses in Leicester. He now sought a reconciliation with his wife and children—to which, amazingly, Mrs Chhokar eventually agreed—with the consequence that things had now come full circle. Mr Chhokar resumed residence in the original matrimonial home. The Chhokars were once again living *en famille* under the same roof. One suspects, nonetheless, that the balance of power in the Chhokar household had altered for ever and that Mr Chhokar was made keenly aware that his whole domestic existence rested on the leave and licence of his incredibly long-suffering wife.

The only trouble was that the roof under which the Chhokars were living now belonged at law to someone else, ie Parmar. However wrongful the actions of Mr Chhokar—and no matter how complicit Parmar was in Chhokar's dishonest design—the transfer of the matrimonial home had indeed been effective to pass the registered (ie the 'legal' or 'paper') title to Parmar. This consequence followed from the fact that, unlike equity, the common law focuses simply on the outer form of transactions. Here there had been a duly executed transfer of title perfected by the registration of Parmar as the new proprietor. And Parmar, on becoming aware that the Chhokars had been restored to a state of family life within his own house, was inevitably concerned to terminate what he perceived as a trespass upon his property. The newly reconstituted Chhokar family was equally determined to resist Parmar's attempts to deprive them of their home. These competing concerns translated themselves into a number of legal questions which eventually required to be decided by the Court of Appeal.

Some Legal Realism

Now it is highly likely that you have already reached some preliminary view of the intrinsic merits of the *Chhokar* case. Anyone who engages seriously with this miserable narrative of treachery and double-dealing has probably decided that the scales of justice tilt rather more heavily in favour of Mrs Chhokar than of Parmar. But this, of course, is to state merely a moral preference as distinct from a reasoned legal conclusion. Yet there has long been a branch of jurisprudential theory (promoted largely by the 'American Realists' of the 1930s and 1940s) which tends towards the view that instinctive ethical assessments of given fact-situations play a hugely formative role in the process of judicial decision. Much has been written about the function of the judicial 'hunch' in the determination of legal outcomes; and there may well be a residual truth in the idea that legal decisions are governed, in some degree or other, by the judge's perception of the relative moral merits of the opposing parties. In effect, the judge first decides which party he or she wants to win and then crafts a judgment (ie manipulates the legal 'rules') so as to bring about precisely this result. On this basis, a judge's ruling in any particular case is little more than a semantic ploy aimed at achieving the desired conclusion; the ruling is simply an *ex post facto* rationalisation of an intuitively preconceived solution. In the words of one of the Realists, court judgments should be seen, not as mirroring the actual process of deciding cases, but 'rather as trained lawyers' arguments made by the judges (after the decision has been reached), intended to make the decision seem plausible, legally decent, legally right, to make it seem, indeed, legally inevitable' (Karl N Llewellyn, 'Some Realism about Realism' (1931) 44 *Harvard Law Review* 1222 at 1238–39). The student of the law is always well advised to look closely at what judges are *really doing*, rather than merely at what judges *say* they are doing.

Let us bear this injunction in mind as we examine the various questions posed in the *Chhokar* case and the responses made by the court. The case was heard first by Ewbank J as a single judge in the High Court and then, on appeal, by Cumming-Bruce LJ and Reeve J in the Court of Appeal.

Did Mrs Chhokar Still Own Any Share in the Home?

In *Chhokar* an initial question obviously arose as to whether, in the aftermath of the dishonest transfer of the house to Parmar, Mrs Chhokar retained any *equitable* entitlement in the property. In other words, had her beneficial half-share in the matrimonial home been destroyed by the sale of that home to a stranger? If that were so, not only would Mrs Chhokar have lost any right to live in the house, but she would also have lost the money value of her substantial investment in its acquisition. Her sole remedy would have been a futile action in damages against her indigent husband for breach of trust. Accordingly, it was vital for Mrs Chhokar to be able to show that her beneficial half-share had survived the transfer of the registered title to Parmar. But there arises here a technical difficulty which originates in a much more general principle of land transfer under English law.

It is a major objective of English law to ensure that, in so far as possible, the transferee of a registered title (such as Parmar) takes the land free of all pre-existing interests. The transferee thus starts, as it were, with a clean sheet. He or she is unencumbered by adverse entitlements belonging to others which might impede the enjoyment or profitable exploitation of the land or might act as a disincentive to long-term planning, strategic investment and future marketability. Fundamental economic motivations underpin this concern to liberate the new registered proprietor from interests which could otherwise operate as a drag (or, in more old-fashioned terminology, a 'clog') upon his or her title. A healthily functioning economy requires that land should remain open to efficient processes of sale or other disposition. It is important, so to speak, that land is kept on the move: the fewer the burdens that inhibit market transfer, the better.

It follows that the statute law which governs registered transfers has always placed strict limits on the interests which are allowed to continue to affect a registered title *after* its transfer. A few kinds of entitlement survive the transfer precisely because they are recorded very obviously on the face of the transferor's register of title and are therefore deemed to have been perfectly apparent to any potential transferee. Otherwise, however, the basic rule is that every new registered proprietor is immediately released—in all but a small number of specially defined circumstances— from the burden of pre-existing rights belonging to other persons. In the *Chhokar* case the normal expectation would therefore have been that the new legal owner, Parmar, took his title free of any adverse claims made by others (including the claim by Mrs Chhokar to a 50 per cent beneficial share in the home by way of implied trust). However, such an outcome would have spelt complete disaster for Mrs Chhokar and her vulnerable family.

The Protection of Actual Occupation

At this point we look more closely at the text of the Land Registration Act, which carefully details the exceptional cases where pre-existing entitlements continue to bind the transferee of a registered title. One such exceptional case relates specifically to the proprietary rights of anyone who, at the time of the transfer, was a 'person in actual occupation' of the land concerned. It has long been clear that the proprietary rights of actual occupiers—albeit unrecorded on the face of the Land Register—are protected on a transfer of the legal title. These rights are said to 'override' the transfer and to fetter the land in the hands of the transferee (Land Registration Act 1925, section 70(1)(g); Land Registration Act 2002, section 29, Schedule 3, paragraph 2). This significant exception to the normal rule reflects the enormous respect which English law has traditionally accorded to the entitlements of those who, at any given time, have established a physical presence on the ground. Precisely the same impulse underlies the ancient maxim that 'an Englishman's home is his castle', as also the longstanding distaste of the common law for any form of violent seizure or forcible eviction. Moreover, the statutory protection of those 'in actual occupation' of registered land is widely viewed as striking a fair balance between all parties concerned. Even though their rights are not apparent from the Land Register itself, actual occupiers can justifiably claim that the sheer fact of their physical occupancy sends a powerful signal to any potential transferee that they may own propri-etary rights in the land which merit further investigation. It seems not entirely unfair that an intending purchaser who fails to inquire into the possibility of their entitlement should therefore take the land subject to any interests held by persons whose presence was so blatantly obvious.

Herein, of course, lay a significant difficulty for Mrs Chhokar. It was painfully apparent that, although she had undoubtedly held proprietary 'rights' in the land (ie her beneficial half-share), she was absent from that land at the precise moment of the transfer of the legal title to Parmar. She had been in the maternity ward of the local hospital. Could it really be said that, for the purpose of the statutory exception, she was a 'person in actual occupation' of the land?

Some Statutory Interpretation

Here we must learn something about the art of statutory interpretation. By virtue of the sheer indeterminacy of language, words can convey only a crude approximation of meaning: they are the distorted echoes of ideas. Words, declared Oliver Wendell Holmes, are not transparent crystals: they are merely 'the skin of a living thought' and they may 'vary greatly in color and content' according to the context in which they are used (*Towne v Eisner* (1918)). In particular, statutory words have a flexibility of application (or plasticity) which almost always enables the judge to work towards an ethically satisfying solution of the legal prob-lem before the court. Thus, in the *Chhokar* case, the first instance judge adopted an expansive interpretation of the phrase 'actual occupation'. True it was that Mrs Chhokar had not been physically present in the home at the date of transfer. But what, on closer analysis, does 'actual occupation' really mean anyway? The phrase surely cannot be inter-preted in such an arbitrary or quixotic fashion that people forfeit their rights simply because, on some vital date, they are rushed off to hospital with a broken leg or happen to go away on holiday or even—come to that—pop out of the house for five minutes to buy a pint of milk. Lord Wilberforce once claimed, slightly incautiously, that the phrase 'actual occupation' comprises 'ordinary words of plain English' (*Williams & Glyn's Bank Ltd v Boland* (1981)). It became readily apparent, however, that these innocuous words conceal some rather difficult questions relating to the required substantiality or continuity of the presence concerned. In this example—as in so many others—the intrinsic frailty of legislative language is rapidly exposed. Statutory words are indeed blunt instruments in the communicative process and it is hardly surprising that the angle, force and range of their impact often need to be controlled by an actor somewhat closer to the scene than the legislator. The process of statutory communication cannot be allowed to be erratic—and indeed it is not. The statutory bludgeon becomes the judge's chisel; the dull blow of the parliamentary draftsman is converted into the judicial craftsman's more finely fashioned legal solution.

Thus, at first instance in the *Chhokar* case, Ewbank J found no difficulty in construing the relevant statutory formula so as to catch circumstances where—as in the present case—the home still contained furniture and other items belonging to the absent Mrs Chhokar. The statutory requirement of 'actual occupation' could not (and did not) exclude occupation which was symbolised, or established vicariously, by the presence of personal paraphernalia associated with the claimant 'occupier'. In this way statutory language can be seen as the tool of the judge, rather than the judge as a mere tool of the legislative process.

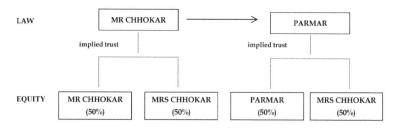

Figure 5.2 The transaction between Mr Chhokar and Parmar

And the end result—not contested before the Court of Appeal—was that Mrs Chhokar's beneficial half-share in the matrimonial home was held to 'override' the transfer of the registered title to Parmar. He effectively took that title subject to an implied trust under which he now shared the beneficial ownership on equal terms with Mrs Chhokar. In reality, Parmar had simply stepped into the shoes of his vendor, Mr Chhokar. In graphic form, the history of the entire transaction now appears as shown in figure 5.2.

Could Parmar Force a Sale of the Home?

Of course, the conclusion that Mrs Chhokar still held an equitable interest did not necessarily foreclose a number of other claims which Parmar wished to advance in respect of the house. Having grudgingly accepted that Mrs Chhokar's beneficial rights had survived the transfer, Parmar predictably sought to salvage what he could from the débâcle by requesting the court to order a sale of the home in which the Chhokar family were now residing. (The court has a discretionary power, now formalised in the Trusts of Land and Appointment of Trustees Act 1996, to order the sale of land which is the subject of a trust.) Such an order would have involved a mandatory disposal of Parmar's registered title on the open market, Mrs Chhokar's beneficial share in the home being compulsorily converted into a half-share of the sale proceeds. At least in this way Parmar could recoup the value of his own beneficial half-share in the property.

At first instance Ewbank J ordered that a sale of the Chhokars' home be effected within nine months and that the sale proceeds be divided between Parmar and Mrs Chhokar. Ewbank J's decision was based on his belief that it was 'quite wrong' that Parmar should provide the Chhokars, free of charge, with a relatively valuable house as their home for the indefinite future. This conclusion was consistent with a long line of cases in which the courts had tended to order the sale of a co-owned home where sale was being pressed for by some complete stranger to the family relationship (such as a creditor who had lent money which he now wished to recover from the sale proceeds).

Ewbank J's ruling in favour of sale was, however, reversed on appeal. In giving the principal judgment in the Court of Appeal, Cumming-Bruce LJ indicated that, although the 'scoundrel Parmar' had no 'matrimonial privity' with Mrs Chhokar, he had sought by his 'monstrous fraud' to 'intermeddle in the wife's interests in the family home'. Parmar was not therefore truly a 'stranger to the marriage'. Accordingly, the discretion to order sale fell to be exercised with reference to the criteria normally applicable where, no 'stranger' being involved, a family home is held on trust for a number of co-owners who cannot agree between themselves whether a sale should occur. These criteria have always placed a heavy emphasis on the question whether the original underlying purpose of the trust remains capable of substantial fulfilment. Ironically, in view of the extraordinary reconciliation achieved between the Chhokars, this original purpose—ie the provision of a home for the Chhokar family—still seemed eminently capable of fulfilment. Nor could the Court of Appeal now see any reason for frustrating the Chhokars' initial intention to use the property as their matrimonial home. But it is also interesting to note that the refusal of the sale so desperately sought by Parmar was explicitly linked to the Court's perception that '[e]verything that [Parmar] did from first to last in connection with the transaction is stamped with immoral stigma'. Cumming-Bruce LJ declared it difficult to 'find language which, with becoming moderation, describes the moral turpitude of every step taken by Parmar throughout'. To the judge it seemed quite plain that, on the question of sale, the voice of the 'innocent' Mrs Chhokar should 'prevail over the voice of the scoundrel who, as the accomplice of [Mr Chhokar], attempted by fraud and diverse devices to frustrate and destroy the wife's overriding interest'. Parmar had been 'caught' in his 'deceit' and could not therefore succeed.

The Court of Appeal accordingly declined to order any sale of the family home. Cumming-Bruce LJ observed that Mrs Chhokar might 'very well be entitled' to 'enjoy her beneficial interest in the matrimonial home, in consortium with her husband or otherwise, for the rest of her life'. Of course, it always remained open to Parmar to reapply to the court for an order for sale in the event of some major change in the parties' circumstances, but Cumming-Bruce LJ (with whom Reeve J expressly agreed) thought it unlikely that such an application could or should be made for 'many years ahead'.

Could Parmar Insist on Sharing Residence in the Home?

If an immediate sale of the Chhokars' home was no longer an outcome available to Parmar, there arose some question as to whether Parmar could at least insist on sharing residence in that home alongside the entire Chhokar family. In English law, after all, a co-owner is presumed to be equally entitled—together with any other co-owner—to enjoy physical possession of each and every part of the co-owned land. However, when the *Chhokar* case reached the Court of Appeal, even Parmar's counsel shrank from pressing such a claim on his behalf. As Cumming-Bruce LJ pointed out, Parmar was a married man himself and 'no court would allow him to try to occupy the matrimonial home in common with Mrs Chhokar'. Indeed, said the judge, 'Mrs Parmar might have something to say about it too, if he tried to do so.'

Could Parmar Exact any Payment of Rent?

Deprived of the possibility of either sale or shared residence, Parmar then argued before the Court of Appeal that Mrs Chhokar should be required to pay him a money rent by virtue of the Chhokar family's exclusive occupancy of the house. Parmar was, after all, a beneficial co-owner and he plainly thought it not improper to extract some rental income in recognition of his equitable half-share in the property. There is, however, a general principle of English law that no rent obligation arises between co-owners merely on the ground that one of these co-owners happens to enjoy sole possession of the co-owned land. This rent immunity flows from the intrinsic entitlement of all the co-owners to share simultaneous physical possession of the land. In effect, no rent can be demanded by a co-owner whose absence from the premises is simply the result of his own voluntary choice. Over the years the courts have been compelled to recognise certain exceptions to this principle, as for example where one co-owner's absence is precipitated by a wrongful act of forcible eviction or domestic violence committed by a co-owner now in possession. Indeed, in modern times it is highly likely that the question whether an occupation rent is due from a co-owner in sole possession has come to rest on a simple test of 'fairness'. Would it be 'fair' to impose such an obligation in all the circumstances of the case?

In *Chhokar* it could, of course, be said that Parmar's absence from the co-owned premises was not immediately a matter of his own choosing: the courts had explicitly denied him any chance of shared occupancy. The historic rationale for rent immunity between co-owners supposedly rests on the freedom of each to occupy the co-owned property at will. Yet the Court of Appeal showed no detectible sign of regret that this freedom was presently unavailable to Parmar. In view of Parmar's 'crooked deceptions' and 'fraudulent conspiracy', the Court considered that it was now wholly *unfair* to cast any rental burden on Mrs Chhokar. In the result Parmar was condemned to stand idly by while the Chhokars enjoyed, for the indefinite future, rent-free occupation of his property. It was quite irrelevant, said Cumming-Bruce LJ, that Mrs Chhokar had currently decided to share this rent-free accommodation with her 'unsatisfactory' husband.

CONCLUSION

All in all, the *Chhokar* case provides a superb cautionary tale couched in the improbable language of the law of realty. It comprises a modern *conte morale*, in which human weakness is countered and ultimately redeemed by the magnanimity of a courageous and determined woman. Powerful forces of lust and cupidity are brought low. There is an eventual triumph of good over ill. There is an ethically satisfying conclusion. A confused and feckless husband is rescued by an act of forgiveness and reconciliation; an avaricious and unscrupulous intermeddler suffers a reversal of his fortunes. Indeed, by the conclusion of the Court of Appeal hearing in the *Chhokar* case, the wrongdoer Parmar began to cut a rather woebegone figure—but the Court seemed disinclined to temper justice with much mercy. Parmar ended up owning a half-share in a house which he could neither occupy nor sell and from which he could derive no rental income. He still owed £65,000 to an estate agent who had lent money towards his conspiratorial purchase. He was ordered to pay a further £21,500 to Mrs Chhokar and her children by way of damages for their wrongful eviction. For Parmar the only morsel of comfort lay in the fact that when the house finally came to be sold at some (as yet unknown) future date, he would receive credit for the original mortgage debt which had been discharged by Mr Chhokar out of the proceeds of their conspiratorial transaction.

By contrast Mrs Chhokar (with the help of legal aid) had vindicated her original entitlement to a half-share in her family's home. Furthermore she was guaranteed rent- and mortgage-free accommodation in that home for the indefinite future, together with the possibly more dubious benefits of continued cohabitation with her reconciled husband. It would have required the skill of a consummate playwright to craft so ironic a conclusion to this remarkable human drama. But, as the Court of Appeal observed, there was no room for 'crocodile tears' on behalf of Parmar merely because his unlawful enterprise did not succeed. Indeed, Cumming-Bruce LJ professed himself able to see 'no reason for giving him anything more than the court in an unreported case gave to the money-lender who had rights over a debtor'. The proceedings, said the judge, 'are recorded in a play of Shakespeare'.

Cases

Chhokar v Chhokar [1984] 5 FLR 313
Pettitt v Pettitt [1970] AC 777
Towne v Eisner 245 US 418, 62 L Ed 372 (1918) (Holmes J)
Williams & Glyn's Bank Ltd v Boland [1981] AC 487

Further reading

Gray and Gray, *Land Law*, 7th edn (Oxford, Oxford University Press, 2011)
A Bottomley and H Lim, 'Feminist Perambulations: Taking the Law for a Walk in land', in H Lim and A Bottomley (eds), *Feminist Perspectives on Land Law* (Abingdon, Routledge-Cavendish, 2007) 1–30
J Dewar, 'Land, Law, and The Family Home', in S Bright and J Dewar

(eds), *Land Law: Themes and Perspectives* (Oxford, Oxford University Press, 1998) 327–55

Louise Tee, 'Co-ownership and Trusts', in L Tee (ed), *Land Law: Issues, Debates, Policy* (Devon, Willan Publishing, 2002) 132–68

6

Equity

Graham Virgo

Charles Dickens' *Bleak House*, first published in 1852, contains this description of equity as practised in the courts of the time:

> On such an afternoon, some score of members of the High Court of Chancery bar ought to be—as here they are—mistily engaged in one of the ten thousand stages of an endless cause, tripping one another up on slippery precedents, groping knee-deep in technicalities, running their goat-hair and horse-hair warded heads against walls of words, and making a pretence of equity with serious faces, as players might.

Dickens adds that all the people in the court are yawning 'for no crumb of amusement ever falls from JARNDYCE AND JARNDYCE (the cause in hand), which was squeezed dry years upon years ago'. That case involved a disputed inheritance and, as Dickens says: 'this scarecrow of a suit has, in course of time, become so complicated, that no man alive knows what it means'. By the end of the novel, judgment is given but the legal costs which have been incurred are so great that they devour most of the estate which was disputed in the first place.

This is the equity of the nineteenth century, which was concerned with death and succession, taxes and debts. This is dry and technical law. But equity today is very different. Although the modern subject is built on the old cases, the principles which underpin those cases have been refined over the years and are of real significance today, often in contexts very different from inheritance disputes. For example, a lot of modern commercial law, especially company law, has been dramatically influenced by equity. Equity is a subject which is intellectually challenging but provides solutions to some important and difficult current problems. This is shown by the case on which this chapter will focus: *Foskett v McKeown*—a case which arose from a father's greed and stupidity. At its heart the House of Lords was concerned with the question: 'Should the sins of the father be visited on his children?' This raises difficult questions about what justice demands, especially when all the parties before the court are innocent of any wrongdoing. But the case raises even bigger questions than this, involving the very nature of legal reasoning and legal method. When judges, especially judges in the appeal courts, have to decide a case, they are faced with a dilemma. Should they be concerned primarily with the merits of the case and focus on the facts, or should they have regard to the bigger picture, by ensuring that the rules and principles of law are clear and coherent to resolve both the present dispute and also future cases? This dilemma can be caricatured as being a choice between a just and fair result (colloquially called an equitable result), which might be uncertain, and a clear and principled result, which might be unjust on the facts. It is a dilemma which underpins much legal decision-making, but it was particularly marked in *Foskett v McKeown.*

But before that case is considered we need to examine what this body of law known as equity actually involves.

WHAT IS EQUITY?

Much of the law which you have been reading about in this book so far is called the common law. It has been developed by the judges in the courts over hundreds of years. But there is another stream of judge-made law known as equity, which was considered in chapter 5 as well. To understand why we have two different streams of judge-made law we need to go back in time to the medieval age. This was the period when judge-made law started to develop rapidly. Legal principles, some of which are still relevant today, started to emerge. However, the general attitude of the judges was strict and inflexible. Although there was room for judicial creativity, the judges tended to interpret the law rigidly and developed it through the elaboration of ever more complicated rules. In particular, claims brought by individual litigants had to fall within clearly established categories and, if they did not, they would fail. If no remedy was awarded or was even available, it was possible to petition the King to seek justice. The King delegated this function to his principal minister, the Chancellor, who exercised his judgment according to his conscience. Equity in this period was discretionary and vague, as was famously described by John Selden, a legal author in the seventeenth century:

> Equity is a roguish thing: for law we have a measure, know what to trust to; equity is according to the conscience of him that is chancellor, and as that is larger or narrower, so is equity. [It is] as if they should make the standard for the measure we call a foot a chancellor's foot; what an uncertain measure would this be! One chancellor has a long foot, another a short foot, a third an indifferent foot. 'Tis the same in the chancellor's conscience.

Eventually a separate court was established, known as the Court of Chancery, to deal with petitions to the Chancellor and it was the law which was developed and applied in this court which became known as equity. The purpose of this body of law was to temper the rigidity in the application of the law by common law judges. From the seventeenth century onwards this body of law became more systematic.

Equity is still sometimes described as operating to modify the rigidity of the common law. But, to the extent that this indicates that equity is vague and unprincipled, it is untrue, for much of equity today is rule-based and certain. But it does not follow that equity is, as it is sometimes quaintly put, 'past the age of child-bearing'. Equity can still be used to create new doctrines and to develop existing ones to provide solutions to problems which are ignored by the common law.

THE CONTRIBUTION OF EQUITY

Equity has had a profound contribution in many areas of the law, especially as regards the identification of rights and the development of important remedies, such as the order of *specific performance* to make the defendant perform his or her obligations under a contract, or *injunctions* to stop the defendant from committing a wrong. The role of equity in creating rights to land was examined in chapter 5. The creative function of equity is particularly well illustrated by an important remedy developed in the 1970s to deal with the problem of a defendant who seeks to hide his or her assets or take them out of the jurisdiction to prevent the claimant from enforcing a judgment for damages against him or her. To avoid this problem equity was relied on to create a new form of injunction, known then as a *Mareva* injunction (after the case which first recognised it, which concerned a ship of that name) and now known as a freezing order. This is an injunction which can be used by judges to freeze some or all of the defendant's assets to ensure that any judgment can be enforced against the defendant. For example, the order might mean that the defendant would not be able to gain access to money which has been credited to his or her bank account. This is an injunction which has proved to be a significant feature of the English law of civil procedure.

Equity has been influential in many other ways. For example, there is a body of law where equity can be used to regulate exploitative transactions, such as where one party unduly influences another to enter into a disadvantageous contract or to make a gift. Equity is also responsible for the recognition and regulation of certain types of relationship which are called fiduciary relationships. A fiduciary is somebody who is in a relationship of trust and confidence with somebody else, known as the principal. The fiduciary is expected to be loyal to the principal and to maintain the highest standards of behaviour in looking after the principal's interests. Typical fiduciary relationships are those of company directors who are in a fiduciary relationship with their company, and solicitors who are in a fiduciary relationship with their clients. The importance of fiduciary law is illustrated by *Attorney-General of Hong Kong v Reid*, a decision of the Privy Council. Reid was a public prosecutor in Hong Kong. Having been bribed by a gang to obstruct the prosecution of some of its members, he invested the bribe money in land in New Zealand. The Hong Kong government sought to recover this land. The Privy Council held that Reid was a fiduciary, because he was in a relationship of trust and confidence with the state; that he had breached his fiduciary duties in accepting the bribe money; and this money should be treated as belonging to the state, which therefore owned the land in New Zealand because it had been bought with the bribe money.

Despite the significant contribution of these different equitable remedies and doctrines to English law, the most important contribution of equity is undoubtedly the *trust*. The crucial feature of the trust is that property is held by one person for the benefit of another. This is recognised through the division of property rights. One person holds the legal title to the property. This is the *trustee*. As far as the common law is concerned that person is the sole owner. But equity can see that the legal owner holds the property for the benefit of somebody else, the *beneficiary*. That beneficiary therefore has an equitable interest in the property. The trustee is obliged to look after the property for the benefit of the beneficiary. If the trustee fails to do this, he or she will have breached the trust and will be liable to the beneficiary.

TYPES OF TRUST

English law recognises a variety of different trusts. The main form is the express trust, which is created intentionally by the settlor (if the trust is created by somebody, while he or she is alive, who 'settles' property on trust) or the testator (if the trust is created by somebody in a will). The express trust can either be fixed or discretionary. In a *fixed* trust the interests of the beneficiaries are established at the time the trust is created. For example, a father may put in his will that, if he dies before his three children attain the age of 18, his property should be transferred to trustees for the benefit of the children. If the father died before the children were 18 the trustees would have legal title to the property, but they would not be able to benefit from it since they would have to manage the property for the children until they attained 18. Each child would have a fixed equitable interest in one-third of the property until they became 18, when the legal interest in their share of the property would be transferred to them. Alternatively, in an express *discretionary* trust the trustees own the property at law but no beneficiary has an existing interest in the property. Rather, the trustees have a discretion to distribute the property as they see fit to people from a particular class of potential beneficiaries. So, for example, the trust may give the trustees a discretion to use the trust property to pay for the education of children of employees from a particular business. The trustees would be free to decide how they could allocate trust funds to such children in such amounts as they consider to be appropriate.

There are a number of reasons why a settlor or testator might wish to establish an express trust. There may be a particular advantage in having trustees managing and administering the property. This might be because the beneficiaries are too young to do so or cannot be trusted with the property. Or the trust might be a convenient way of holding the property for the mutual benefit of a group of people. This is one of the main reasons why the trust is used in the commercial world. For example, it is used as a mechanism for managing pension funds for the benefit of many employees, or as a mechanism for a group of people investing their funds by means of a unit or investment trust. Another purpose of the trust is that it can provide a means for avoiding tax, by transferring property to somebody whose tax liability might be smaller. But here the trust might be open to abuse and there is a lot of complex law to ensure that the trust is not used as an illegitimate method of tax evasion.

Another type of trust is known as the *constructive* trust. This arises through the application of legal rules rather than being expressly created by a settlor or testator. It is relevant, for example, where a defendant has obtained property by fraud. Even though the common law might say that the property belongs to the fraudster, equity will say that the property is held on constructive trust by the fraudster for the victim of the fraud.

Normally the trust works well, but sometimes the temptation of the trustee to benefit personally from the property is too great and there is an abuse or breach of trust. It was a breach of an express fixed trust which triggered the litigation in *Foskett v McKeown*.

THE FACTS OF *FOSKETT v McKEOWN*

A group of businessmen decided that they wished to invest in property on the Algarve in Portugal, which they wanted to develop as a golf course.

They agreed that their money should be held on trust for them, so that the money was managed by somebody else on their behalf. The money was therefore transferred to a trustee. He had legal title to the property but, because he held it on an express trust for the businessmen, they had an equitable interest in the money.

Some time earlier the trustee had set up a life insurance policy on his own life. The terms of the policy were such that, if he died, the sum of £1 million would be paid to his children. He was required to pay annual insurance premiums of about £10,000. These premiums were invested to obtain units and it was the value of these units which was used to pay for the maintenance of the policy. The trustee paid the first three premiums from his own money. He then stole £10,000 from the trust to pay for the fourth premium and did the same the following year. This constituted a breach of trust. He then committed suicide. The fact that he died at his own hand did not invalidate the policy. It followed that his children were eligible to receive a lump sum payment of £1 million from the insurance company (see figure 6.1 below).

Year	1	2	3	4	5 →	suicide →	£1m
Trustee's own money	×	×	×				
Beneficiaries' money				×	×		

Figure 6.1 Sources of payments of the insurance premiums

However, the beneficiaries of the trust discovered that the trustee had stolen £20,000 from the trust and that he had used this money to pay two of the premiums. The beneficiaries argued that, since their money had been used to pay two of the five premiums which had contributed to the payment of £1 million, it followed that they should have two-fifths of that sum, amounting to £400,000. The children contested this on the basis that the money belonged to them and either they should keep the whole £1 million or they should simply reimburse the beneficiaries for what they had lost.

THE POSSIBLE SOLUTIONS

Despite the somewhat complicated facts of *Foskett v McKeown*, the basic issue was straightforward: should the businessmen beneficiaries recover a proportionate share of the £1 million? There were essentially four solutions to this dispute:

1 As the beneficiaries argued, since the money which had been used to pay the fourth and the fifth premiums belonged to them in equity, they should get a two-fifths share of the £1 million.

2 Since the beneficiaries had only contributed £20,000, that is what the children should be required to reimburse, plus interest to compensate the beneficiaries because they had not been able to use their money for a period of time.

3 The beneficiaries should recover nothing. This argument, which was also made by the children, was dependent on the peculiar nature of the insurance policy. The premiums which were paid were not automatically used to maintain the policy. Rather, the premiums were used to purchase units. The first three premiums had purchased sufficient units to mean that, even if the fourth and the fifth premium had not been paid, the insurance policy would not have lapsed and the £1 million would still have been paid. Consequently, it was argued that the beneficiaries' money had not contributed to the receipt of the £1 million in any way.

4 There is a further solution which was not argued in the case, namely, that, because the fourth and the fifth premiums had been stolen from the trust, which was a criminal offence, it followed that the £1 million was the proceeds of crime. English law has long recognised that recipients of the proceeds of crime should be required to give up those proceeds to the victim and cannot be seen to benefit from them. Consequently, even though the children were innocent of the crime themselves, they could not be seen to benefit from their father's crime in any way and so the beneficiaries should recover the whole of the £1 million.

IDENTIFICATION AND APPLICATION OF RULES AND PRINCIPLES

Although the five judges in the House of Lords were divided by three to two as to the appropriate result, there was a great deal of consensus amongst them as to the proper mode of analysing a problem such as this. The judges identified the following principles and steps in their reasoning.

Principle and Not Discretion

In determining whether the businessmen beneficiaries or the children should win, one approach is to determine what is the just and fair result by reference to the facts of the case. This is a discretionary approach. Such an approach may have a variety of benefits, but it is subject to the drawback that it results in uncertain and unpredictable law. Where there is a dispute between parties it is preferable to resolve that dispute outside the courts through a settlement between the parties, if only because it is quicker and cheaper to do so. If the law is certain and predictable it makes it much easier for a settlement to be reached because the parties can predict how a judge might decide the case. Even where a settlement may not be possible, perhaps because there is a dispute as to the facts and the case goes to trial, there are major advantages in having law which is certain and predictable. This is because it enables the judge to apply the law more easily and ensures that there is consistency in that application, for otherwise the result of the case may become a lottery, depending on which judge hears the case.

In *Foskett* the majority recognised that vague notions of justice and equity, in the sense of fairness, were not appropriate when considering who had an interest in the £1 million. That should be resolved through the application of established principles. The relevance of principles was identified by one of the judges as follows:

> This case does not depend on whether it is fair, just and reasonable to give the [beneficiaries] an interest as a result of which the court in its discretion provides a remedy. It is a case of hard-nosed property rights.

Certainty and clarity in the law were considered to be more important than the application of judicial discretion.

The Proprietary Base

It was therefore necessary for the judges to consider what the applicable principles were. For the beneficiaries to show that some, if not all, of the £1 million received by the children belonged to them, they needed to show that the money which was stolen from the trust was their money. This has been called the *proprietary base* on which the claim is built. This proprietary base was very easy to establish on the facts of the case because it was clear that the money was stolen from an express fixed trust. This trust was significant for two reasons. First, because it showed that the beneficiaries had a property interest in the money. Secondly, because it meant that this interest was equitable. The nature of the interest is very important for a number of reasons. Legal property interests are governed by the common law, whereas equitable proprietary interests are governed by equity. The source of the interest will be particularly important as regards the nature of the remedy which is awarded. This is because, where somebody has taken your property, the common law's response is almost always to require the defendant to pay the claimant the value which that property had when it was stolen. This is called a 'personal' remedy. However, equity is more willing to require the defendant to transfer the property itself back to the claimant by means of a proprietary remedy. This is often a much more attractive remedy, especially where the value of the property has increased, as it had in *Foskett*.

Following and Tracing

Once the beneficiaries could show that money which belonged to them in equity had been used to pay two of the premiums, they then needed to be able to link this money to the eventual payment of the £1 million. This involved the application of a complex body of law known as the *following* and *tracing* rules. The application of these rules can be illustrated by the following examples. First, imagine that your car has been stolen by a thief who gives it to the defendant. In order to make a claim to the car you need to be able to show that the car which was stolen from you was the same car which was received by the defendant. You would establish this by following the car from you to the thief to the defendant. Following involves identifying the original property in somebody else's hands. This is easy. But things become a lot more difficult where the car was stolen by a thief who sold it and used the proceeds to buy a motorbike which he gave to the defendant. Let us also assume that the car has been destroyed. In those circumstances you cannot follow the car because it no longer exists. But you can show that the value which was within the car has been used to purchase the bike. You should then be able to make a claim to the bike on the basis that the bike now represents your car. To make such a claim you need to trace the value which was within the car into the bike. The application of tracing rules enables the owner of property to claim a substitute for that property or its product.

The reason why the law in this area is so complex is because the rules relating to tracing are interpreted differently depending on whether you are tracing property at law, where the claimant has a proprietary base recognised by the common law, or in equity, where the proprietary base is equitable. The common law adopts a restrictive approach to its tracing rules, especially because the common law says that where the claimant's property is mixed with other property it is no longer possible to identify the claimant's property and so tracing fails. The equitable tracing rules are different, since equity is willing to trace property into and through a mixture. This difference between tracing at law and in equity is most important as regards money credited to a bank account. This can be illustrated by the following example. Imagine that the claimant has two bags, one containing £1,000 and the other containing £2,000. The first bag belongs to the claimant at law; but the second bag is held on trust for the claimant, so that she has an equitable but not a legal interest in it. Both of the bags are then stolen by the defendant who takes them to a bank where the money is credited to the defendant's existing bank account. When you pay money into a bank account, those particular notes and coins are not paid physically into a particular account. Rather, the money is credited to that account. This means that the bank owns the actual notes and coins, but the credit to the account means that the bank owes the account-holder the amount of money which was credited. In other words, the relationship between the account-holder and the bank is one of creditor and debtor. Even though there is no physical money in the account, the debt which is owed by the bank is itself a piece of property which can be owned and transferred. This debt is sometimes known as a 'thing in action' or a 'chose in action'. Whatever it is called, it is a piece of property in its own right which is distinct from the original cash.

Returning to our example (see figure 6.2 below), when the defendant took the two bags to the bank, let us assume that he already had £500 credited to his account. So when the money in the two bags is deposited it will mean that the defendant has £3,500 credited to his bank account, as shown in figure 6.2 below.

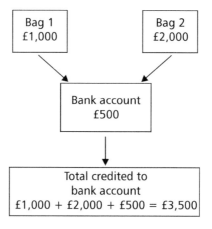

Figure 6.2 Tracing and following

Can the claimant trace his money in such circumstances? As regards the £1,000 which belongs to the claimant at law, tracing is not possible because that money is transformed into a debt worth £1,000 but this has become mixed with the existing £500 which was already credited to the account, so that it is no longer possible to say which money belongs to the claimant and which to the defendant. It is like mixing the claimant's bag of peas in a saucepan with the defendant's bag of peas; it is no longer possible to say which peas belong to the claimant and which to the defendant. Consequently, the common law throws up its hands and says 'we cannot unpack this mixture because the peas all look the same' and so tracing into the mixture will fail. It follows that all the peas will belong to the defendant. Of course, the answer would be different if the claimant's peas were green and the defendant's peas were yellow, because they could be easily distinguished. Even if the peas were the same colour, however, equity, which is more creative than the common law, is willing to separate the mixture into its constituent parts. So, if the claimant knew that his bag contained 1,000 peas he would be able to recover any 1,000 peas from the mixture, even though some of the peas may actually have been contributed by the defendant. Equity is able to do exactly the same as regards money credited to a bank account. In our example there will be £3,500 credited to the defendant's bank account. £500 of this will belong to the defendant, since that was the amount which was already credited to the account. £1,000 will represent the money which belonged to the claimant at law, and which will have lost its identity because it was paid into a mixture. But the remaining £2,000 will represent the money in which the claimant had an equitable interest and which will not have lost its identity because equity can see it represented within the mixture. So the claimant will be able to recover this amount in equity. This example shows how important it is to distinguish between interests in property which exist at law and those which exist in equity, because different tracing rules apply.

Although these examples are very basic, they form the foundation for the intervention of equity in cases involving millions of pounds. Some of these cases may involve massive corporate fraud or money laundering where it is important to show that the value of money which belonged to the claimant can be identified in different property which is now in the hands of the defendant money-launderer.

The importance of the tracing rules is especially well illustrated by the facts of *Foskett v McKeown*. Once the beneficiaries had established that the money which had been taken from the trust belonged to them in equity they needed to show that this money existed in the £1 million.

They could not follow their money into the £1 million, because it was not the same money as that which had been stolen from the trust, so they had to rely on the tracing rules and, because they had an equitable proprietary interest in the trust fund, they relied on the equitable tracing rules.

The judges in the majority in the House of Lords clarified what the function of the tracing rules was, by emphasising that tracing was concerned with identifying the value which was originally in the trust fund and locating it in the £1 million. This involved two different steps. First, it was necessary to establish that the money which had been taken from the trust could be traced through various bank accounts and into the fourth and fifth premiums which were paid to the insurance company. Equity was willing to do this even though the money had been mixed in various bank accounts.

Secondly, and this was the most difficult part of the claim, it was necessary to show that the value of the money which had been taken from the trust could be traced from the premiums into the £1 million. This was difficult to establish because of the peculiar nature of the insurance policy which meant that, even had the fourth and fifth premiums not been paid, sufficient value had been contributed by the first three premiums to mean that the £1 million would have been paid anyway. How then could it be shown that the fourth and fifth premiums contributed to the £1 million? For one of the dissenting judges this was the reason why the beneficiaries' claim failed, because it was not possible to show that the payment of the fourth and the fifth premiums had caused the £1 million to be paid. But, for the majority, it was possible to trace into the £1 million despite this feature of the insurance policy. This was because it was sufficient that the value of the money which had been taken from the trust could be attributed to the £1 million, even though this value had not caused the £1 million to be obtained. This attribution was established by reference to a very technical argument which derived from the terms of the insurance policy. That policy said that the death benefit would be paid 'in consideration for' all of the premiums which had been paid. What this meant was that, in return for the payment of the premiums, £1 million would be paid once the person whose life had been insured died. In other words, although £1 million would have been paid even had the fourth and fifth premiums not been paid, the £1 million was paid with explicit reference to all the premiums, which included the contribution from the beneficiaries.

The consequence of the approach of the majority was that the value which was recognised by equity as belonging to the beneficiaries in the trust fund could be traced from that fund, through various bank accounts, into the fourth and fifth premiums and from there into the £1 million.

Identification of the Remedy

Even though the beneficiaries could show that they had an equitable proprietary interest in the £1 million, it certainly did not follow that they could recover the whole amount. This was because the beneficiaries had only contributed two-fifths of the premiums which had been paid, with the remaining three-fifths being contributed by the trustee himself. It was therefore necessary for the court to determine what the appropriate remedy should be. This was the crucial part of the case and the part which proved to be most controversial.

Once a claim or cause of action has been established this means that the claimant has a right which needs to be protected or remedied in some way. In *Foskett v McKeown* the businessmen beneficiaries were able to show that they had a property right which needed protecting. There are two general types of remedy which can be used to protect property rights. The first is called a *personal* remedy. This requires the defendant to pay to the claimant the value of the property which has been received. In other words, it creates a debt. The other type is a *proprietary* remedy. This can operate in a number of ways, but the simplest is to require the defendant to transfer the actual property received to the defendant. Personal and proprietary remedies have different advantages and disadvantages.

The main advantage of personal remedies is that, if the property is lost or falls in value, the defendant is still liable to pay money to the claimant which represents the value of the property at the time it was received. However, if the property still exists and has increased in value, it is preferable to get a proprietary remedy, because the claimant will get the benefit of that increase in value. Proprietary remedies have another advantage which is relevant where the defendant has few, if any, assets. Such a defendant may be declared bankrupt, if they are an individual, or insolvent, if they are a company. The defendant will typically owe money to a number of creditors and there may not be enough to go around, so with a personal remedy the claimant may end up with nothing. However, if the claimant is awarded a proprietary remedy he or she would rank above other creditors and would be able to claim the relevant property in priority to their claims. This might prove to be highly significant, depending on the defendant's financial circumstances.

We have already seen that one of the key differences between legal and equitable remedies is that the common law, for the most part, awards only personal remedies, to restore the value of the property received, whereas equity can award both personal and proprietary remedies. In *Foskett v McKeown* the beneficiaries sought a proprietary remedy to recover a proportionate share of the £1 million, amounting to £400,000.

This remedy had not been awarded in the Court of Appeal. Rather, that court held that the children were liable to repay only £20,000 because the beneficiaries' contribution of that amount was not used to acquire the £1 million, but operated only to maintain the insurance policy. An analogy can be drawn with reference to money being spent on a house. If the claimant's money was used to acquire the house, either completely or partially, the claimant should have a property interest in the house to the extent of that contribution. If, however, the money was used simply to maintain the house which already belonged to the defendant, eg by enabling the defendant to paint the external walls, it would not be appropriate to say that the claimant had a property interest in the house itself because the value in the claimant's property had not been used to acquire the house. Rather, the claimant should only be reimbursed the cost of maintaining the house. The cost of maintaining the policy was held by the Court of Appeal to be £20,000, representing the value of the fourth and fifth premiums.

The House of Lords accepted this distinction between acquiring and maintaining property, but reached the opposite conclusion when applying this distinction to the facts. The majority in the House of Lords concluded that the beneficiaries' money was used to help acquire the £1 million rather than simply to maintain the policy and so it was held that the children were liable to pay £400,000 of the £1 million to the beneficiaries.

This conclusion needs to be considered carefully. Is it really fair that the beneficiaries should have recovered such a large amount of money? This may have been appropriate had the fourth and fifth premiums actually been necessary to obtain the £1 million. But that was not the case on the facts. It was one thing to conclude that the beneficiaries had a property interest in the £1 million. It is a very different matter to conclude that this interest should be valued at two-fifths of the fund where the beneficiaries had not actually contributed to that amount being obtained. Against this you might wish to argue that it is not fair that the children should get £1 million minus £20,000, when their father had stolen money from the beneficiaries and when that money would have been necessary to obtain the £1 million had the father lived a bit longer. When it comes to criticising a decision such as this it is difficult to avoid introducing questions of justice and fairness – and even to ask, 'what would be the equitable result?'

Defences

Some of the judges went on to consider one other matter relating to property claims in equity, even though this was not relevant on the facts. Once it has been concluded that the claimant has a proprietary base in property, that the value in this property can be traced into the property held by the defendant and that the appropriate remedy is a proprietary one, it may also be necessary to consider whether the defendant should be given a defence to protect him or herself from the claim. The most important defence which might be available is one which has been called the defence of change of position. At its most basic this defence is relevant where, for example, the claimant paid £1,000 to the defendant by mistake but the defendant, without knowing or suspecting that there had been a mistake, spent £800 of it on a holiday. When the claimant sues the defendant for the £1,000, the defendant is not liable to pay back £800 because his or her position has changed. It follows that, if the defendant had spent all the money, he or she would not be liable to pay anything to the claimant.

The issue which was canvassed in *Foskett v McKeown* was whether this defence of change of position should be available even where the claimant wishes to recover his or her property. The issues of principle and policy which this raises can be illustrated by the following hypothetical problems:

- A trustee steals £1,000 from a trust and gives this money to the defendant. The defendant is a poor student who, thinking that the money belonged absolutely to the trustee, spends all of it at various pubs and clubs. The beneficiaries of the trust would not be able to bring a claim against the defendant to recover the money. But this is not because of the application of the defence of change of position as such. It is simply because, if the defendant no longer has assets in which the claimant has an equitable proprietary interest, the claimant cannot recover any property since the defendant does not have any property which belongs to the claimant. In such a case the claimant would have to sue the trustee for breach of trust in stealing the money in the first place. This is the easy case. The following scenario is more difficult.

- Again, the trustee steals £1,000 from the trust, which he gives to the defendant. But this time money is credited to the defendant's bank account. Since the defendant is richer than he was before, he decides to sell some shares which had been left to him by his grandmother. He sells them for £1,000 and uses this to pay for a holiday to the Caribbean. In this situation the defendant still has assets in which the claimant has a proprietary interest, in the form of the money which is credited to his bank account. But the defendant has changed his position in good faith as a result of receiving this money, since he sold the shares and spent the proceeds. In this situation whose interests should prevail? Should it be the claimant beneficiary, who can show that the defendant still has property which belongs to the claimant in equity? Or should it be the defendant, who is now in no better position after having sold the shares, which would not have been sold had the defendant not received the money from the trustee?

Lord Millett in *Foskett v McKeown* indicated, in part of his judgment which did not relate to the issues arising in the case and so is called *obiter dicta*, that the defence of change of position should not be available where the claimant wishes to recover his or her property and where that property or its substitute or product remains identifiable. Whether you like such a result will depend, to some extent at least, on the general approach which you want to adopt to the structure and operation of the law. If you would prefer the legal system to operate to obtain a just result at all costs you might prefer the defence of change of position to operate in such a scenario. For the defendant did nothing wrong in selling the shares and we can show that those shares would not have been sold had the £1,000 not been received. Against this, a stricter, more principled, approach would focus on the fact that the claimant's property is still in the defendant's hands. Property rights are particularly strong rights in English law and perhaps they should not be defeated by changes in the defendant's circumstances, save where that change has the effect of destroying the property in which the claimant has the right. The rejection of the defence of change of position is consistent with this idea that property rights are strong, or, as Lord Browne-Wilkinson described them in *Foskett v McKeown*, they are 'hard-nosed' rights. According to this approach it is tough luck that the defendant changed his or her position and, anyway, the defendant did at least have the benefit of the holiday in the Caribbean.

CONCLUSIONS

The analysis of *Foskett v McKeown* tells us a lot about the nature of that body of law known as equity, but also forces us to think rather more deeply about our approach to legal method. It can be seen that this body of law is technical, but it is a vital part of being a law student that you are able to apply legal rules and principles logically and go on to consider whether the interpretation of the law is acceptable and workable.

But this case raises some bigger questions. First, is the fundamental distinction between the common law and equity defensible today? We have seen that equity developed as a distinct stream of law hundreds of years ago for reasons which are no longer relevant today. We have seen that the maintenance of two distinct streams of judge-made law makes for very complex exposition of that law. This is especially well illustrated by the fact that we have different tracing rules at law and in equity. Is this defensible today? Indeed, a number of the judges in *Foskett v McKeown* suggested that these two sets of tracing rules should be merged. But if such a merger did occur, where should it stop? Should we get rid of equity completely? If so, we would lose many vital mechanisms in the law, especially the trust. Perhaps we need closer co-operation between law and equity, but this should not extend to total assimilation.

Finally, we are left with the big theme which runs throughout *Foskett v McKeown*. Should our approach to law and legal method be principled or discretionary? Justice, equity and common sense are vital attributes of any coherent legal system, but the importance of principles must not be forgotten. This was expressed most eloquently by Lord Goff in a lecture called *The Search for Principle*:

> When we talk about the desired result, or the merits, of any particular case, we can do so at more than one level. There is the crude, purely factual level—the plaintiff is a poor widow, who has lost her money, and such like. At another level there is the gut reaction, often most influential. But there is a more sophisticated, lawyerly level, which often consists of the perception of the just solution on legal terms, satisfying both the gut and the intellect. ... The judgment so exercised should not be, and is not, a purely personal judgment. It is an informed and educated judgment, formulated in public discussion and founded not merely upon a shared experience of the practical administration of justice, but also upon an accepted basis of systematic legal principle.

There is a role for the gut reaction in our approach to the law, but it is the identification of principles which is at the heart of the study of law as an intellectual discipline.

Cases

Attorney-General of Hong Kong v Reid [1994] 1 AC 324
Foskett v McKeown [1998] Ch 265 (CA); [2001] 1 AC 102 (HL)
Lipkin Gorman (a firm) v Karpnale Ltd [1991] 2 AC 548

Mareva Compania Naveira SA v International Bulk Carriers SA [1975] 2 Lloyd's Rep 509

Additional reading

Dickens, *Bleak House* (1852)

Lord Goff of Chieveley, *The Search for Principle: Essays in Honour of Lord Goff of Chieveley*, ed Swadling and Jones (Oxford, Oxford University Press, 1999) 313–29

Virgo, *The Principles of the Law of Restitution*, 2nd edn (Oxford, Oxford University Press, 2006) part V

Worthington, *Equity*, 2nd edn (Oxford, Oxford University Press, 2006) ch 1

.

7

Constitutional Law

Mark Elliott

INTRODUCTION

A Rude Awakening

Imagine that, in the dead of night, you are awoken by the sound of your front door being smashed in. Your first thought is that your house is being burgled; but there seem to be an awful lot of sets of boots pounding up the stairs. Before you know it, your bed is surrounded by police officers, and children who were sleeping in other bedrooms are screaming in fear as you are handcuffed and bundled into a police car. Are you under arrest? 'No,' says one of the police officers. Are you being charged with committing a criminal offence? 'No.' Why, then, are you by now in prison cell? 'Suspected involvement in terrorism,' you are told. But why has this suspicion arisen? 'Can't say—national security reasons.' And how long might it be before you are released? 'Can't say—you are being indefinitely detained by order of the government.' Will you at least have a chance to put your side of the story—to show why you think the government's suspicions are groundless? 'Yes.' But then it turns out that the government will not tell you in any meaningful detail why it is detaining you, so you do not know how to defend yourself: the hearing you are given is nothing more than a sham. Years later, you are still in prison, and you still don't know why.

This is the stuff of nightmares. It is the sort of thing that happens in countries run by dictators and shady military juntas. But it does not happen in civilised, enlightened societies, and it is unthinkable that people could be treated in this way in the United Kingdom. Isn't it?

The World Trade Center, New York, and Belmarsh Prison, London

This chapter on UK constitutional law begins in two very different locations: Belmarsh prison in south-east London and the World Trade Center in New York. On 11 September 2001, Al-Qaeda terrorists hijacked four airliners in the USA, two of which were flown into the twin towers of the World Trade Center. More than 2,600 people died as a result. Of the two remaining planes, one was flown into the Pentagon in Washington DC, costing nearly 200 lives, while the other airliner, possibly destined for the White House, crashed in Pennsylvania, killing all 40 passengers and crew. The consequences for those who were killed, injured and bereaved were as obvious as they were horrific. But the wider ramifications of the 9/11 attacks were also immense. Shockwaves were felt around the world—including in Belmarsh high-security prison in London. There, as a direct response to the events of September 11, a number of men suspected by the British government of being involved in international terrorism were detained for over three years without ever being accused of, let alone tried for or convicted of, any criminal offence. The treatment of the suspects was later held by the Council of Europe's Committee for the Prevention of Torture to amount to 'inhuman and degrading treatment'.

What, then, does all of this have to do with the constitutional law of the UK? And why, in any event, does this book contain a chapter on that subject, when it is often said that the UK does not have a constitution? The purpose of this chapter is to answer the latter question—by explaining that the UK *does* have a constitution, albeit not a 'written' one—through engaging with the former. As we will see, the legal and constitutional aftermath in the UK of the 9/11 attacks casts a bright light on the nature of Britain's constitutional arrangements. Looking at what happened in the wake of 9/11 will help to illustrate some of the key features—and peculiarities—of the UK constitution.

The Response to 9/11: Detention without Trial

Although no strangers to terrorist violence—more than 3,000 deaths resulted from Northern Ireland-related terrorism—people in the UK unsurprisingly felt vulnerable after 9/11. Given the close relationship between the UK and the USA, there was a strong sense that a group antagonistic to the US might be equally ill-disposed towards its smaller ally. (Indeed, these anxieties proved well-founded when, on 7 July 2005, over 50 people were killed as a result of an Al-Qaeda sponsored attack on London's transport network.) It was against the background of such fears that, shortly after 9/11, the UK Parliament enacted a new law known as the Anti-Terrorism, Crime and Security Act 2001. It was intended to provide greater legal powers for fighting terrorism. For instance, it sought to enhance aviation, nuclear and biological security, to extend police powers in terrorism-related investigations, and to make it easier to freeze terrorists' assets (eg by preventing access to funds in bank accounts). But our particular concern is with a different, and truly extraordinary, part of the Act.

Part 4 of the Anti-terrorism, Crime and Security Act 2001 ('the Anti-terrorism Act') was enacted in order to contain the perceived threat posed by foreigners who were suspected of involvement in terrorism, but who could not be dealt with in either of two more conventional ways. As we have seen in chapters 1 and 2 of this book, the first way of dealing with those suspected of criminal activity is to *prosecute them in the criminal courts*. However, the government felt that in respect of certain suspected terrorists prosecution would be either impossible (eg due to an insufficiency of evidence) or unwise (eg because bringing a prosecution would require the presentation in court of evidence that might compromise intelligence sources). A second way of addressing the risk posed by foreign nationals considered to be dangerous is to deport them—ie to *expel them from the country*. However, as the law currently stands, the government cannot do this if there is a real risk that the person, when sent to another country, would be subjected to torture or to inhuman or degrading treatment. This created a significant difficulty from the UK government's perspective, since many of the people it regarded as presenting a terrorist threat came from countries whose governments are known to practice torture.

For these reasons, the government considered itself to be between a rock and a hard place: some foreign terror suspects could neither be prosecuted nor deported. Part 4 of the Anti-terrorism Act was designed to address this problem. It applied to any foreign national whom the Home Secretary—a government minister—had reason to believe was involved in terrorism. When such a person could not be deported, he could instead be detained indefinitely: in other words, put in jail for an open-ended, potentially limitless, period of time. For the government, this represented the best of both worlds. On the one hand, the criminal justice process was bypassed, so there was no need to gather or disclose to a court enough evidence to secure a conviction (which would have required proof beyond reasonable doubt). On the other hand, the ban on deportations when torture abroad was a real possibility was rendered practically irrelevant: the perceived threat posed by foreign suspects could be contained by incarceration in the UK, rather than by physical removal from the country.

It would be hard to exaggerate the exceptional nature of the powers which Part 4 of the Anti-terrorism Act conferred on the Home Secretary. Allowing someone to be imprisoned for an open-ended period on the say-so of a politician involves a major departure from the standards that are normally expected in a civilised society. You do not need to be a legal expert to know that locking people up in this way contradicts basic principles of justice and human rights, such as the right to a fair trial, the presumption of innocence and the liberty of the individual. As Baroness Hale—one of the judges involved in hearing the detainees' legal challenge, to which we turn below—put it, 'We have always taken it for granted in this country that we cannot be locked up indefinitely without trial or explanation.' The Bush administration in the US was widely condemned for the way in which it held suspected terrorists without trial at its military base in Guantanamo Bay, Cuba. What is less well-known is that something fundamentally similar—in that it involved imprisonment of suspects without charge or trial on the say-so of the executive government—went on at Belmarsh Prison. It was there that the suspects detained under Part 4 of the Anti-terrorism Act (of whom there were fewer than 20: Belmarsh was no Guantanamo in terms of numbers) were held for several years.

What happened here is really very simple. The government, acting, as it saw it, for the general public good, decided to sacrifice the interests of a very small minority in pursuit of the majority's security. In one sense, there is nothing particularly startling about this. Governments have to strike a balance between competing sets of interests all the time. For instance, if employees' interests are favoured by raising the national minimum wage, employers may argue that their interests are thereby compromised; if spending on public services is increased in order to benefit the less well-off, the wealthy may suffer through higher taxes. However, the effect of Part 4 of the Anti-terrorism Act was different in an important respect: an absolutely fundamental right—the right to personal liberty—was suppressed in the interests of the majority. You would be forgiven for thinking that this is just the sort of thing that a constitution is supposed to stop from happening. This is a good point, then, at which to step back from the Belmarsh detainees—we will pick up their story later—to consider what constitutions are, and what they are for.

CONSTITUTIONS

What Are Constitutions For?

Any organisation—whether a school, company or country—needs a set of ground-rules which determines basic things about how it is to operate. Who is in charge? How do they get to be in charge? What powers do they have? What are the limits on their powers? Who enforces such limits? And what can people do if they do not like how the organisation is being run? These are exactly the sort of questions which, in relation to countries, constitutions are supposed to answer. Unpacking these points a little further, it can be said that, at least in most countries, constitutions serve four main functions.

First, they *allocate power to the government*. Classically, this is done according to the 'separation of powers' principle, whereby the constitution creates three institutions—or 'branches'—of government, giving each a different job. For example, the first three articles of the US Constitution create a legislative branch, which is responsible for making law; an executive branch, which implements the law; and a judicial branch whose job is to interpret and apply the law in particular cases. These three institutions of government recognisably exist in Britain—there is a national legislature in the form of the UK Parliament at Westminster; an executive government, headed by the Prime Minister and the Cabinet; and a judicial system—although, as we will see below, the dividing lines between the three branches are far from distinct in the UK. It is also often the case that constitutions divide power between different tiers of government—local, regional, national and so on. For instance, in the UK, there is a local tier of government (eg district and county councils), devolved government (in Scotland, Northern Ireland and Wales), national government and a further layer in the form of the European Union.

Secondly—and this point follows from the first—constitutions generally *limit the powers of the government*. Another way of putting this point would be to say that constitutions determine where government power ends and individual freedom begins. Many constitutions do this by setting out people's fundamental rights and stipulating that the government is not allowed to do anything which interferes with such rights. Within such a constitutional system, if the executive was to adopt a policy or if the legislature was to pass a law which conflicted with an individual's constitutional rights, that policy or law would be invalid, and the courts would be able to strike it down. The constitution therefore stands as an important brake on government power, and as a crucial safeguard of the individual's rights.

Thirdly, constitutions normally put in place arrangements for ensuring that *governmental powers are exercised responsibly*. This is normally done in two (mutually complementary) ways. On the one hand, the *separation of powers* principle recognises that there is truth in the view expressed by Lord Acton—a nineteenth-century commentator and historian—that 'power tends to corrupt, and absolute power corrupts absolutely'. In the light of this, the separation of powers principle says that no one should have a monopoly on power, and that it should, instead, be shared among different bodies. This, then, is the thinking that lies behind our first point, above. On the other hand, constitutions often provide for a system of *checks and balances*. This may, for example, involve requiring two branches of government to agree before certain things can be done, or giving one branch powers to scrutinise the work of another.

Fourthly, constitutions—or good ones, at any rate—aim to provide a structure for government and its relationship with individuals that *reflects widely shared values*, such as a commitment to democracy, human rights and so on. Constitutions therefore tend to confer a *degree of permanence* upon the arrangements which they contain. If those arrangements are animated by deep-seated values, it stands to reason that they should not be capable of being casually cast aside. Constitutions are therefore often *entrenched*, meaning that they are hard to change, such that arrangements, rights and values set out in a constitution can be altered only in limited circumstances. For example, an amendment to the US Constitution can be made only if it is proposed by a two-thirds majority of both chambers of the national legislature and then approved by three-quarters of the individual states' legislatures. (There is an alternative process that is even harder to comply with, but which has never been successfully used.)

The UK's Peculiar Constitution

The previous section was concerned with things that constitutions typically do. But Britain's constitution, as we are about to discover, is far from typical. The most obvious respect in which it is unusual is in its being 'unwritten'. Although this adjective is often applied to the UK's constitution, it is important to be clear about what it means in this context.

First, it does *not* mean that there is no such thing as a British constitution. We observed above that any organisation, including any country, must have a set of ground-rules if it is to have any prospect of working effectively rather than descending into utter chaos. The UK is no exception: it simply could not function without a constitution.

Secondly, when we say that the UK lacks a written constitution, this does not mean that none of its constitutional arrangements exists in written form. There is a great deal of legislation which deals with constitutional matters—human rights, the division of power between local, regional, national and European tiers of government, and so on. In this sense, large swathes of Britain's constitutional arrangements are actually written down, even though there is no single document entitled 'The Constitution'.

Does this mean, then, that the UK's constitution is atypical, but in a relatively unimportant sense? That it might be harder to deduce its content—because it is scattered around various pieces of legislation—but that it otherwise conforms to the norms considered in the previous section? The short answer to this question is 'no'. To give a longer answer, we need to return to Belmarsh Prison. Using Part 4 of the Anti-terrorism Act as a reference point, we consider, in the remainder of this chapter, a number of respects in which the British constitution is highly unusual. In particular, three questions need to be asked. First, why was it possible to enact such a draconian piece of legislation as the Anti-terrorism Act? Secondly, what was the role of the courts in all of this: were the detainees able to contest the legality of their detention in the courts? And, thirdly, does this extraordinary episode reflect well or badly on the British constitution: are the eccentricities it highlights a cause for concern or celebration?

BRITAIN'S CONSTITUTIONAL ARCHITECTURE

The answer to the first of those questions lies in the unusual (many would say highly defective) nature of Britain's constitutional architecture—ie the fundamental way in which the system works and in which the various parts of it fit together. In two crucial respects, the UK's constitution differs markedly from the model set out above. Taken together, they help to explain why British governments are peculiarly well-placed to secure the enactment of legislation—even if, like Part 4 of the Anti-terrorism Act, it rides roughshod over fundamental rights.

Executive Control of Parliament

We noted above that constitutions classically allocate distinct functions
to the three branches of government in order to ensure that power is
not concentrated in one set of hands. This will sometimes mean that
it is harder to get things done because one branch can be thwarted by
another. For instance, the executive government may wish to adopt a
given policy, but the legislature may be unwilling to enact the necessary
legislation (either at all or in the precise terms the executive wants); or
the executive might contend that it already has sufficient legal powers
to implement the policy in question, but the courts might rule otherwise. From one perspective, this may seem undesirable: a dynamic
government intent on introducing radical reforms might be prevented
from doing so. But the upside is that no one branch of government is
all-powerful: the powers of each branch are held in tension with those
of the others, and so (the theory goes) it is more difficult for any one
government institution to exercise its powers in an abusive, oppressive
or otherwise improper way.

So much for the theory of the separation of powers. The reality is that
(in at least one crucial respect) the UK constitution does not adhere to
that theory. This, in turn, helps us to understand why it was relatively
straightforward for the executive government to persuade Parliament to
give it the extraordinary powers that were contained in Part 4 of the Anti-
terrorism Act. In the UK, there is no real separation of powers between
the executive government and the legislature. This is not to say that the
executive and Parliament do not exist as distinct *institutions*. Crucially,
however, there is a high degree of overlap in terms of *membership*. This
is no accident: it is an inevitable consequence of the nature of the UK
system of *parliamentary government*.

Under this system, members of the executive government are not
directly elected: whereas, for instance, individuals stand for election
to the office of President of the USA, no one puts themselves forward
in the same way for the post of British Prime Minister. Barak Obama
became US President in 2009 because he won the presidential election.
But there is no such thing as a British prime ministerial election. In
the UK, the explicit function of a general election is to determine who

becomes a Member of Parliament and is thereby entitled to sit in the House of Commons and (among other things) participate in the enactment of legislation. However, general elections also indirectly determine who becomes Prime Minister, because that position is held by the person best able to command the confidence—ie the support—of the House of Commons. Normally, one party secures more than half the seats in the Commons, meaning that its leader becomes Prime Minister. He then appoints members of his party to other positions within the government. As a result, around 100 MPs—roughly a sixth of the total membership of the House of Commons—are government ministers. However, the influence of the government over the House of Commons is even greater than this simple statistic implies. The Prime Minister can rely not just on the support of his 100 or so ministers who sit as MPs in the House of Commons: he can also rely on the support of the other—'backbench'—MPs from his party. And while government backbench MPs are ultimately free to vote as they wish, most vote as the government tells them to—not least because any ambitious backbencher will want to curry favour with senior members of the government in order to bolster his or her chances of being appointed in the future to a government position.

What we have said so far presupposes that one political party 'wins' the general election, meaning that it secures more than half the seats in the House of Commons. However, that was not what happened when a general election was held in 2010. Instead, a 'hung Parliament'—in which no party had an outright majority—resulted. The Conservatives secured 47 per cent of the seats in the House of Commons, making them the biggest party—but not quite big enough to form a majority government on their own. As a result, they joined with the Liberal Democrats (who won 9 per cent of the seats) to form a coalition government. As leader of the bigger of the two coalition parties, and therefore the person best-placed to command the confidence of the House of Commons, David Cameron became Prime Minister, while the leader of the Liberal Democrats, Nick Clegg, became Deputy Prime Minister. Coalition government is clearly different from single-party government: it involves two parties, perhaps with very different views in some areas, working together and therefore compromising. But the distinctiveness of coali-

David Cameron and Nick Clegg outside No 10 Downing Street.
© Prime Minister's Office; Crown Copyright

tion should not be overstated. Most parties, and most governments, have to accommodate people with differing points of view; coalition simply means that those differences may be sharper and more obvious, in that the presence of two formally distinct parties emphasises the existence of political and ideological divisions. There is no doubt a greater risk of a coalition government being derailed by disagreements, and it may be harder for the government to impose discipline if the members of one or other of the coalition parties are being asked to vote for legislation with which they fundamentally disagree. However, if the coalition partners have agreed on a package of policies that are mutually acceptable, such a government—whose parties will, of course, account for more than half the MPs—at least has the potential to dominate the House of Commons in much the same way as a single-party government.

Governments, whether composed of one party or a coalition of parties, are therefore generally in a commanding position when it comes to getting Parliament to enact legislation. And so it proved with the Anti-terrorism Act 2001. The then Labour government, whose MPs accounted for 63 per cent of membership of the House of Commons, faced almost no real opposition in the Commons. Indeed, many opposition, as well as government, MPs were willing to support the legislation (being tough on terrorism was very much in vogue in the aftermath of 9/11), and it received little genuine scrutiny in the House of Commons: only 16 hours were spent considering the legislation, which was comprised of 126 clauses and eight schedules covering over 120 pages. This is striking, bearing in mind the extraordinary nature of the powers conferred, in particular, by Part 4 of the Act.

The House of Commons is only one half of the legislature: there is also the House of Lords. The general principle is that in order for legislation to be enacted, it must be approved by both Houses—and the Lords is often willing to subject legislation to more thoroughgoing, objective scrutiny than the Commons is. This is largely because the Lords, at least for the time being, is not dominated in the same way as the Commons by party politics—partly because a substantial minority of peers (as members of the Lords are known) are not affiliated to any party (the so-called 'cross-benchers'), and partly because even those who are members of political parties are less likely than their MP colleagues to follow the party line slavishly. The chief reason for this is that few peers are career politicians looking to advance their own prospects by doing what their party leaders would wish. Ultimately, these characteristics of the House of Lords are attributable to the fact that peers are unelected (most are appointed by the monarch on the advice of the Prime Minister) although it may well be that elections to the House of Lords will be introduced in the foreseeable future. In any event, the House of Lords took a much closer, and more critical, look at the Anti-terrorism Act than the Commons had done. In relation to Part 4, the Lords insisted that the text should be amended so as to require the Home Secretary's belief that a person was involved in terrorism to be an objectively reasonable one. This was a small but important concession: it meant that the Home Secretary could not claim to have an absolute discretion to detain anyone who he subjectively believed to be a terrorist.

At the end of the day, however, the Commons and the Lords are unequal legislative partners. In recognition of the fact that (at least for now) the Lords has no democratic legitimacy, a special mechanism—under the Parliament Acts 1911 and 1949—can be invoked if the two Houses cannot agree. The upshot is that the most the House of Lords can do is to delay, by one year, the enactment of legislation (and it does not even have this delaying power in respect of financial legislation). This is not an insignificant power. If, as was the case in relation to the Anti-terrorism Act, the executive government is anxious to see legislation enacted rapidly, the House of Lords' delaying power is a useful bargaining chip—hence the government's willingness to concede a requirement of objective reasonableness in relation to Part 4 rather than waiting a year to enact the legislation in its preferred form. Nevertheless, it remains the case that the executive government in the UK is in an unusually strong position. It exerts considerable influence—control would not be an exaggeration—over the House of Commons, such that, in most circumstances, it is assured by virtue of its majority of being able to get the Commons to do more or less whatever it wants. And while the House of Lords may be a source of more critical scrutiny and greater opposition, the legal limits on its powers are such that it is ultimately unable to block the enactment of legislation which the House of Commons—at the instigation of the executive government—is intent on pushing through.

The Constitution as Ordinary Law

We can see, then, that the nature of the relationship between the executive and legislative branches in the UK is such that its constitution does not strictly adhere to the separation of powers principle set out earlier in this chapter. That, in itself, might be thought to be a cause for concern. Whereas, under the separation of powers doctrine, the legislature should be a counterweight to the executive, the British system allows the latter branch to dominate the former, resulting in precisely the sort of overconcentration of authority which the separation of powers seeks to guard against.

It is, however, important to recognise that the separation of powers principle is not an end in itself: it is merely a means to an end. It prescribes a form of government which, it is said, will prevent, or at least reduce the risk of, the abuse of power. The key question, then, is not whether a given constitution rigidly adheres to the detailed requirements of the separation of powers; rather, it is whether whatever arrangements are actually adopted adequately guard against the misuse of power. Notwithstanding the lack of a clear distinction in the UK between the executive and legislative branches, other features of the constitution might compensate for this by adequately guarding against the risk of power being used in an oppressive or otherwise improper way.

For example, if Parliament (for the reasons considered above) is unable or unwilling to stand up to the executive by preventing it from getting its way in relation to the enactment of legislation, perhaps some other body—the courts, for instance—might step in. In many countries, this is precisely what happens: courts are able to set aside legislation which conflicts with the constitution. So if, for example, the legislature (as a result of executive persuasion or otherwise) enacted legislation that cut across fundamental rights protected by the constitution, the courts would be able to rule that the legislature had exceeded its authority and strike down the legislation as unconstitutional. However, although commonplace elsewhere, arrangements of this sort are not embodied in the UK's constitution. Here, then, we encounter the second architectural feature of the British constitution that makes it strikingly unusual.

If there is one key to understanding what sets the British constitution apart from almost every other constitution in the world, it is that it *consists only in ordinary law*. What we mean by this is that legislation (eg the Human Rights Act 1998, which we consider below) dealing with fundamentally important constitutional matters has the same legal status in the UK as any other piece of legislation (eg the Driving Instruction (Suspension And Exemption Powers) Act 2009, which made modest changes to the system for regulating driving instructors). This has two absolutely crucial consequences.

First, it means that *the UK constitution is unusually flexible*. Constitutional laws, being ordinary laws, can be changed as easily as all other laws. As a result, fundamentally important constitutional arrangements can be changed with the same ease—by passing an Act of Parliament—as amending the law on more mundane matters. This stands in stark contrast to most countries' constitutions, which are usually much harder to change than ordinary laws. It follows that in the UK, nothing is legally sacrosanct. For instance, the Conservative Party was able, in its 2010 election manifesto, to propose scrapping the Human Rights Act, safe in the knowledge that even a constitutional change as substantial as this could be achieved simply by enacting a normal Act of Parliament. (In fact, the Act has not been scrapped; the Conservatives' coalition partners, the Liberal Democrats, are strong supporters of it.)

Secondly, most countries' constitutions are regarded not just as a *different* (and harder-to-change) form of law: they are regarded as a *superior* kind of law. In many countries, all other law exists in the shadow of constitutional law. What this means in practice is that any law that is inconsistent with the constitution—eg a law that tries to take away fundamental rights protected by the constitution—will be invalid, and so vulnerable to being struck down by the courts. But precisely because its constitution is contained in ordinary laws—such as regular Acts of Parliament—this is not so in the UK. Because constitutional law does not have a special status (in the sense of being hierarchically superior to ordinary law), it cannot override other law.

These two defining features of the UK's constitution—flexibility and absence of hierarchy—are really two sides of the same coin, the key point being that Parliament's power to make and change the law is legally unlimited. Or, as constitutional lawyers like to put it, Parliament is *sovereign*. This simply means that Parliament is always legally free to enact any legislation it wishes (even if this involves tearing up long-standing constitutional principles) and that the courts are powerless to intervene. This explains why, once the executive had persuaded Parliament to enact Part 4 of the Anti-terrorism Act providing for indefinite imprisonment of terror suspects, the government could be confident that the courts could not set it aside as invalid, even though it was at odds with suspects' basic rights.

One final point should be made in this regard. The principle of parliamentary sovereignty is only relevant to Acts of Parliament made at Westminster by the UK legislature. It has no application to other types of law (eg rules enacted by the executive government and laws made by devolved legislatures such as the Scottish Parliament), and courts therefore *can* strike down such laws if they are contrary to fundamental constitutional principles (including human rights). Similarly, decisions and policies of the executive government are not covered by the principle of parliamentary sovereignty, meaning that they, too, can be struck down by the courts in appropriate circumstances. If, then, the executive government wishes to ensure that something is placed beyond interference, it must enshrine it in an Act of Parliament. This can only be done with Parliament's agreement—but, as we have seen, the executive is very well-placed to secure such agreement.

Taking Stock: The Story So Far

A picture thus emerges of a set of constitutional arrangements in Britain that is strikingly unusual. Most of the things that were said above about how constitutions typically work turn out not to be accurate descriptions of the position in the UK. In particular, what has been said so far suggests that the British constitution lacks the careful balance of powers between the three branches of government that is supposed to guard against the oppressive or otherwise improper use of authority. Instead, what seems to exist is an executive branch of government which, in effect, controls the legislature, and a legislature which is uncontrollable by the courts. It is unsurprising, then, that a major concern for writers about British politics and the British constitution is that the executive government is too powerful.

Clearly, these fears are not wholly ill-founded: that much is demonstrated by the simple fact that the executive was able to get Parliament to give it the power to lock people up whenever a government minister (reasonably) thought that they might be involved in terrorism. You might wonder, then, why the UK is—the likes of the Anti-terrorism Act notwithstanding—a largely free society in which people's fundamental rights are generally respected. If the executive government has, in the way described above, its hands on all the key levers of power, why does Britain not more closely resemble a dictatorship in which basic freedoms are denied to people? One possible explanation is that the people with their hands on the levers of power might not *want* to do things like this—they might be decent people, determined to govern in a way that is fair and just. But is that it? Does freedom in the UK ultimately depend on the integrity of politicians (which, history suggests, cannot always be relied upon)? Or are there other factors which help to explain why those who run the country—and who, for the reasons considered above, have legally unlimited powers—nevertheless generally exercise such powers in ways that respect people's basic rights and freedoms? Happily, as we explain in the next section, the answer to this question is yes.

THE ROLE OF THE COURTS

Back to Belmarsh

The Belmarsh detainees were eventually released. And although the courts did not compel their release—because their detention was authorised by an Act of Parliament—the courts were nevertheless instrumental in securing the detainees' freedom. This, then, is the point at which to tell the detainees' story—and, in particular, the part of it in which they mounted a legal challenge to their detention—in more detail. The case is formally known as *A and others v Home Secretary*, but we will simply call it the *Belmarsh* case. Although the case was heard at a number of judicial levels, our concern is mainly with the decision of the House of Lords. (When *Belmarsh* was decided in 2004, the Appellate Committee of the House of Lords was the highest court in the UK—although, as explained in chapter 1, it has now been replaced by the UK Supreme Court.)

The decision of the House of Lords in *Belmarsh* was a trail-blazing one. As we shall see, it demonstrates that, in spite of what has been said so far, the UK government is not truly free to do exactly as it pleases. If the significance of *Belmarsh* can be reduced to a single proposition, it is that it shows that while, under the UK constitution, the executive-con-

Belmarsh protest.
© Gareth Fuller/Press Association Images

trolled Parliament may have *theoretically* unlimited powers, there are
nevertheless *practical* limits to what it can do. In order to explain why
this is so, we need to consider two interlocking aspects of the *Belmarsh*
case.

The First Question: Had the Detainees' Human Rights Been Breached?

The first aspect concerns the surprisingly bold way in which the House of
Lords assessed the detainees' claim that Part 4 of the Anti-terrorism Act
breached their human rights. Until the passage of the Human Rights Act
1998, such arguments were rarely made—and, when they were, courts
tended to adopt a highly reticent approach, attaching great respect to
the government's views, particularly if arguments such as national security were deployed. The significance of *Belmarsh* is that the House of
Lords took a strikingly different approach, subjecting the government's

attempts to justify the detention of the suspects to searching and critical scrutiny—and, as we shall see, ultimately finding the government's arguments unconvincing. To explain all of this properly, however, we need to step back and explain, in legal terms, what the issue in *Belmarsh* was.

The detainees took the government to court, alleging that, by imprisoning them under the Anti-terrorism Act, the government was denying them their rights under the European Convention on Human Rights (ECHR). The ECHR is an international agreement, or treaty, under which many European countries, including the UK, have committed to respect basic human rights and freedoms. And, under international law—ie the system of law which regulates the behaviour of countries—there is a legal obligation upon countries to abide by their treaty commitments. We explain in the following section exactly how the ECHR, as a piece of international law, is relevant as a matter of national constitutional law. But for now our focus is simply on the question whether the detainees were right—was the government doing something forbidden by the ECHR?

The detainees' principal argument was that detention on the say-so of a government minister was contrary to the right to liberty under Article 5 of the ECHR. Article 5 says that '[e]veryone has the right to liberty and security of person' and that '[n]o one shall be deprived of his liberty' except in certain limited circumstances spelled out in Article 5 (eg detention following conviction of a criminal offence). None of those circumstances applied to the detainees, and so it was clear that they were, as they asserted, being denied their rights under Article 5. The House of Lords had no difficulty in reaching this conclusion, which was later confirmed by the European Court of Human Rights when, in *A v United Kingdom*, it considered the case of the Belmarsh detainees. (The European Court of Human Rights is based in Strasbourg: we will simply call it the 'Strasbourg court' in this chapter.)

However, the case was more complex than this. The government had anticipated that precisely this sort of argument might be made—and that it might be accepted (as indeed it was) by the courts. The government had therefore sought to take advantage of other provisions of the ECHR to allow the detainees to be denied the right to liberty which they would otherwise have been entitled to under Article 5. It had done so by attempting to invoke the special power contained in Article 15 of the ECHR, the first two paragraphs of which read as follows:

> (1) In time of war or other public emergency threatening the life of the nation any [State] Party may take measures derogating from its obligations under [the ECHR] to the extent strictly required by the exigencies of the situation, provided that such measures are not inconsistent with its other obligations under international law.
>
> (2) No derogation from Article 2, except in respect of deaths resulting from lawful acts of war, or from Articles 3, 4(1) and 7 shall be made under this provision.

Even though it uses technical language, the general thrust of Article 15 is reasonably clear: it confers a 'derogation power', meaning that, in certain circumstances, it allows things to be done even though they would normally be forbidden by the ECHR. With this in mind, two more specific points should be noted.

First, Article 15 *only applies to some rights*. One of the rights to which it does not apply is the right to be free from torture and inhuman and degrading treatment under Article 3. This explains why the UK government could not simply derogate from Article 3 and then return foreign terror suspects to their home countries irrespective of whether they would face a real risk of torture there. In contrast, Article 15 does allow the right to liberty under Article 5 to be derogated from.

But, secondly, even if a right can in principle be derogated from under Article 15, *it will only be lawful to derogate if the two conditions laid down in Article 15 are satisfied*: (1) there must be a 'war or other public emergency threatening the life of the nation'; but (2) even if there is such a war or emergency, this does not enable the government to do whatever it likes: it can do things which would otherwise be incompatible with the right in question only to the extent that this is necessary. Deciding whether these two conditions had been satisfied was the main question which the court had to answer in the *Belmarsh* case.

First, then, was there a *'war or other public emergency threatening the life of the nation'*? The government's case, in effect, was that, bearing in mind the close and long-standing relationship between the two countries, the 9/11 attacks in the USA indicated a heightened risk of a devastating terrorist attack in the UK. One of the judges, Lord Hoffmann, refused to accept that this gave rise to a 'public emergency' in the Article 15 sense. The 'life of the nation', he said, is not to be equated with 'the lives of its people': only a threat of violence so serious as to threaten 'our institutions of government or our existence as a civil community' would be sufficient to trigger the derogation power. In a scathing critique of what had been done in relation to the Belmarsh detainees, Lord Hoffmann said:

> The real threat to the life of the nation, in the sense of a people living in accordance with its traditional laws and political values, comes not from terrorism but from laws such as these. That is the true measure of what terrorism may achieve.

The other eight judges disagreed. (Panels of five judges normally decide cases at this level: the fact that nine judges sat in the *Belmarsh* case underlines its importance.) They did so mainly because they took a broader view of what might constitute a 'public emergency', accepting that that category was wide enough to include the threat of a large-scale terrorist attack even if it did not jeopardise the existence of civil society. Those eight judges went on to hold that the government had been entitled to conclude, on the basis of the 9/11 attacks and the intelligence information to which it had access, that the terrorist threat was sufficient to fall within the definition, as they saw it, of 'public emergency'. In reaching this conclusion, the eight judges in the majority on this point accepted that, under the separation of powers, it was not for courts to second-guess delicate decisions made by the executive government drawing on expert advice from the intelligence services. (Lord Scott, however, could not resist pointing out that the latter had hardly acquitted themselves with distinction in their assessment of the threat posed by Saddam Hussein's regime in Iraq.)

So far—Lord Hoffmann's approach excepted—this hardly looks like a radical assertion by the courts of their constitutional duty to protect individuals' fundamental rights. However, the court's assessment of the second question raised by Article 15 proceeded along very different lines. That question (which was considered by the eight judges who accepted the existence of a public emergency) was *whether the government's response to that emergency was 'strictly required by the exigencies of the situation'*. In other words, was the indefinite detention of foreign terror suspects really necessary—or could the government have achieved its objective of protecting public safety in a way that would have involved restricting suspects' rights to a lesser degree, or even not at all? In the past, whenever the government had pleaded that something needed to be done in the interests of national security, the courts had generally been willing to take it at its word. Not so in the *Belmarsh* case. Seven of the eight judges who considered this point held that the government had failed to establish that imprisonment without charge or trial was a necessary response to the terrorist threat. Here, two crucial points need to be made, concerning, respectively, the House of Lords' *general approach* to the necessity question and the *consequences* of that approach when applied to the specific facts of the case.

The court's general approach was to dismiss unthinking judicial deference to the government's views on such matters as national security as a relic of the past. While courts would attach appropriate respect to the opinions of the government when it was particularly well-qualified in relation to the given matter (eg gathering and assessing intelligence so as to predict the level of the terrorist threat), such deference was no longer to be the norm. The Human Rights Act 1998—to which we turn shortly—required courts to examine precisely the sort of matters raised in the *Belmarsh* case, meaning that it was no good arguing that such issues were somehow inappropriate for judicial consideration. 'The 1998 Act,' said Lord Bingham, 'gives the courts a very specific, wholly democratic, mandate' to determine the legality of government action that interferes with human rights. Moreover, the right to liberty, which was at stake in the *Belmarsh* case, was an absolutely fundamental right—meaning, as Lord Hope put it, that 'any interference with [it] must be accorded the fullest and most anxious scrutiny'.

How, then, did this approach play out in the particular circumstances of the case? The judges noted that it would only be necessary to take a particular step if the goal being pursued could not be achieved in some other way. The question was therefore whether the objective of protecting the public could be secured in a way that did not involve taking the draconian step of locking people up without giving them anything resembling a fair trial. For two reasons, the House of Lords was not satisfied that the government had established that the answer to that question was 'yes'.

First, Lord Bingham noted that there were many other ways in which terrorist activity might be disrupted. For example, the government could have introduced a system whereby suspects would be monitored in the community through the use of such measures as electronic tagging, curfews, bans on associating or otherwise communicating with other suspects, and so on. The government had not demonstrated to the court that such measures—which would of course seriously interfere with suspects' freedoms but not as gravely as outright deprivation of liberty—would fail adequately to contain the threat allegedly posed by the suspects.

Secondly, as explained above, the detention regime provided for by Part 4 of the Anti-terrorism Act applied only to foreign nationals. No comparable provision was made in that Act or elsewhere for the detention of UK nationals suspected of involvement in terrorism. This fatally undermined the government's claim that the detention powers contained in Part 4 were necessary. As Baroness Hale acerbically pointed out:

> The conclusion has to be that it is not necessary to lock up the nationals. Other ways must have been found to contain the threat which they present. And if it is not necessary to lock up the nationals it cannot be necessary to lock up the foreigners. It is not strictly required by the exigencies of the situation.

All but one of the judges who considered this aspect of the case agreed that Part 4 of the 2001 Act had not been shown to be necessary. This led to the conclusion that the conditions for suspending the right to liberty were not satisfied. Given the traditional timidity of British judges in the face of government claims of national security, the significance of this decision is hard to overstate. It showed a new boldness on the courts' part, and a new willingness to hold the government to account. This aspect of the *Belmarsh* case therefore goes some way towards allaying fears that might otherwise be justified by the close relationship between Parliament and the executive. Earlier, we noted the concern that the executive's control over the legislature risks an overconcentration of power which makes it possible for the executive to have its own way too easily. *Belmarsh*, however, highlights the fact that the courts are capable of being—and are willing to be—a real counterweight to the other branches of government.

The Second Question: So What?

This is all very well. But it begs an obvious question: 'So what?' If the UK Parliament is sovereign, meaning that it can enact any law it likes, what practical relevance, if any, could the *Belmarsh* ruling have? The detention of the suspects was sanctioned by an Act of Parliament—and, as we already know, courts must, because Parliament is sovereign, accept and apply the legislation it produces. What, then, was the point of the court in *Belmarsh* pronouncing on whether the anti-terrorism legislation breached the detainees' human rights?

In order to answer this question, it is necessary to be clear about exactly what the court was being asked to do in *Belmarsh*—which, in turn, requires an explanation of the constitutional status of human rights in UK law. We noted earlier that the UK is bound, as a matter of international law, by the ECHR. This means that if the Strasbourg court finds that UK law is inconsistent with one or more of the rights contained in the ECHR, the UK is required by international law to remove the inconsistency by amending national law—unless, that is, it decides that it would prefer to cease being a party to the ECHR. However, international treaties like the ECHR do not automatically become part of UK law. Essentially, this means that they are only enforceable by national courts to the extent (if any) that national law provides.

What, then, does national law have to say on this matter? Until quite recently, it said nothing, meaning that people who wanted to bring legal proceedings alleging a breach of their rights under the ECHR generally had to pursue their case in the Strasbourg court. However, the Labour government which assumed office in 1997 regarded this state of affairs as unacceptable. It felt that people should be able to enforce their rights in national courts, and therefore enacted the Human Rights Act 1998 in order to 'bring rights home'. The Act pursues that objective in a variety of ways, but for current purposes sections 3 and 4 of the Act are the most important. Section 3 says that, whenever it is possible to do so, UK courts must interpret national law in a way that is compatible with the ECHR. Meanwhile, section 4 provides that if this cannot be done—ie if UK law is flatly inconsistent with the ECHR—certain courts may issue a 'declaration of incompatibility'. Such a declaration has no legal effect in that the incompatible national law remains in force and has to be applied by the courts. Rather, its effect is simply to draw the existence of the incompatibility to the attention of the other branches of government (as well as the wider public), leaving those branches to decide whether, and if so how, national law should be amended so as to remove the incompatibility.

In the *Belmarsh* case, the House of Lords, as we have seen, decided that Part 4 of the Anti-terrorism Act was incompatible with the right to liberty. It also held that while there was a public emergency that might in principle be capable of justifying laws at odds with that right, the government had not shown that it was necessary to infringe the right to liberty to the extent that Part 4 did. What this boils down to is that Part 4 was flatly inconsistent with the ECHR. As a result, the House of Lords issued a declaration of incompatibility. In doing so, it did not seek to disguise the fact that such a declaration is not a legally potent remedy. As Lord Scott freely acknowledged, 'The making of such a declaration will not . . . affect in the least the validity under domestic law of the impugned statutory provision.' The detainees therefore won a moral but not a legal victory: the House of Lords condemned their detention as a breach of their fundamental rights, but could not order their release because they were detained under an Act of Parliament whose legality was untouched by the declaration of incompatibility.

This limitation on the courts' powers under the Human Rights Act should not take us by surprise. Indeed, it would have been constitutionally impossible to assign any greater powers to the courts. We saw above that in many countries constitutional laws have a special, higher legal status, meaning that other, lesser laws will be invalid if they are incompatible with the constitution. But that is not the position in the UK, where laws dealing with constitutional matters—for instance, legislation like the Human Rights Act which sets out individuals' fundamental rights—only have the status of ordinary law. Because all Acts of Parliament are equal in legal status, even an Act dealing with important constitutional matters can always be overridden by a subsequent Act. From this, it follows that it would have been impossible when the Human Rights Act was enacted in 1998 for Parliament to have given it a special legal status allowing it to override subsequent legislation that was inconsistent with human rights. Put simply, unless the fundamental principles of the UK constitution change (and no one can even agree on how that might be done), it is impossible to create a legally superior body of constitutional law that has precedence over other Acts of Parliament. The Human Rights Act could not therefore give the courts a power to strike down subsequently enacted legislation, and so Parliament went as far as it could by authorising courts to issue declarations of incompatibility.

THE COURTS' ROLE: BROADER CONSIDERATIONS

This explanation helps us to understand why the Human Rights Act does not give the courts more potent powers—but it does not establish that the necessarily weaker powers given to the courts by that Act are useful. If the most that could be done was to authorise courts, in effect, merely to *say* that legislation is incompatible with human rights, was passing the Human Rights Act a worthwhile endeavour? The answer is 'yes'. What, then, is the *positive* case for giving courts the type of powers conferred upon them by the Human Rights Act?

A helpful way of approaching this question is to consider what happened after the House of Lords gave judgment in the *Belmarsh* case in December 2004. Even though, as explained earlier, the declaration of incompatibility issued by the court had no legal teeth—it did not require anybody to do anything—the detainees had been released, and Part 4 of the 2001 Act repealed (scrapped, in other words), by March 2005. Why? The beginnings of an answer lie in an observation made by Lord Scott in his judgment in *Belmarsh*. The fact that declarations of incompatibility issued under the Human Rights Act are not legally binding does not make them irrelevant: their significance, he pointed out, is 'political not legal'. The government's strategy of subjecting terror suspects to imprisonment without trial was already a highly controversial one before the House of Lords' ruling: but the judges' decision in the *Belmarsh* case redoubled the pressure under which the government found itself to put an end to the Part 4 detention system. Indeed, whenever a declaration of incompatibility is issued, the government is placed under pressure to remove the incompatibility by amending the legislation in question. There are two reasons for this.

The first is a *legal* one. Although, as we know, UK courts are powerless to compel the government to do anything when an Act of Parliament is found to conflict with the ECHR, the same is not true of the European Court of Human Rights. If that court finds UK law to be deficient, the UK, as noted earlier, is obliged as a matter of international law to put things right. Crucially, if someone 'wins' a case in the UK courts, in the sense of getting a declaration of incompatibility, it is likely that, unless the government caves in and amends the relevant law, the person concerned will take their case to the Strasbourg court. And it is likely that, armed with a declaration of incompatibility, they will win: while the Strasbourg court is in no way bound by national courts' opinions, it generally takes account of them. There is therefore little point in the government refusing to act in response to a declaration of incompatibility, given the likelihood that it would lose in Strasbourg. This is no doubt a large part of the reason why the government habitually legislates in response to declarations of incompatibility, even though it is under no national legal obligation to do so.

Secondly, independently of the prospect of being taken to, and losing in, the Strasbourg court, a declaration of incompatibility piles *political* pressure on the government to remove the incompatibility. In the *Belmarsh* case, the declaration was issued, by a majority of eight to one, by the UK's highest court. It signalled very clearly that, in the opinion of that court, UK law fell short of the minimum human rights standards guaranteed by the ECHR in 50 European countries, stretching from Ireland and Portugal in the west to Russia and Turkey in the east. Why, people unsurprisingly asked, was the UK peculiarly unable or unwilling to adhere to such standards? It would be going too far to say that the political pressure created by a declaration of incompatibility is always irresistible—but it is certainly hard for a government to justify a refusal to accord to people in the UK the minimum human rights standards that operate across Europe. Against this background, the Home Secretary told Parliament that he 'accept[ed] the Law Lords' declaration of incompatibility' in the *Belmarsh* case. He later stated that the legislation introduced to replace Part 4 of the Anti-terrorism Act was 'designed to meet the Law Lords' criticism that the previous legislation was both disproportionate and discriminatory'. The new legislation sought to contain the threat posed by both British and foreign terror suspects by allowing the government to subject them to 'control orders' (eg providing for curfews and preventing association with other suspects). Such an order can undoubtedly constitute a major limitation upon a suspect's freedom to live his life as he wishes—as one judge put it, the cumulative effect of the restrictions imposed by such an order may result in a situation 'not far short of house arrest'—although the control order regime is at least less draconian than the detention without trial system which it replaced. Many of the Belmarsh detainees were subjected to control orders as soon as they were released from prison.

Legal and Political Constitutionalism

What does all of this tell us? It suggests that the fact that nothing in the UK is set in legal stone—because any law, even one concerning fundamental rights or basic constitutional principles, can be undone or changed by a subsequent law—should not lull us into thinking that the government can therefore do as it pleases. In countries which adhere to the more normal sort of constitutional model sketched earlier in this chapter, the emphasis is on *legal constitutionalism*. The constitution lays down hard and fast lines which the branches of government are legally impotent to cross. And if they try to do so—for instance, by enacting laws that seek to take away people's constitutional rights—the courts can intervene by striking down such laws. The position in the UK is different. The UK approach relies more heavily on the notion of *political constitutionalism*: that is, on the capacity of political considerations to prevent or at least dissuade those in authority from using their powers oppressively or abusively. Often, the simple fact that British governments periodically have to submit themselves (in the rather indirect way considered above) for re-election will be enough: politicians' instincts for self-preservation will generally lead them to avoid doing things which will upset large numbers of people.

More problematic are situations in which a government is inclined to do something that disadvantages a small group of people—suspected foreign terrorists, for instance—in order to benefit everyone else. Here, other things being equal, the electoral calculus may favour behaving in precisely such a way. It is in such circumstances that political constitutionalism risks failing—if, that is, we judge success in terms of treating everyone fairly and equally. Crucially, however, the UK's constitution is not a *purely* political one. Legal standards exist (for instance in the form of the ECHR) and there are courts which can adjudicate on whether those standards have been adhered to. The UK system, then, is an amalgam of legal and political constitutionalism. Politicians—because they control Parliament, and because Parliament is sovereign—ultimately have the upper hand. But the business of politics is conducted within a system that possesses legal benchmarks and courts that are prepared to say whether they have been met. *Belmarsh* is a case in point. The House of Lords' ruling that Part 4 of the Anti-terrorism Act fell short of the *legal* standards laid down by the ECHR made a decisive contribution to the *political* debate about whether it was acceptable to detain suspects without trial—and ultimately resulted in the government giving in to pressure to put an end to that system. It is, therefore, in the interaction of law and politics that the immense powers of the British government are subjected to a generally effective form of control.

SOME CONCLUSIONS

The main conclusion which our discussion points towards is that the UK's constitution is unusual because it is contained in ordinary laws that can be changed or scrapped simply by enacting further such laws. This means that everything is up for grabs in a way that is not so in a legal system with a constitution that is very hard to amend. It means, too, that such things as fundamental rights, which would normally be protected by provisions in a hard-to-change constitution, are not legally secure.

Like any other part of the British constitution, such rights can be limited—even removed in their entirety—by enacting ordinary legislation. Yet, while these things are true and important to anyone trying to understand what the UK constitution is and how it works, they are only part of the story. There are, as we have seen, powerful reasons, both political and legal, which explain why people in the UK generally enjoy basic rights and freedoms notwithstanding the government's ultimate constitutional freedom to remove them.

The question that remains is whether this situation is acceptable. Here, there is a wide variety of views. Some people argue that the UK is still too reliant on politicians exercising self-restraint, and that fundamental constitutional matters, such as the protection of human rights, should be placed on a more secure legal footing. The most obvious way in which this could be done is by adopting a written constitution that adheres more closely to the model sketched near the beginning of this chapter. Others contend that British courts already have too much power—in particular, that the Human Rights Act 1998 has given judges a licence to interfere in matters that should be left to politicians. It has been argued, for instance, that the House of Lords overstepped the mark in the *Belmarsh* case: that the judges should have respected the government's view about what steps were necessary to try to make people safe.

This is not the right place to examine the merits of these different perspectives. Rather, for current purposes, the point is simply that the choice represented by these divergent views is an important one. It goes to the heart of how we are governed by determining who ultimately has the final word: judges or politicians. What is better: a constitution that leaves politicians free to do whatever they like (even if that involves sacrificing the fundamental rights of minorities in order to protect, or secure the votes of, the majority) or one that allows unelected judges to strike down such laws (even if they are supported by the vast majority of people)? Questions of this sort are undoubtedly big ones, and may appear rather abstract. But, in reality, they are of acute practical relevance. They ultimately determine (for example) whether it is legally possible for people to be left to rot in jail because a politician thinks they might present a risk to public safety or, putting the same matter in different terms, whether the government is free to take what it regards as necessary steps to prevent suspected terrorists from flying airliners into skyscrapers.

It is questions such as these with which constitutional law is concerned—and, as we have seen in this chapter, the answers which *British* constitutional law supplies are in many ways atypical. This does not mean that people in the UK do not enjoy comparable rights and freedoms to those in similar countries around the world—but it does mean that those rights and freedoms rest on a legally fragile foundation thanks to the unusual flexibility of the British constitution. To some, a constitution which can be changed with the breathtaking ease with which the British constitution can be altered is a contradiction in terms—is not the whole point of a constitution to safeguard fundamental, enduring values and principles? For others, its malleability is the UK constitution's principal virtue, not least because it allows the government to act in the public interest free from constitutional constraints that may be outdated or otherwise inappropriate. Whether the much-vaunted flexibility of the UK constitution is its greatest strength or its biggest weakness is not a question with a right answer: like many of those you will encounter should you decide to study law, it is one about which you will ultimately have to make up your own mind.

Cases

A and others v Home Secretary [2004] UKHL 56, [2005] 2 AC 68
A v United Kingdom (2009) 49 EHRR 29

Further reading

Bogdanor, *The New British Constitution* (Oxford, Hart Publishing, 2009)
Elliott and Thomas, *Public Law* (Oxford, Oxford University Press, 2011)
Feldman, 'None, One or Several? Perspectives on the UK's Constitution(s)' [2005] *Cambridge Law Journal* 329
Leyland, *The Constitution of the United Kingdom: A Contextual Analysis* (Oxford, Hart Publishing, 2007)

8

European Union Law

Catherine Barnard

INTRODUCTION

I bet you aren't neutral about the European Union: you are bound to be
either (strongly) for or against it. And perhaps 'against' is more likely,
given the often hostile media coverage in this country about the EU.
You might have heard that the EU has tried to ban prawn-cocktail crisps,
home-made jam, round cheese, donkeys from beaches, and darts from
pubs—none of which is true. You might also have heard that the EU
lets foreigners claim social security benefits and receive free healthcare
when they come to the UK—some of which is true. And you might have
heard that the institutions of the EU (the Commission, the Council, the
European Parliament, the European Council, the Court of Justice) are
full of people feathering their own nests but who are incapable of organ-
ising a party in a brewery let alone a major international organisation
which affects the lives of nearly half a billion people.

But what you do not often hear about are the EU success stories:
that thanks to EU intervention we can travel (and live) in the 27 different countries of the EU with virtually no restrictions, that we can get
there cheaply with low-cost airlines such as Ryan Air and EasyJet, that
using your mobile phone abroad is now a lot cheaper, and that pasta and
café latte have become the standard fare of the British high street. Most
importantly, thanks in part to the creation of the European Union, states
like France, Germany, Spain and the UK, which have been enemies for

much of the past 1,000 years and which fought two world wars in the last century, have not been to war with each other since the EU was founded over fifty years ago.

Love it or loathe it, the EU is a fundamental part of our daily existence and European Union law has a profound effect on every aspect of national law, since EU law is part of our law and takes precedence over our law. This so-called *doctrine of supremacy* of EU law is what Eurosceptics rail against. For example, the Referendum Party, campaigning to secure Britain's withdrawal from the European Union in 1996, took out a full-page advert in a national newspaper filled with the words 'John Major is impotent'. This referred not to the sexual health of the then British Prime Minister but to the fact that he was 'completely powerless in the face of diktats from unelected European bureaucrats'. The advert continued: 'Yet again it demonstrates that Brussels [the seat of most of the European Union institutions], not Westminster [the seat of the British Parliament], now decides how we must lead our lives.' A similar point is made in the cartoon on page 189. It is an issue which has bedevilled the British relationship with the EU.

But EU law is not just about economics, politics and constitutional issues. Like contract, tort, and equity, it is also about individuals who have suffered some harm and want the courts to give them a remedy. But what makes EU law exciting for lawyers is the fact that the doctrine of supremacy of EU law, so mistrusted by Eurosceptics, gives lawyers a trump card to win their case. If a point of EU law is successfully raised it will defeat arguments based on *national* law, where the two laws conflict. This is exactly what the lawyers did in *Bosman*, the case discussed in this chapter. Jean-Marc Bosman was a Belgian footballer, not a very good one, but a footballer with the sense to hire good lawyers to challenge the rules of URBSFA (the Belgian football association) and UEFA (the Union of European Football Associations) which prevented him from playing for a French club, as being contrary to EU law. The legal case he fought—which ended up before the Court of Justice of the European Union— tells us much, not only about the rather murky world of professional football, but also about the nature of EU law, its relationship with national law, the legal reasoning of the Court of Justice and the broader political context in which the Court operates. These issues form the heart of this chapter. But first the facts of *Bosman*.

THE DISPUTE

Bosman was a Belgian national employed by the Belgian first-division club RC Liège. When his contract expired he wanted to play for the French second-division club US Dunkerque. However, UEFA and URBSFA had two rules which stood in the way of Bosman playing for US Dunkerque.

The first, the so-called '3+2 rule', said that national football associations could allow each first-division team to field up to three foreign players and two 'acclimatised' foreigners (players who have played in the country for an uninterrupted period of five years) in domestic league matches, but no more than five foreign players in total.

The second concerned transfer fees. According to these rules, on the expiry of a contract with club A (RC Liège), a professional footballer could not play for club B (US Dunkerque) until club A (RC Liège) had released his registration. This would be done only on the payment of a transfer fee. Since RC Liège did not think that US Dunkerque would be able to pay the high transfer fee it had put on Bosman's head, Bosman found himself without a club for the following season. He did eventually manage to sign two short contracts with French clubs before ending up at Olympic de Charleroi, a Belgian third-division club. There was strong circumstantial evidence that Bosman was being boycotted by all the European clubs that might have engaged him because, as a result of the litigation he brought, he was seen as a trouble-maker.

INTRODUCTION TO KEY PRINCIPLES OF EUROPEAN UNION LAW

The Relevant Rules

The Treaties

But what did European Union law have to do with Mr Bosman's tale of woe? Well, quite a lot. He argued before his national court that UEFA and URBSFA's rules contravened Article 45 TFEU, giving workers the right to move freely around the EU, and Article 101 TFEU prohibiting anti-competitive agreements (these are agreements between companies and/or individuals which restrict the free operation of the market in some way).

Both Articles 45 and 101 can be found in the (inelegantly named) Treaty on the Functioning of the European Union (TFEU). The TFEU is the renamed successor to the European Community (EC) Treaty, which, in turn, was the renamed version of the original European Economic Community adopted in 1957. The EC Treaty, together with the Treaty on European Union (TEU) which was adopted at Maastricht in 1992, were to all intents and purposes the 'constitution' of the European Union, as the Court of Justice has acknowledged (see eg *Kadi and Al Barakaat*, paragraph 281). Indeed, the fact that the Treaties were no longer simply international agreements but formed the constitutional backbone of the EU was recognised by the 'Treaty establishing a Constitution for Europe' (sometimes referred to as the 'Constitutional Treaty'), agreed by the heads of the EU states in 2004. This Treaty was intended to simplify the complex arrangements laid down by previous Treaties. However, many people thought that the express reference to a 'constitution' went too far and made the EU more like a state than it actually was. Eventually, the French and Dutch voters rejected the Treaty in 2005 and so it never came into force.

However, the Lisbon Treaty of 2007 emerged from the ashes of the Constitutional Treaty. The Lisbon Treaty was largely a carbon copy of the Constitutional Treaty, albeit shorn of many of its 'constitutional' trappings (eg the reference to the EU flag, the EU day and the EU anthem). Confusingly, the Lisbon Treaty amended the two pre-existing Treaties, the EC Treaty and the TEU, renamed the EC Treaty the Treaty on the Functioning of the European Union (TFEU), and declared the TEU and the TFEU to have equal value. Nevertheless, read together, the two Treaties are still a constitution of sorts. And, as with any 'federal' constitution, state laws or the equivalent, such as the rules of other public bodies such as UEFA, can be checked against the constitution to see if they are compatible with it. This is what happened in *Bosman*: the Court of Justice checked the compatibility of UEFA and URBSFA's rules with the EU Treaties, in particular the Treaties' rules on free movement of workers.

The Four Freedoms

The free movement of workers is one of the 'four freedoms' at the heart of the European Union. The others are the free movement of goods, services and capital. Together, these freedoms form the core of the 'common' or 'single' market project, begun by the European Economic Community (EEC) Treaty in 1957.

The four freedoms share a common feature—that goods, persons, services or capital moving from one Member State of the European Union to another should not suffer discrimination simply because they are foreign. In other words, it should be as easy to trade or move between London and Budapest as it is between London and Birmingham. So, the big idea behind the single market is market integration: the removal of barriers to trade and to migration between states. But what are the advantages of market integration? In the case of free movement of persons, there are benefits both for individual migrant workers and the 'host' state where they go to work. From the host state's point of view, workers coming from other Member States often take up jobs which cannot be filled by national workers. Migrants also bring new talents and skills which the national workforce cannot offer. For the individual migrants, moving to a new job in another Member State means escaping from possible unemployment at home, bettering their personal circumstances and broadening their range of experience.

So far, so win–win. When times are good, workers from other Member States do help to fill a skills gap, as we saw in the UK with the arrival of hundreds of thousands of Polish, Hungarian and other Eastern European workers when those countries joined the EU in 2004. But when times are bad, migrant workers are seen to threaten jobs for nationals (see, eg: Milland, 'Jobless up 92,000 as Poles flood in', *Daily Express*, 17 August 2006, 1; Whitehead, '92,000 East Europeans Milk Our Benefits', *Daily Express*, 23 May 2007, 1, Little, 'Migrants Rob Young Britons of Jobs', *Daily Express*, 19 August 2010) and it is then that host governments, bowing to domestic political pressure, may decide to make life more difficult for migrant workers. They might, for example, limit the number of foreigners who can do a particular job (as with the 3+2 rule in *Bosman*). Or they might ban foreigners from working in the host state altogether. A famous example of this was the call by Gordon Brown, then British

Pickets protesting at the Lindsey oil refinery.
©Anna Gowthorpe/Press Association Images

Prime Minister, at the Labour Party conference in September 2007, for 'British jobs for British workers'. His words came back to haunt him: on the picket line at the Lindsey oil refinery in Lincolnshire protesters used his words to justify their strike in January 2009 over the fact that IREM, an Italian company, had brought Italian and Portuguese construction workers in to fulfil a contract on the site. This is where European Union law comes into play: Article 45 TFEU can be invoked by migrant workers or Article 56 TFEU can be invoked by service providers (such as IREM) to challenge such unjustified barriers created by laws and practices of the host Member State.

But removing barriers (sometimes referred to as *negative integration*) may not be enough to achieve free movement of goods, persons, services and capital. Sometimes additional rights are needed to achieve free movement (referred to as *positive integration*). These additional rights take the form of legislative measures adopted by the institutions of the European Union to help facilitate free movement. Most commonly, these measures take the form of *Regulations*, which automatically form part of domestic law, or *Directives*, which must be implemented by Member States by passing legislation in their own national systems. Regulations and Directives are proposed by the European Commission, the executive arm of the European Union (the officials in Brussels who run the Union day to day), and then adopted (usually) by a combination of the Council of Ministers (meetings of Ministers from each of the Member States) and the European Parliament (the only directly elected body in the EU).

One such legislative measure, Regulation 1612/68 on the free movement of workers in the EU, was agreed as early as 1968 to allow workers to move freely with their families. The Regulation says that workers have to enjoy an equal chance with nationals of getting a job and to benefit from equal treatment once employed. It also says that the worker's family members should be able to join the worker in the host state and work there themselves. These latter provisions have been replaced by the Citizens' Rights Directive 2004/38 which has, more fundamentally, overhauled the system of free movement rights. We shall return to this Directive later. For now remember that, as he began to challenge the 3+2 nationality rules, Bosman relied on not only the Treaty provision, Article 45 TFEU, but also on the provisions of the legislative measure, Regulation 1612/68.

The Principles of Supremacy and Direct Effect

The Principles

But how can these *EU* rules be raised in a *national* court given that you might expect that national courts to apply national law only? The Court of Justice of the European Union answered this question in two seminal cases decided in the 1960s, *Van Gend en Loos* and *Costa v ENEL*. In these cases the Court, adopting a *teleological* approach to interpretation (looking at the purpose of the Treaties rather than the literal meaning of the words used), developed two key principles: direct effect and supremacy.

Direct effect means that unconditional and precise European Union law rules, including provisions of the Treaties, can be enforced by litigants before their national courts. *Supremacy* or *primacy* of European Union law means, as we have already seen, that EU law takes precedence over any conflicting national law. The two principles go hand in hand: without supremacy there is no point in having direct effect (otherwise national law would trump EU law) and, conversely, without direct effect there is no point in having supremacy (otherwise supreme EU law could not actually be enforced in national courts).

Criticism of the Principles

The upshot of the principles of direct effect and supremacy is that Mr Bosman could rely on the provisions of the Treaties to challenge the football authorities' rules in his local (Belgian) court and, if the local court found in his favour, EU law would prevail over the conflicting UEFA/URBSFA rules.

This is what makes the Eurosceptics angry: why should national rules give way to European Union law? Well, the answer is that the Member States agreed to this on accession to the EU. Take the case of the UK. The British government signed up to the EEC Treaty when it acceded to the EU in 1973 and the EEC Treaty, as interpreted by the Court of Justice, implicitly included the principles of supremacy and direct effect. The UK incorporated these principles, together with the rest of EU law, into British law by the European Communities Act (ECA) 1972. In principle, this Act, like any other Act of Parliament, is subject to the doctrine of parliamentary sovereignty considered in chapter 7. This means that it can be repealed (ie reversed) by the British Parliament at any stage, thereby freeing the UK of its obligations under European Union law. The doctrine of parliamentary sovereignty should have helped to put the Eurosceptics' minds at rest. In practice, however, the ECA 1972, like the Human Rights Act 1998 incorporating the European Convention on Human Rights into UK law, has assumed a special constitutional status, and will not be repealed lightly. So perhaps the Eurosceptics have a point.

Critics of the EU also complain about the Court of Justice's activism. What right did the Court have to 'invent' principles, such as direct

This cartoon by Gaskill illustrates the concerns expressed by Euro-sceptics about the loss of UK parliamentary sovereignty to 'Brussels'.
© David Gaskill, *The Sun*.

effect and supremacy, which are not actually written down in the Treaties? The Court of Justice argues that it is empowered by the EU Treaties to ensure that 'the law is observed', which, to the Court of Justice, means making sure that EU law is *effective* in practice and that Member States comply with their Treaty obligations. Other federal systems where power is divided between the central (federal) and local (state) levels have equivalent rules to ensure their systems can operate; the Court of Justice has introduced these principles to make sure that the European Union system, while not a federal system in the German or US sense, can function effectively too. There is no point in individuals (ie people and companies) seeing EU law as remote and inaccessible. For it to work they must be able to rely on it before their local courts: in Riga, Rimini and Rotherham.

Express reference to the principle of supremacy (but not direct effect) was in fact made in the Constitutional Treaty in 2004. However, the Lisbon Treaty removed the reference to supremacy but referred to it in a (non-legally binding) declaration. Nevertheless, it is widely accepted that, because the principles of direct effect and supremacy are firmly established and central to the operation of EU law, they will continue to apply.

The Article 267 Reference Procedure

If they feel able, local courts can decide cases such as Bosman's for themselves; if not, as in *Bosman*, they can refer questions to the Court of Justice under the so-called Article 267 TFEU *preliminary reference* or *preliminary ruling* procedure. Under this procedure national courts ask the Court of Justice questions about the interpretation of European Union law. This process, while apparently complex and certainly time-consuming, is one of the great strengths of the European Union legal system. At its best, it sees the national courts and the Court of Justice working in co-operation: the Court of Justice gives a ruling on the meaning of European Union *law* and the case returns to the national court to apply this ruling to the *facts* of the case. In the UK the rulings of the Court of Justice form part of the system of precedent and, in recognition of the supremacy of Union law, take precedence over the rulings of all British courts, including the Supreme Court.

The Court of Justice's ruling should always be clear enough for the national court to follow. It helps that there is only ever one judgment—there are no dissents—and each judgment contains a *dispositif* (closing section) at the end summarising the Court's findings. However, the downside of a single judgment is that it is often hard to get all the judges to agree on its wording. Whether the Court of Justice sits as a Full Court (all 27 judges, a rarity), as a Grand Chamber (13 judges), or as a Chamber of three or five judges, the judgment must be agreed by all the judges. The judgment is drafted in French (the working language of the

Court) by the *juge rapporteur* (reporting judge). At times, controversial paragraphs on which agreement cannot be secured are removed from the final version, with the result that the judgment may be difficult to follow in places.

Originally, the decisions of the Court of Justice were short, following the French model which sees cases as merely expounding the law, not justifying or developing it. However, in recent years the decisions of the Court of Justice have grown in length and, reflecting the increasing common law influence (following the accession of the UK and Ireland to the EU in 1973), discuss and distinguish other cases more fully. Unlike common law, though, there is no doctrine of precedent in EU law, although in practice the Court of Justice does tend to follow its earlier decisions.

More detail can often be found in the Advocate General's opinion. The Advocate General, a judge at the Court of Justice, writes an advisory opinion to assist the Court. This reads more like a common law judgment (and so is generally much longer than the Court of Justice's decision). The Court of Justice is not obliged to follow this opinion but, in many cases, it does so. In *Bosman* the Court of Justice did reach the same conclusion as its Advocate General but, while the Advocate General placed much emphasis on the challenge to the football associations' rules as being anti-competitive under Article 101 TFEU, the Court's sole focus was on the free movement of workers provisions under Article 45 TFEU.

Having introduced you to some of the nuts and bolts of EU law, it is now time to consider what the Court of Justice actually said in *Bosman*.

THE COURT OF JUSTICE'S DECISION

The 3+2 Rule

The Judgment

You will remember that Bosman's first claim was that the 3+2 rule (ie that there could only be five 'foreign' players in a team at any one time) directly discriminated against him contrary to Article 45 TFEU on the free movement of workers and Regulation 1612/68; had Bosman been French there would have been no limit on his right to play. The Treaties prohibit discrimination on the grounds of nationality because such discrimination is irrational: employers, including football clubs, must make selection decisions based on the rational criterion of merit, rather than on the irrational criterion of nationality. With the opening up of the single market, this means that employers have a much bigger pool of candidates to choose from; using nationality as a criterion to narrow that pool undermines the purposes of the single market.

The Court of Justice recognised this point in *Bosman*. It said that the 3+2 rule related to the essence of the activity of professional players: if EU law did not apply to this situation, then Article 45 TFEU would be 'deprived of its practical effect and the fundamental right of free access to employment which the [Treaties confer] individually on each worker in the [Union] rendered nugatory'. The 3+2 rule was therefore unlawful.

Three points are worth noting about the Court of Justice's observations. First, the Court relied on the 'effectiveness' argument (the argument used by the Court to develop the principles of direct effect and supremacy) to buttress its reasoning (Article 45 TFEU would be 'deprived of its practical effect' if it did not apply to Bosman's case). Secondly, the Court said that Article 45 satisfied the criteria to be direct effective (the 'right of free access to employment which the [Treaties confer] individually on each worker').

Thirdly, this right of free access to employment was described as 'fundamental'. Traditionally, the epithet 'fundamental rights' is attached to civil and political rights such as the right to life and freedom of expression. It is not usually attached to *economic* rights such as the right to free movement. However, it will be recalled that the European Union was originally established as the European *Economic* Community: economic freedoms—the free movement of goods, persons, services and capital— lay at the core of the EEC and therefore achieved 'fundamental' status. In the past this has led to a certain imbalance between economic freedoms and other fundamental rights. However, as the EEC has evolved from European Economic Community to European Union, greater recognition has been given to fundamental civil and political rights. The adoption of the Charter of Fundamental Rights 2000, which put both civil/political rights and economic/social rights into a single document has helped to redress the initial imbalance. The Charter is now legally binding since the Lisbon Treaty came into force in December 2009.

So, the Court of Justice held that the 3+2 rule was directly discriminatory: it overtly discriminated against non-nationals such as Mr Bosman. Direct discrimination is considered the worst type of discrimination— because it is so obviously connected with the prohibited ground of nationality. However, the Treaties do provide defences for the defendant Member States/sporting associations. These defences, known in EU law as 'derogations', concern public policy, public security and public health. These derogations are all narrowly interpreted and it is only in the rarest of cases that the defendant successfully relies on one of them. *Bosman* was not such a case.

The football associations also tried to defend themselves by pointing out that the European Commission had been involved in the drafting of the 3+2 rule: surely, they argued, if the EU's own Commission had said the 3+2 rule was acceptable, that amounted to a good defence. But the Court of Justice said 'no', dryly observing that the Commission did not have the power 'to authorise practices which are contrary to the [Treaties]'.

The Implications

In light of the Court of Justice's ruling in *Bosman*, how then do national sports teams (ie England, France, Germany) get away with fielding a team of only national players? This question had been addressed in the earlier case of *Donà v Mantero* where, in respect of *national* teams, the Court of Justice essentially created a new exception to the rule prohibiting non-discrimination. Relying on the rather contentious justification that *national* games are not commercial in nature, the Court said that Union law did not prevent the adoption of rules 'excluding foreign players from participation in certain matches for reasons which are not of an economic nature'. Therefore, in the context of matches which are of sporting interest only, such as matches between national teams (eg

England v Germany), Union law does not apply and so discrimination is permitted.

The upshot of *Bosman* and *Donà* is that clubs (eg Manchester United and Chelsea) are subject to Union law in respect of the nationality of players that can be fielded, while national sides (eg England and France) are not. The decision in *Donà v Mantero* shows that the Court of Justice has rather well-tuned political antennae and decided not to make itself, and EU law, a laughing stock by requiring national teams to field a mixed nationality squad (no matter that some national sides would benefit from the injection of some foreign blood).

One final question. Given that Article 45 TFEU stops sports associations from limiting the number of *EU* nationals that can play for club sides, what is the position in respect of nationality rules for players coming from non-Member States of the European Union, so-called 'third-country nationals' (TCNs)? Well, if the EU has an agreement with the third country, and that agreement contains a non-discrimination clause, then discrimination can be prohibited. This can be seen in *Simutenkov*. The Spanish football association had a rule limiting to three the number of TCN players who were allowed to participate at any time in the Spanish first division. Following *Bosman*, Simutenkov, a Russian footballer who played for a Spanish club, challenged this rule as being contrary to Article 23(1) of the European Communities–Russia Partnership Agreement which prohibited discrimination against Russian nationals legally employed in the territory of a Member State. He won his case. Had there been no such agreement, discrimination against TCNs would be a matter for national and not EU law.

The Transfer Fee Rule

Establishing a Breach of European Union Law

Jean-Marc Bosman challenged not only the 3+2 rule but also the requirement to pay transfer fees. As we discussed earlier, on the expiry of a contract with club A, a professional footballer could not play for club B until club A had released his registration. This was usually conditional on club B paying a transfer fee to club A. Did this rule breach EU law?

The problem facing the Court was that this rule, unlike the 3+2 rule, was not discriminatory on the grounds of nationality because it applied equally to transfers between clubs belonging to different national associations within the same Member State (eg between Manchester United and Celtic) and was similar to the rules governing transfers between clubs belonging to the same national association (eg between Manchester United and Chelsea). Nevertheless, the Court of Justice concluded that the transfer rules did breach Article 45 TFEU because they 'directly affect[ed] players' access to the employment market in other Member States' and were 'capable of impeding freedom of movement for workers'.

This was an important ruling because the Court of Justice now recognised that Union law was no longer simply about removing *discrimination* (as the Treaties provide) but it was also about ensuring that goods and people from other Member States enjoyed *access to the market* of other Member States, even where the rule was non-discriminatory. The Court said that Bosman should have had free access to the football market in other Member States unless there were 'objectively justifiable' (ie good) reasons why he should not.

The Court of Justice's new approach has serious implications for the Member States. Under the *discrimination* model, Member States/sporting associations had the freedom to set their own rules and these rules would not be challenged under EU law unless they were discriminatory either directly (such as the 3+2 rule in *Bosman*) or indirectly (a rule which on its face applies to all workers but which in fact imposes a particular burden on the migrant, such as a residence requirement). By contrast, under the *market access* approach, nearly all national rules risk being challenged as interfering with the Union rights to free movement because, by their nature, most national rules interfere with trade or free movement in some way.

The difference between the discrimination and market access approaches can be seen in the following example. Greek law prohibited qualified opticians from operating more than one optician's shop. This rule was challenged by the European Commission as being contrary to EU law because the rule interfered with the right of opticians from other Member States to set up a chain of opticians in Greece. If the Court of Justice had applied the discrimination model the Commission would have lost its case because Greek law treated Greek and foreign opticians the same: nobody could set up a chain of opticians shops. The rule therefore would not have breached the Treaties and was therefore lawful.

In fact, the Court of Justice applied the market access approach and found the Greek rule did breach the Treaties because the rule interfered with the right of opticians from other Member States to set up a chain of opticians' shops in Greece. The fact that Greek opticians also could not set up a chain of opticians' shops was irrelevant. The Court's focus was instead on the restrictions experienced by traders and entrepreneurs from other Member States trying to break onto the Greek market. Because such restrictions existed, they breached the Treaties and were thus unlawful unless they could be justified which they could not be on the facts. So it followed that the national rule had to be set aside so that opticians from other Members States could set up a chain of opticians' shops in Greece.

This choice between the discrimination and the market access approaches as the underpinning theory regulating free movement has troubled not only the EU but also other international organisations such as the World Trade Organisation (WTO). While, on the one hand, the market access test risks doing more damage to social, environmental and consumer legislation enacted by democratically elected national governments, on the other hand, it is more likely to achieve market integration (ie the creation of a single market) since it strikes down—often antiquated—provisions such as the Greek single optician's shop rule. By contrast, the discrimination approach is less likely to interfere with national regulation but it is also less effective in achieving market integration.

In the field of free movement of persons, the Court of Justice has opted very much in favour of the market access approach, now increasingly referred to as the 'obstacle' or 'restriction' approach. In many cases the Court simply asks the question 'Does the national rule being challenged constitute an obstacle or restriction on free movement?' If, as in *Bosman,* the answer to this question is 'yes', then the national rule breaches the Treaties. The burden then shifts to the defendant state to come up with a good reason to justify the existence of the rule.

Justification, Proportionality and Fundamental Human Rights

What, then, are these justifications? They are an open-ended list of 'good' reasons for the rule developed by the Court of Justice on a case-by-case basis. These justifications (or public interest requirements as they are sometimes called) supplement the express derogations (defences)—public policy, public security and public health—laid down by the Treaties. The price for adopting the broad market access test is that the Court has had to recognise an ever-wider range of justifications (including consumer protection, environmental protection and worker protection) available to the Member States to prevent the wholesale dismantling of national rules.

However, Member States cannot just point to a good reason for the existence of the rule. They must also show that any steps taken to achieve one of the derogations or justifications are proportionate (ie the measures must be *suitable* for securing the attainment of the objective and must not go beyond what is *necessary* to attain it), and the measures must respect fundamental rights. The case of *Carpenter* provides a good illustration of how these principles work together.

Mrs Carpenter, a Filipino national, overstayed her entry permit to the UK. She then married a British national. The UK tried to deport her for overstaying her visa. In contesting her deportation, Mrs Carpenter came up with an ingenious argument. Since she was Filipino (a so-called TCN) she could not invoke EU law herself. However, she said that if she was deported this would restrict her British *husband's* ability to carry on business as a service provider in other Member States since she looked after his children while he was away. Her deportation therefore contravened Article 56 TFEU on freedom to provide services. The Court of Justice accepted Mrs Carpenter's argument and said that her deportation would in principle constitute an obstacle to Mr Carpenter's ability to provide services under EU law.

In its defence, the UK argued that Mrs Carpenter's deportation could be justified on grounds of public policy. While recognising that the UK had a point, the Court of Justice said that the UK had to balance the public interest in deporting Mrs Carpenter with the fundamental rights of Mr and Mrs Carpenter, in particular the right to family life under Article

8 of the European Convention on Human Rights (ECHR) (the Court of Justice of the European Union regularly refers to the ECHR to guide its own case law and the Lisbon Treaty now requires the EU to accede to the ECHR). While the right to family life is not itself unlimited, the Court said that the decision to deport Mrs Carpenter was disproportionate: even though Mrs Carpenter had infringed UK immigration laws (by overstaying her entry visa) she did not constitute a danger to public order and safety. Therefore, as a result of European Union law, Mrs Carpenter was entitled to stay in the UK.

Establishing Justification and Proportionality in Bosman

So how did the principles of justification, proportionality and human rights apply in *Bosman*? Well, the Court of Justice began by recognising that transfer fees might be justified. It said:

> In view of the considerable social importance of sporting activities and in particular football in the [Union], the aims of maintaining a balance between clubs by preserving a certain degree of equality and uncertainty as to results and of encouraging the recruitment and training of young players [the transfer fees] must be accepted as legitimate.

In other words, the Court of Justice recognised that sport was special and different because it was based on a notion of mutual interdependence. To help explain the significance of the Court's observation, one academic commentator, Stephen Weatherill, contrasts the sport 'market' with the 'widget' market (the term 'widget' is used in legal texts to denote non-specific products). On the 'widget' market, producers aim to gain the largest market share, if necessary by driving their rivals off the market. By contrast, in sport, opponents are there to be beaten but the whole point of the endeavour is destroyed if opponents are beaten out of sight.

Having recognised that sport was special, the Court of Justice said that there were good reasons to justify the existence of transfer fees: as a way of transferring funds from rich clubs to poor clubs and as a way of providing incentives to clubs to invest in the training of young players. This seemed to suggest that the football associations were going to win.

However, the Court of Justice then turned to the question of the proportionality of the transfer fee rules and found them to be disproportionate (it never got to the question of fundamental rights). It said that the transfer fee rules were not an adequate means of maintaining financial and competitive balance in the world of football because they neither precluded the richest clubs from securing the services of the best players nor did they prevent the availability of financial resources from being a decisive factor in competitive sport. It also said that the prospect of receiving transfer fees was neither a decisive factor in encouraging the recruitment and training of young players nor an adequate means of financing such activities. The Court of Justice therefore concluded that the transfer fee rules, like the 3+2 rule, breached EU law and so were unlawful. Jean-Marc Bosman had won his case.

THE IMMEDIATE CONSEQUENCES OF THE *BOSMAN* RULING

The Consequences for Mr Bosman

So, what happened next? Well, the Belgian football authorities paid Jean-Marc Bosman £312,000 in damages and he in turn agreed not to pursue the case any further. This happened in December 1998, more than eight years after the expiry of his contract with RC Liège. But in reality Bosman did not benefit from the litigation. He was left heavily in debt as a result of his legal fight with the football authorities and, with his professional career over and his marriage in tatters, he moved back in with his parents. In early 1997 some of the world's top players planned a testimonial for him involving Barcelona and a Europe XI. However, the Spanish FA and FIFA objected to the match, blaming Bosman for the large number of foreign players in the Spanish league (Oliver, 'Sport Around the World: Bosman out in the cold in Spain', *Daily Telegraph*, 1 March 1997, 18). The match did eventually go ahead but Bosman's name was not officially connected with the event.

Jean-Marc Bosman at home with his career over.
© Gary Carlton, 2006.

The Consequences for Football

The *Bosman* ruling had ramifications for the world of professional foot-ball going way beyond the immediate circumstances of Jean-Marc's case. With the abolition of the 3+2 rule, the nationality composition of many teams has changed dramatically (look at who now plays for teams such as Chelsea, Arsenal and Liverpool). With the abolition of trans-fer fees for players whose contracts have come to an end, clubs have responded by hiring stars on longer contracts, with money previously used for transfer fees being diverted into wage packets. This has made multi-millionaires out of many European players. The football industry has also revised its rules on transfers of players. These new rules include a system of training compensation to encourage and reward the effort of clubs, especially small clubs, in training young players, as well as the creation of a restricted transfer period prior to each season, and a further limited mid-season window, with a maximum of one transfer per player per season.

Furthermore, UEFA has introduced a 'home-grown player rule' which applies to games in the Champions League and the UEFA cup. Clubs competing in these competitions must include in a 25-man squad 8 locally trained players (ie players who, regardless of their nationality, have been trained by their club or by another club in the same national association for at least three years between the age of 15 and 21). Clubs are not obliged to play these home-grown players in any match. UEFA sees this rule as one step towards addressing the problem created by the *Bosman* ruling, namely that 'the richest clubs have been able to stock-pile the best players, which makes it easier for them to dominate both national and European competitions'.

The home-grown player rule, while potentially indirectly discrimina-tory (ie it disadvantages in practice those from other Member States), is more carefully tailored than the 3+2 rule. The Commission has there-fore indicated that it thinks the rule can be justified. It has said that the objectives of the rule, namely promoting training for young players and consolidating the balance of competitions, seem 'legitimate objectives of general interest, as they are inherent to sporting activity' and are pro-portionate.

However, there remains considerable disquiet in the world of football that EU law should apply to it at all. There is a strong feeling of resent-ment that EU law rules which were intended to apply to 'public' laws of the Member States (eg Acts of Parliament and statutory instruments) have been extended by the Court of Justice to the 'private' world of football. Those in charge of football argue that, because sport is special, it should be exempted from the EU's free movement rules altogether (Blitz, 'EU labour movement rules threaten football, says Platini', *Financial Times*, 21 May 2007). Football, they argue, should be left to footballers and not 'unelected bureaucrats' such as European Commissioners (those in charge of the European Commission) and the Court of Justice who have 'never played sport'.

THE LONGER-TERM CONSEQUENCES OF *BOSMAN*: THE DEVELOPMENT OF UNION CITIZENSHIP

The Position of the Non-economically Active and Union Citizenship

For better or for worse, *Bosman* has changed the face of European football. *Bosman* was also an important staging post in another more fundamental political transformation occurring in the European Union. As we saw in the earlier part of this chapter, the original EEC Treaty gave rights to those who were 'economically' active (such as workers) who could move from one country to another to take up a job. By contrast, those who were not economically active had no rights to move to another Member State. In a European *Economic* Community this distinction made sense: those who were economically active were able to contribute to the economy of the host state, largely through paying taxes. They would therefore be a benefit, not a burden, to the economy of that state. The same would not be true for those who were not economically active (eg the unemployed). These individuals risked becoming a financial burden on the social welfare system of the host state.

However, the Court of Justice began to erode the distinction between the economically and the non-economically active by extending the Treaty rights to those who were not economically active, in the traditional sense, such as work-seekers and tourists. This led some to suggest that the Court of Justice was developing a concept of EU 'citizenship', ie giving rights of free movement to anyone holding the nationality of a Member State regardless of their economic status. This in turn reflected a changing attitude by the Court of Justice towards the EU: the EU was no longer just a glorified free trade area but it was also a *political* body assuming state-like qualities. One key aspect of any state is having a 'people', ie its own citizens; and citizens have human rights which need to be protected. Cases such as *Carpenter* can be understood as part of this development.

The adoption of the Maastricht Treaty in 1992 helped reshape the understanding of what 'Europe' was about. Not only was this Treaty responsible for the name change from European Economic Community to European Community, but it also introduced the concept of the European Union. This shift from a purely *Economic* Community to a European *Union*, with a political as well as an economic dimension, was given real substance by the inclusion at Maastricht of new Articles on EU citizenship. These provide that all those holding the nationality of one of the Member States of the Union are Union citizens, which, according to Article 21 TFEU, gives them the right to move to, and reside in, another Member State, subject only to the limits laid down by the Treaties (such as the public policy, security and health derogations) as well as the right to vote and stand as a candidates in municipal and European elections in the host state under Article 22 TFEU.

The *Bosman* case was an important marker in this changing perspective from economic community to political union. Mr Bosman was relying on his economic rights as a worker. Yet the Court talked of him not just as a worker but also as a citizen. For example, it said that the provisions of the Treaties relating to freedom of movement for persons were intended 'to facilitate the pursuit by [Union] *citizens* of occupational activities of all kinds throughout the [Union], and preclude measures which might place [Union] *citizens* at a disadvantage when they wish to pursue an economic activity in the territory of another Member State' (emphasis added).

But what is now the position of those who, unlike Bosman, are not economically active? Are they entitled to enjoy the rights of free movement too? And, if so, are they entitled to enjoy social welfare benefits in the state they move to (the host state) on the same terms as nationals? In the leading case of *Grzelczyk* the Court suggested that the answer was a qualified yes.

Grzelczyk was a French student studying at a Belgian university. Having supported himself financially for the first three years of his studies he applied for a *minimex* (a Belgian social security benefit guaranteeing a minimum income) at the start of his fourth and final year. While Belgian students could receive the benefit, migrant students could not, and so Grzelczyk complained that he was being discriminated against, contrary to European Union law. However, the difficulty with his claim was that, under the relevant EU law rules on students, he was supposed to have sufficient resources to support himself during his studies and so not become reliant on the Belgian social welfare system.

The Court did a remarkable thing. It elevated Union citizenship to 'the fundamental status of nationals of the Member States, enabling those who find themselves in the same situation to enjoy the same treatment in law irrespective of their nationality, subject to such exceptions as are expressly provided for'. Those 'exceptions' included the need to have sufficient resources. However, having elevated the status of Union citizenship, the Court used this to justify a narrow reading of the exceptions. So the Court said that the requirement to have sufficient resources had to be read subject to the principle of proportionality, and that it would be disproportionate to deport Grzelczyk during his fourth and final year of study. Furthermore, and more controversially, the Court said, given the 'solidarity' (ie the sense of common feeling) that now exists between migrant students (such as Grzelczyk) and the Belgian taxpayer, due to the existence of a common EU citizenship, the Belgian authorities should pay him the minimex for so long as he did not become an unreasonable burden (a phrase which was not explained) on Belgian public finances. As a result, Grzelczyk, a migrant EU citizen, did enjoy a certain amount of equal treatment in respect of social security benefits in Belgium.

Citizens' Rights Directive

The position of individuals such as Grzelczyk has been strengthened by the adoption of the Citizens' Rights Directive 2004/38. In part this Directive consolidates the secondary measures, like the Workers' Regulation 1612/68, adopted in the 1960s to encourage free movement. However, the Directive goes further than these earlier measures because it expressly gives rights to those who are not economically active. For example, the Directive provides that any national can move to another Member State for up to three months, whether they are economically active or not, and that they will enjoy equal treatment with nationals in the host state once there. However, the Directive contains an important limitation: they will not enjoy equal treatment in respect of social welfare or student benefits. This helps to reduce immediate concerns about 'welfare tourism'.

For periods beyond three months, migrants also enjoy the right to move but only if they are engaged in economic activity in the host state as a worker or a self-employed person; or they have sufficient medical and financial resources for themselves and their family members; or they are students. These individuals also enjoy the right to the same treatment as nationals of the host state, including in respect of social assistance but not student support. After five years, Union citizens do not need to show they are workers, self-employed, students or adequately resourced. Thus, after five years, the link with economic activity is truly severed. These migrants are deemed to be sufficiently assimilated into the life of the host state that they are considered, for all practical purposes, to be nationals, with the result that they enjoy equal treatment not only in respect of social assistance but also as regards student maintenance in the form of grants or loans.

Developments in the field of citizenship prompt further, more fundamental, questions: where is the EU to go from here? Should it continue down the path of further integration, giving the EU ever more state-like qualities (a defence force, a foreign policy, a social security system?). Should the EU stand still, draw breath and take stock? Or should the EU look to retrench and focus again on the four freedoms? The period of reflection following the rejection of the Constitutional Treaty by the Dutch and French voters was supposed to give the prime ministers and presidents of the Member States time to think these thoughts but the Lisbon Treaty indicates there was little appetite to engage with these difficult issues.

CONCLUSIONS

Bosman is an important case. At a legal level, its importance lies in the shift from a non-discrimination model to a market access approach and in the Court of Justice's willingness to embrace 'Union citizenship'. At a practical level, *Bosman* is important for Jean-Marc himself, in that the Court of Justice sent out a very strong message that he had been wronged, and for the world of professional football where the rules on nationality and transfer fees have been radically overhauled. For the purpose of this book, the case is important because it shows us how Union law works and it tells us about the method of reasoning of the European Court of Justice.

The EU is a political entity and a legal system that you may—or may not—agree with but it is exciting, dynamic and transformative. The debates about the EU matter, not least because so much is yet to be decided. As lawyers, we have an important role in the continuation of this debate.

Cases

Case C-415/93 *Union Royale Belge des Sociétés de Football Association ASBL v Bosman* [1995] ECR I-4921

Case 26/62 *Van Gend en Loos v Nederlandse Administratie der Belastingen* [1963] ECR 1

Case 6/64 *Costa v ENEL* [1964] ECR 585

Cases C-402/05P and C-415/05P *Kadi and Al Barakaat* [2008] ECR I-6351

Case 13/76 *Donà v Mantero* [1976] ECR 1333

Case C-265/03 *Simutenkov v Ministerio de Educaión y Cultura, Real Federación Española de Fútbol* [2005] ECR I-2579

Case C-140/03 *Commission v Greece (opticians)* [2005] ECR I-3177

Case C–60/00 *Mary Carpenter v Secretary of State for the Home Department* [2002] ECR I–6279

Case C-184/99 *Grzelczyk v Centre public d'aide sociale d'Ottignies-Louvain-La-Neuve* [2001] ECR I-6193

Comment

S Weatherill, '"Fair Play Please". Recent Developments in the Application of EC law to Sport' (2003) 40 *Common Market Law Review* 51

Websites

The EU's own website is at http://europa.eu.

European Union legislation can be found at http://eur-lex.europa.eu/en/index.htm

The European Court of Justice's website is at www.curia.europa.eu.
UEFA's website is at www.uefa.com/uefa/footballfirst/protectingthe
game/youngplayers/index.html

Further reading

Introductory reading:

Rosas and Armati, *EU Constitutional Law: An Introduction* (Oxford, Hart Publishing, 2010)
Ward, *A Critical Introduction to European Law*, 2nd edn (London, Lexis Nexis Butterworths, 2003)
Weatherill, *Law and Integration in the European Union* (Oxford, Clarendon Press, 1995)

More detailed reading:

Barnard, *The Substantive Law of the EU: The Four Freedoms*, 3rd edn (Oxford, Oxford University Press, 2010)
Chalmers, Davies and Monti, *European Union Law: Text and Materials*, 2nd edn (Cambridge, Cambridge University Press, 2010)
Craig and De Búrca, *EU Law: Text, Cases and Materials*, 4th edn (Oxford, Oxford University Press, 2007)

9

Conclusions: Drawing Some Threads Together

Janet O'Sullivan, Catherine Barnard and Graham Virgo

So, what about law? You should, by now, have a pretty good idea of the sorts of issues studied by students in an academic law course at a good university. This chapter aims to take a step back and reflect on some of the themes and ideas that you will have encountered throughout the rest of the book. Its aim is to provide some further insights into legal problems and legal reasoning, and ultimately to help you decide what *your* answer is going to be to our title question, what about law?

First of all, you have probably spotted that, like it or not, there is no getting away from the fact that you have to acquire the building blocks of the subject. Studying law involves a lot of hard work, reading, understanding and learning difficult rules, and much of this will be the result of *independent* study. Law will not be spoon-fed to you in bite-sized pieces. A good analogy is perhaps with the study of architecture. An architect must spend years learning the basics of his profession—rules about materials, geometry, mathematics, the history of design and so on. But, like architecture, there is *so* much more to mastering the law than merely learning the rules and assembling building blocks. In this chapter, we will give you a taste of some deeper, more creative ideas and questions that await you, once you have mastered the basics of law.

For example, you may have noticed something surprising throughout this book about the sort of process judges are engaged in when applying the law to decide a case. Students often think mastering the law is all about learning all the laws, like memorising lots of encyclopaedias. They assume that, having learnt them all, they will be able to scroll through their mental index and produce the 'right' answer to any legal problem: a bit like putting the facts into the top of a vending machine and expecting the 'right' answer to pop out of the bottom. As you will have realised by now, happily, the process of legal reasoning is much more complex and *much* more interesting than this, particularly in a common law system built on precedent. Simmonds explains the point very clearly in the first edition of his book, *Central Issues in Jurisprudence*:

> But if the law consists of rules which have been positively established and which can be ascertained without difficulty, how does it come about that expert lawyers frequently disagree? Rival QCs or law professors may disagree about what the existing law is. Many appellate decisions adjudicate between rival views of the existing law. But how can this be if the law is so unproblematic? When Professor X and Professor Y disagree about the law of tort, does that show that one of them has not done his homework, and has overlooked some statute or case that the other one has discovered? But we know that in most disputes all the statutes and cases are, as it were, on the table and known to both parties. So why can they not just *see* what the rules are?

Perhaps our notion of a doctrine of precedent lulls us into a false sense of confidence that the law will always be clear-cut and easy to identify: surely new cases are simply to be decided in accordance with past *authority*, in other words, decided following an earlier binding decision on the same facts? But there's the problem: it is extremely rare for the facts of a case to be *exactly* the same as the facts of an earlier precedent. This rarely matters at all, because usually the differences between a new case and the earlier precedent are obviously irrelevant when it comes to applying the earlier legal rule. The following example illustrates this point.

In 1975 the Court of Appeal established in *Froom v Butcher* what should happen when a car driver is injured in a head-on collision caused by the defendant's negligent driving, but whose injuries are exacerbated because the driver was not wearing a seat-belt. The court decided that, where the driver sued the defendant in tort, the driver's damages should be reduced by 20 per cent because of the driver's *contributory negligence* (a partial defence under the Law Reform (Contributory Negligence) Act 1945). This became a precedent for what should happen in such cases in future. Now, in *Froom* the victim's car happened to be a Jaguar, but it is obvious that the rule *Froom* established (about deducting 20 per cent for contributory negligence) does not apply only to unbelted *Jaguar* drivers, but to unbelted drivers of any sort of car. So obvious, in fact, that after *Froom*, cases involving drivers of Fords, Volvos and Toyotas whose injuries were exacerbated because they failed to wear seatbelts were straightforwardly treated as governed by the same precedent. More to the point, the question would never have been argued in court in those cases, because the lawyers acting for both parties would know precisely what the applicable law said about contributory negligence and would readily agree to a 20 per cent reduction in damages.

However, sometimes it is nowhere near this obvious whether an earlier precedent should apply or not. In such a case, the judge has to decide whether the differences between the facts of the earlier precedent and those of the new case are insignificant or important. Sticking with the seatbelt example, a judge might have to decide whether the *Froom* rule should apply if the unbelted driver was pregnant or suffering from a medical condition that made wearing a seatbelt dangerous. What if the driver was obese and so found wearing a seatbelt uncomfortable? And what if the unbelted victim was a passenger not the driver? It is quite plausible that different judges might come to different conclusions about the significance of these distinctions. One judge might regard them as significant enough to distinguish *Froom*, while another judge might decide that *Froom* should apply because the difference did not really matter. Sometimes, both points of view will surface in the same case, with decisions reversed on appeal or with an appellate court divided into majority and minority views. Yet all the judges reached their views in accordance with and using the same legal texts and rules.

You will have noticed many instances throughout this book of judges having to decide whether to apply or distinguish an existing legal rule, based on their view about the importance of factual differences between the precedent and the case in front of them, as well as many examples of judges disagreeing about what the law is in a given situation, what it means and how it should be applied.

The potential for disagreement is not confined to judges—commentators and law students often disagree too. The following two examples will give you a sense of where the disagreements might lie when facts differ, even slightly. The first involves the serious criminal offence of rape. Most people know what 'rape' means and could make a good attempt at working out what the essential elements of the criminal offence are likely to be (the *actus reus* and the *mens rea,* to recap from chapter 2). In essence, the offence of rape involves sexual intercourse with a victim without the victim's consent. You probably imagine that working out whether a particular set of facts falls within this definition is unlikely to be problematic (although *proving* those facts is often extremely difficult). But in 1923 the Court of Criminal Appeal had to consider the case of *R v Williams*. Williams was a singing teacher, who was giving singing lessons to a naïve 16-year-old girl. He told her that she had problems with her breathing and that he could improve it by using his body to 'make an air passage'. He then had sex with her. She consented to what he was doing, not realising that it was sexual intercourse. Was Williams guilty of rape?

His barrister argued that as the girl had consented to penetration, Williams could not be guilty of rape (although he might be guilty of a less serious offence). This forced the court to confront exactly what the word 'consent' means in the definition of rape and, unsurprisingly, found that Williams was indeed guilty of that serious crime, despite the fact that his actions were not quite as obviously within the definition as the stereotypical situation of rape by a stranger on an obviously unwilling victim. But would the same apply if a slightly less naïve woman consented to penetration, knowing the 'facts of life' but having been led to believe that intercourse would nevertheless improve her singing voice? This is even further away from the stereotypical rape situation, and subtly different again from the facts of *Williams*. So has such a victim given consent within the definition of rape or not? (There is a similarity here with the victims who were infected with HIV in *Dica*, discussed in chapter 2.) It is entirely plausible to imagine two lawyers disagreeing about whether *Williams* should be applied or distinguished in such a case, yet both views might be equally consistent with existing law and logically reasoned. As you will discover, lawyers frequently read majority decisions of the appellate courts and find, disconcertingly, that the dissenting speech is just as convincing as the majority speeches and it is very difficult to decide which side to support.

Interestingly, nowadays the offence of rape is defined in a statute (the Sexual Offences Act 2003) and its provisions deal with the problem in *Williams*. The victim will not be considered to have consented to sex where 'the defendant intentionally deceived the complainant as to the nature or purpose of the relevant act' or where 'the defendant intentionally induced the complainant to consent to the relevant act by impersonating a person known personally to the complainant'. But this statutory wording brings its own grey areas about interpretation. What if a defendant agrees to have sex with a prostitute, intending not to pay her? Has he intentionally deceived her as to the nature of the act? What if the defendant is desperate to have sex with the victim, who tells him that she will only agree to have sex with him if he says that he loves her? He does not love her but tells her that he does in order to have sex with her. Has he intentionally deceived her as to the nature of the act? What if the defendant pretends to be a famous pop star and he has sex with the victim? Has the defendant impersonated somebody 'known personally' to the victim? What does 'personally' mean here? For example, what if she has met the pop star on a number of occasions or merely attended all his UK concerts?

The second example of reasonable disagreement is much more recent and, as the House of Lords' 3:2 decision shows, much more difficult to resolve.

Moore Stephens (a firm) v Stone & Rolls Ltd (in liquidation) concerned Mr S, a fraudster, who set up a one-man company (in other words he was effectively its sole shareholder and director) called S&R. He then used S&R to defraud various banks out of large sums of money. Eventually the fraud was detected and the banks sued S&R and Mr S for damages (using a tort called 'deceit'). The banks' claims were successful, but the problem was that neither Mr S nor his company S&R had any money left to pay what the judgment demanded. So the banks had achieved a hollow victory.

Shortly afterwards, S&R went into liquidation—this is the equivalent for a company of an individual going bankrupt, meaning it had no assets or money to pay all the debts it owed. When a company goes into liquidation, professional insolvency practitioners ('liquidators') take over control of the company, with the task of gathering in all the company's assets and paying out as much as possible to the people who are owed money by the company (known as 'creditors'). The liquidators act in the *name* of the company, but with the sole purpose of maximising the amount available to pay the creditors.

What happened next was that S&R (being controlled by its liquidators of course) sued a firm of accountants called Moore Stephens. Moore Stephens had been S&R's auditors for many years, which means every year they checked S&R's accounts and produced an audit report. The gist of the claim brought against them was that they had negligently failed to spot the fraud being perpetrated by S&R and therefore allowed it to rack up huge liabilities to the banks—in other words, the allegation was that if Moore Stephens had done its job properly, it would have spotted the fraud sooner and nipped it in the bud.

If you take a step back, you might be struck by the audacity of S&R's claim, which is effectively, 'I want damages from you to compensate me for the financial consequences of *my own fraud*'! But S&R argued that it was also the victim of the fraud—the real perpetrator was Mr S—and that part of the auditors' role was to be on the lookout for the controller of a company using it for fraud.

What does the law have to say? There are two important principles of relevance here. First, the law does not allow someone to rely on their own illegality in legal proceedings. This is a vital principle of public policy, usually expressed in Latin as, no cause of action can arise '*ex turpi causa*'. The easiest example is to imagine someone who has paid an assassin to murder his wife—if the assassin pockets the fee but does not go ahead with the murder, the husband's attempt to sue the assassin for breach of contract will be prevented by the principle of illegality. He will not be allowed to plead or enforce his own illegal contract. Unfortunately, most examples are not so clear cut and illegality is a difficult concept, not least because by declining to assist a claimant whose claim is tainted with illegality, the effect of the principle is often to leave the other (equally culpable) party, like our assassin, having made a profit from the illegality. But as the courts sometimes say, preventing someone relying on their own illegality is a principle of public policy not of justice.

The second principle that arises on the facts of *Moore Stephens* concerns companies and how they are treated by the law. Crucially, a company is an entirely separate 'person' in the eyes of the law from the individuals who set it up and run it. A company can make contracts, borrow money and buy things itself; more to the point, it can incur liabilities and debts which do not bind the people actually running the company. Now that is all very well in theory, but a company is just a legal notion, existing on paper—what the law needs is a set of rules to determine which acts by the people running the company are deemed to be the acts of the company and which are not, known as principles of *attribution.* These also tell us whether wrongdoing by the people in the background who control the company is treated as wrongdoing *by* the company or *against* the company.

Anyhow, back to the litigation. Moore Stephens applied to strike out the company's claim at a preliminary stage, on the basis of *ex turpi causa*—S&R could not benefit from its own fraud. The majority of the House of Lords agreed and struck out the claim, explaining that Mr S's fraud was attributed to S&R since it was a one-man company and thus was effectively the perpetrator and not the victim of the fraud. This meant that S&R was attempting to rely on its own illegality, something prohibited by the *ex turpi causa* principle.

Whilst this at first glance might appear self-evidently the right answer, the two Law Lords in the minority were troubled by the fact that, since S&R was already insolvent, Mr S would not gain a penny from an award of damages. So if Moore Stephens could plead *ex turpi causa* to defeat the claim, the real losers would be S&R's innocent creditors, including of course the defrauded banks! As Lord Scott, one of the two dissenters, said:

> In a case, such as the present, where the company is insolvent and will stay so whatever damages are recoverable from the auditors, the need to ensure that the delinquent director does not benefit from the damages does not present a problem. There is no possibility of Mr S benefiting from any damages recoverable from Moore Stephens. So, I repeat, why should the *ex turpi causa* rule, a rule based on public policy, bar an action against the auditors based on their

breach of duty? The wielding of a rule of public policy in circumstances where public policy is not engaged constitutes, in my respectful opinion, bad jurisprudence.

Once you appreciate that all five Law Lords in *Moore Stephens* agreed on the applicable legal rules and principles, you are forced to think carefully about *why* those judges disagreed about the result in the case. Essentially, the answer is that they had to make *value judgments* about whether those rules should be applied or distinguished, and how they should be interpreted, as lawyers invariably have to do when faced with a new factual situation.

When doing so, some of the considerations taken into account are obviously legal (such as whether extending an existing rule to this new situation would 'flood' the courts with too many new claims or disrupt existing legal rights too drastically), but many other sorts of question are relevant too, such as considerations of morality, economic theory and ethics. For example, you will recall from chapter 2 that all the judges in *R v Brown* made certain assumptions about the moral framework underlying the criminal law—if the judges hadn't made a value judgment (one way or the other) on that non-legal issue, it would not have been possible to decide the case 'according to the law'. In chapter 3 we saw that economic assumptions underpin much of the law about remedies for breach of contract, based on the functioning of a market in a capitalist economy. And in the failed sterilisation cases discussed in chapter 4 the courts came face-to-face with ethical judgments about the value of human life and questions of distributive justice in a society such as ours with a publicly funded health service.

Precisely the same sorts of disagreements arise about the proper interpretation of European Union law and other international legal texts. In this context other issues also come into play—such as the multilingual environment in which the texts were drafted and different cultural norms. Some of these issues can be seen in *P v S*, a decision of the Court of Justice where the Court's interpretation was swayed less by a literal reading of the text and more by underlying values. P, a male-to-female transsexual, was dismissed on the grounds that she was undergoing a sex change (or 'gender reassignment' as it is properly known). Because, at that time, English law did not prohibit discrimination on grounds of gender reassignment, P argued that European Union law, in particular the Equal Treatment Directive 76/207 (now Directive 2006/54), did cover her situation. The question for the Court of Justice was whether the word 'sex', in the phrase 'there shall be no discrimination whatsoever on the grounds of sex' used by the Directive, was broad enough to include 'change of sex'. The Court of Justice said yes. Its judgment was influenced by the passionate opinion of the Advocate General who urged the Court to take a 'courageous' decision and interpret the word 'sex' to include change of sex because such an interpretation is 'undeniably based on and consonant with the great value of equality'. The result was that P won her case and her victory benefited many other transsexuals, because the UK government adopted the Sex Discrimination (Gender Reassignment) Regulations (now found in the Equality Act 2010) amending British law to prohibit discrimination against transsexuals.

The realisation that judges are often making value judgments prompts the question: are unelected lawyers, judges in particular, the best equipped and most appropriate people to decide these sorts of issue and to mould the law by reference to them? Some people suggest that since judges are predominately from an elite social and educational background, they are not sufficiently representative of the community. To make matters worse, stories about High Court judges not understanding references to pop groups serve only to undermine further the public's trust in them. On the other hand, most people's experience of the judicial system in operation is extremely positive (at least in so far as the intelligence, sharpness and impartiality of the judges is concerned). Some people have argued that recent legislation, especially some of the recent reforms to the criminal law, suggest that our elected representatives cannot always be relied on for common sense and independence and be guaranteed to protect citizens' fundamental rights.

You have probably also noticed throughout this book that some judges are more willing than others to be *creative* when moulding the law. Perhaps the clearest example was the 2003 case of *Rees v Darlington Memorial Hospital Trust* discussed in chapter 4, in which the House of Lords invented a new £15,000 damages award to be given in future to parents of 'unwanted' babies, a remedy that appeared to be plucked out of thin air and with no precedent to support it, as astonished commentators have pointed out.

More recently, the House of Lords disagreed openly about whether another new tort rule could be developed by the judges at common law or whether it was too radical and should therefore be left to Parliament. The case involved an unusual tort called *conversion* which covers taking someone else's property (roughly speaking it is the tort equivalent of the crime of theft, but does not require the same level of fault as the criminal offence). Conversion usually applies to tangible goods, but the House of Lords was pondering whether it should be extended to cover intangible 'things' like contractual rights (see the discussion of 'choses in action' in chapter 6). Under the existing law, conversion does apply if the intangible right is embodied in a physical document like a cheque or a share certificate. So, for this reason, Lord Nicholls thought that the common law could and indeed should extend the law to purely intangible rights. In his view:

> The time has surely come to . . . recognise that the tort of conversion applies to contractual rights irrespective of whether they are embodied or recorded in writing. I would so hold. This would be a modest but principled extension of the scope of the tort of conversion.

In contrast, Lord Walker took entirely the opposite view:

> Lord Nicholls makes a powerful case for extending the tort of conversion so as to cover the appropriation of choses in action. But in my opinion his proposals would involve too drastic a reshaping of this area of the law of tort. . . . It would have far-reaching consequences which this House is not in a position to explore or assess fully. This is an area in which reform must come from Parliament, after further consideration by the Law Commission.

Perhaps the most famous (some would say notorious) exponent of judicial creativity was Lord Denning, a brilliant lawyer who reached the Court of Appeal just after the Second World War at the remarkably young age of 49 and did not retire until the 1980s. His attitude to inconvenient precedents standing in the way of reaching the 'right' result is seen in the following characteristically sweeping passage from *Hill v CA Parsons Ltd*, a 1971 case about whether a court could, in exceptional circumstances, order an injunction to prevent an employer from wrongfully dismissing an employee:

> The judge said that he felt constrained by the law to refuse an injunction. But that is too narrow a view of the principles of law. He has overlooked the fundamental principle that, whenever a man has a right, the law should give a remedy. . . . This principle enables us to step over the *trip-wires of previous cases and to bring the law into accord with the needs of today* [emphasis added].

In stark contrast, other judges take a much more conservative approach to what they can do when faced with a 'problematic' precedent or statute. This is well illustrated by the decision of the House of Lords in *Hicks v Chief Constable of South Yorkshire*, another tort case which arose (like *Alcock*, discussed in chapter 4) from the Hillsborough football stadium disaster in 1989. Almost 100 Liverpool fans were crushed to death against barriers separating the crowd from the pitch when the police negligently opened gates at the rear of the stand, allowing more fans to surge in. Sarah and Victoria Hicks, aged 19 and 15, were among those killed and their parents sued the police for damages in the tort of negligence; they did this, not for financial motives, but as Lord Bridge explained, 'to mark the anger of these parents and other bereaved relatives as to what occurred' (although you will remember that an award of damages is not intended to be punitive).

The Fatal Accidents Act 1976 provides for bereavement damages of £7,500 to be awarded if a claimant's spouse or *minor* child was killed by the defendant's negligence, so this sum was awarded in respect of Victoria's death. (Does it surprise you that a bereaved mother whose young child is killed by the defendant's negligence receives only *half* the amount of damages that *Rees* gives to the mother of a child who would not have been born without the defendant's negligence?) But Sarah was over 18 and so this provision did not apply in her case. However, an entirely separate statute also provides that if a legal claim has accrued to a deceased person during his or her lifetime, most such claims will *survive for the benefit of the deceased's estate*— in practice, this means that the deceased's personal representatives are permitted to bring a claim if the deceased could have done so just before their death. The sisters died without leaving a will, but their parents became their personal representatives (known as administrators) and sued the police on behalf of their deceased daughters' estates, to recover damages for the pain and suffering experienced by the girls before they died.

The problem with this claim lay in existing case law, which said that a distinction had to be drawn between pain and suffering experienced *before* death and the pain and suffering *of* death— the deceased accrued a right of action in respect of the former during his or her lifetime, but (by definition) not the latter, so only the former survived for the benefit of the estate to be claimed by the deceased's personal representatives. The judges in *Hicks* felt compelled to decide that this existing case law prevented any damages being awarded in respect of the deaths, despite expressing 'regret' at this conclusion. Had he been judging the case, Lord Denning would almost certainly have found a way to avoid the 'tripwires' of those existing precedents so as to give damages to the bereaved parents. Very few lawyers and commentators would have objected had that (opposite) result been reached in *Hicks*, but more generally justice is not necessarily better served by judicial creativity— there are sometimes considerable advantages in judicial conservatism, at least where that means that the law is certain and predictable.

In fact, you will have noticed throughout this book that there is invariably tension between two inconsistent characteristics, both of which can claim to make 'good' or 'just' laws, namely certainty and flexibility. It is very important that legal rules are clear, predictable and consistently applied, but too much certainty can bring inflexibility and injustice. On the other hand, although it is vital that the law is flexible enough to produce fair results tailored to the individual merits of a given situation, too much flexibility can bring uncertainty and unpredictability. Getting the balance right is not easy and different areas of law will strike that balance in different ways. For example, the law of contract operates for the most part in the commercial sphere, where businesses need predictable, clear rules so that they can enter into transactions knowing precisely where they stand and what the law's response will be if things go wrong (remember Lord Hobhouse's convincing dissenting speech in the *Blake* case considered in chapter 3). Too much emphasis on tailoring results to the individual merits of a case would be highly undesirable in commercial contracts (less so, perhaps, in consumer transactions). In criminal law, on the other hand, where the liberty of citizens is at stake, flexibility is very much more important—the same sentence for everyone who commits the same offence would be extremely clear and easy to apply, but it would not do justice to the individual defendant for whom there may have been mitigating—or indeed aggravating—factors. But even in criminal law, too much discretion would be a bad thing— no decent legal system could function if, for example, the law gave judges discretion to 'tailor' the elements of offences or the rules of evidence to match the 'merits' of a case.

This tension was particularly evident in chapter 6, when we considered the role of equitable principles in modern society. Equity began as a flexible, discretionary jurisdiction to do justice by reference to the conscience of the parties, in response to the obvious harshness of the early common law's strict, 'letter of the law' attitude. But in the twenty-first century, equitable principles have very important functions in commercial and property transactions, both of which need certainty to ensure the security of investments and proprietary rights.

The same tension is apparent in the tort of negligence considered in chapter 4, especially in setting the standard of care against which the defendant's conduct is judged. You will remember that English law sets an objective standard, comparing the defendant's conduct with that of the hypothetical reasonable person placed in the same situation. This makes for certainty and ease of application— imagine how hard it would be to administer a subjective standard of care requiring evidence of whether the defendant fell short of his or her own normal standard of care— but can lead to apparent unfairness, as when a person of below-average intelligence or ability is judged against a standard that they could not possibly be expected to attain. This is acceptable as a civil law standard of 'wrongdoing', but would be much more controversial if used as a criminal level of fault.

Indeed, if we step back from the detail of the law we can see the same tensions at a more general, theoretical level. It is vitally important for any decent legal system to have clear, publicly ascertainable rules, so that the public can know in advance what they may or may not do, what rights they have and how their disputes will be resolved. This goal is best served by a small number of very basic, rigid rules, not complicated by exceptions or discretionary qualifications, yet this is inconsistent with doing justice in the individual case, also a vitally important goal of a decent legal system. Think, for example, about whether it would be feasible for a western, capitalist legal system to operate its law of contract on the basis that a promise must be kept unless the welfare of the majority of the citizens would be maximised if it were broken. You will briefly have considered this notion of *utilitarianism* in chapter 2. Lawyers really ought to consider general issues of this sort, unless they are content to accept the existing legal regime without questioning it at all.

We are starting to see that identifying, understanding and applying the law involves all sorts of considerations and values that are not straightforwardly legal issues. This should prompt us to ask even deeper, jurisprudential questions about the law: for example, do non-legal considerations and values form part of the law or not? There are echoes here of the discussion in chapter 7 about the fundamental notion of the rule of law. What would happen if English judges started to decide difficult cases by reference to *unacceptable* values or prejudiced considerations? Would those decisions have the status of 'law' or not?

From what you have read in chapter 7, are judges required to apply an obviously immoral statute (eg one which allows the state to lock up citizens without any access to courts) just because it was 'properly' enacted by Parliament? Given the supremacy of Parliament, would it be consistent with the rule of law to apply or refuse to apply such a statute?

Related issues arose in chapter 8, with consideration of what membership of the EU means for parliamentary sovereignty in the UK, and are apparent whenever English courts apply the European Convention on Human Rights. You might be interested to hear the final twist in the tale of George Blake, the notorious traitor we met in chapter 3 whose autobiography provided the opportunity for the House of Lords to introduce the controversial remedy of the 'account of profits' into the English law of contract. Blake subsequently took the UK to the European Court of Human Rights (ECtHR) and succeeded in his claim that the UK breached his human right to have a fair hearing because it took an inordinately long time to resolve the litigation about the profits from his autobiography (over nine years from start to finish). Blake was awarded damages of 5,000 euros by the ECtHR—can you imagine the House of Lords reaching that conclusion if the question had been raised in the domestic courts?

The fundamental question of whether non-legal considerations and values form part of the law takes us to some very difficult debates about the meaning of law and, in particular, its relationship with morality. What does 'law' mean? Is it separate from morality or inextricably linked? Chapter 2 provides a good introduction to some of the different views on this important relationship. Until the nineteenth century, most legal philosophers (influenced by Aristotle) believed that there was an underlying body of *natural law* with a moral content and that the role of lawyers was to unearth and expound it. Later commentators sought to separate the question of whether a particular rule or principle counts as a *valid* law from the equally important question of whether that law is a *good* law— an approach known as *positivism*. Positivists say that it is possible to identify that something is 'law' by reference to its source and whether that source is recognised as legitimate by the population, without making any claim about its *moral* authority. After all, the Nazi government in Germany scrupulously enacted laws to give dubious authority to its barbarous regime. But positivism still doesn't tell us precisely what is going on when a judge is interpreting a given law, in the light of his or her moral, ethical and other values, so as to decide whether the law should be applied to a new situation or distinguished.

Finally, you will have noticed throughout this book that you can never ignore the *context* in which a particular legal problem has arisen. The common law system of precedent sometimes tempts us to look for higher levels of generality than are actually appropriate; common lawyers are always keen to identify general principles that connect diverse situations. Yet, very often, a rule cannot simply be transplanted into a different factual context—the same answer may not be appropriate, even where apparently the same principles apply. For example, you may well have been surprised in chapter 3 to read that a a nineteenth-century case about a fire department from Louisiana failing to provide the contractually agreed level of service was cited to support the creation of an exceptional new remedy for a treacherous breach of a government contract of employment. Lawyers are so used to generalising that they sometimes fail to notice how odd it is to cite and rely on such diverse cases in this way. The same point was made in chapter 8, when discussing the extent to which EU laws made in one context (the promotion of the single market via the free movement of workers) should apply in the very different, rather special, context of sport. You will probably have appreciated too that predicting how precedents will be applied in the future also requires a keen sensitivity to context. For example, was the *Blake* 'account of profits' remedy appropriate only because of the non-commercial, espionage context of the decision itself, or is its rationale potentially wide enough to catch all contracts, even those in a wholly commercial context? Only time will tell.

Context is sometimes the most important aspect of a decision. Think again about *Chhokar v Chhokar*, discussed in chapter 5, with its wholly unusual, indeed shocking, storyline involving collusion between the legal owner, Mr Chhokar, and the third-party purchaser, Mr Parmar. How far do you think the judges in *Chhokar* were influenced by this exceptional factual context when considering the meaning of the crucial statutory phrase 'actual occupation'? If you are not sure, ask yourself how an analogous case should be decided involving an equally wicked husband who, while his wife is temporarily away from the family home, hides most of her obviously feminine possessions, then purports to sell the house to a wholly innocent, if naïve, purchaser who knows nothing about the wife's interest in the house. This time there is no reconciliation between wife and husband (he has disappeared with the proceeds of sale), just a dispute about whether the innocent purchaser is bound by, or free of, the innocent wife's beneficial interest. It would be much harder for a court to justify a conclusion that the wife remained in *actual occupation* in this situation by virtue of the symbolic presence of her belongings. Indeed, a court might well decide in favour of the naïve purchaser here, perhaps by pointing out that the statutory word 'actual' must mean something, arguably the opposite of 'symbolic'? And, in turn, the reasoning chosen to support this conclusion might well depend, as we saw in chapter 7, on whether the judge wants the precedent being set by the case to be confined to its precise facts or to be potentially relevant in a broader context.

In conclusion, as a law student you will spend many hours reading, learning and understanding details, principles and techniques. But, as we have tried to show in this book, you will also spend a lot of time on more creative endeavours—making connections and thinking about the implications of one legal rule (whether from a statute, a case or some other source) in other areas, recognising similarities and drawing distinctions, considering arguments and ideas from all sorts of disciplines outside the law. If you find this an exciting challenge and are ready for lots of reading, thinking and questioning, then we think you will relish studying law at university.

Cases

Blake v UK, Application No 68890/01 [2006] All ER (D) 126 (case law of the European Court of Human Rights can be found at www.echr. coe.int/echr)

Froom v Butcher [1976] QB 286; [1975] 3 All ER 520

Hicks v Chief Constable of South Yorkshire Police [1999] 2 All ER 65

Hill v C A Parsons Ltd [1971] 3 All ER 1345

Moore Stephens (a firm) v Stone & Rolls Ltd (in liquidation) [2009] 4 All ER 431

Case C-13/94 *P v S and Cornwall County Council* [1996] ECR I-2143

R v Williams [1923] 1 KB 340

Further reading

N Simmonds, *Central Issues in Jurisprudence: Justice, Law and Rights*, 3rd edn (London, Sweet & Maxwell, 2008)

JAG Griffith, *The Politics of the Judiciary*, 5th edn (Bodmin, Fontana Press, 1997)

HLA Hart, *The Concept of Law* edited, with a postscript, by Penelope A Bulloch and Joseph Raz, 2nd edn (Oxford, Clarendon Press, 1997)

Epilogue

Now that you have been introduced to some of the key principles of the law, why not take another look at the image on the front cover and see how many legal issues you can identify? (Of course, it is an American street scene, but imagine that it is set in the UK for this purpose.)

Most obviously, it looks as if a criminal offence is being committed in the foreground, where a businessman is being held up and robbed at gunpoint. The robber, if arrested and subsequently prosecuted, is likely to be sent to jail for a substantial period. Can the businessman recover the money which was stolen? What if the money had been paid into the robber's bank account? Does it matter that the robber acquired the money illegally?

Meanwhile, on the left-hand side of the picture, a postman is collecting letters from a postbox. Perhaps one of the letters is a reply to a contractual offer, in which the writer agrees to enter into a contract to buy a rare painting. This reply subsequently gets lost in the post and the painting is sold to someone else. Where, in contract law, does that leave the sender of the letter?

In the background there has been a road traffic accident. This accident may also raise criminal issues (perhaps one or both of the drivers were driving carelessly or dangerously), but the law of tort may also be relevant. Anyone injured might sue the drivers for damages in the tort of negligence. If it was a passenger who was injured, but she wasn't wearing a seatbelt, her damages might be reduced in proportion to her contributory negligence. A relative of the injured passenger might even have a claim for damages, if he or she suffered a recognised psychiatric illness caused by shock on seeing the accident happen or coming upon its immediate aftermath. There appear to be photographers taking pictures of the aftermath of the crash. Are they under any duty to help those who may have been injured? And what about the pedestrians who appear to be ignoring what has happened?

Plenty of people are out and about, but as a matter of land law who owns the highway, the pavement and the land beneath? Not the drivers and pedestrians, that's for certain, yet they have rights of way over the land, to use it for passage to and fro. In fact, there appears to be a gathering of people in the middle of the picture. Is this a protest? If so, it raises issues of constitutional law as well. The European Convention on Human Rights, incorporated into domestic law by the Human Rights Act, protects freedom of assembly and freedom of expression. But these rights are not unlimited. If the protest gets out of hand, the police can intervene to prevent breaches of the peace and other public order offences from being committed. And what if the police discover that some of the protesters are nationals of other EU Member States? As EU citizens they have a right to be in the UK. And EU law will provide them with protection against any police decision to put them on a plane and deport them simply because they have been involved in a breach of the peace.

On the right-hand side of the picture there is a stand where newspapers and magazines are for sale. Perhaps the publications contain sensational and untrue—or true—stories relating to a celebrity's private life. Would the subjects of such stories have any claims against the publishers? Can they do anything to stop publication?

Finally, the picture itself raises important questions of property law. Who owns the picture (and for our purposes the photograph of the picture)? This involves a special type of property law, called intellectual property law, and, in particular, the law of copyright. For your information, the publisher of this book has entered a contract with the copyright holder to reproduce the picture. And you have entered into a contract with the bookseller to buy this book or with the publishers if you ordered the book directly from them. Law is all around you—and that makes it fun and rewarding to study.

Catherine Barnard, Janet O'Sullivan and Graham Virgo

Index